STEPHAN PYLES
NEW TASTES ROM TEXAS

UPDATED AND REVISED

Photography by Ben Fink

Clarkson Potter/Publishers
New York

To the culinary pioneers of Texas

Book Packaging Editorial and Design: Martha Hopkins and Randall Lockridge
Chef for Revised Edition: Mark Kiffin **Photographer:** Ben Fink
Chef for Original Edition: Geoffrey Meeker **Food Stylist:** Trish Dahl
Food Stylist Assistant: Martha Gooding **Prop Stylists:** Molly Terry & Terri Raith **Proofreader:** Carol Boke
Terrace Publishing Assistants: Matthew Stevenson and Erin Kennedy
Photographer of pages 90-1 and 118-9: Matthew Savins **KERA Coordinator:** Jana Sims
Special thanks to Mike Anglin for opening his home to us.

Pyles, Stephan
New Tastes from Texas
Published by Clarkson Potter/Publishers, 201 East 50th Street, New York, New York 10022.
Member of the Crown Publishing Group.
Random House, Inc. New York, Toronto, London, Sydney, Auckland
http://www.randomhouse.com/
CLARKSON N. POTTER, POTTER, and colophon
are trademarks of Clarkson N. Potter, Inc.

Library of Congress Cataloging-in-Publication Data
Pyles, Stephan. New tastes from Texas / Stephan Pyles; photography by Ben Fink;
editing and design by Martha Hopkins and Randall Lockridge
p. cm. ISBN 0-609-80497-9 (pb)
1. Cookery, American—Southwestern style. 2. Cookery—Texas. I. Title
TX715.2.S69P93 1999 841.59764—dc21 99-23443 CIP

Printed in China

10 9 8 7 6 5 4 3
Second Edition

table of contents

influence of mexico on texas cuisine

The recipes in this book are written in the traditional *mise en place* format.
Please take care to read the recipe in its entirety before beginning.

techniques for classic

Preparing the Grill

Grilling food over a fire is probably the oldest form of cooking. A modern grill cooks food both by direct heat and by heat transmitted through the metal bars of the grill itself.

Build a fire in a grill using charcoal briquettes or, preferably, natural lump charcoal. Briquettes, the more readily available option, are composed of charcoal, coal, starch, and some chemical additives to enhance lighting and burning. Lump charcoal, processed from hardwoods such as hickory, mesquite, cherry, maple, or pecan, is the preferred option in my kitchen as it contains no additives. Note that mesquite charcoal, which burns the hottest and lasts the longest, throws out showers of sparks and requires special care.

To start the fire in the grill, use wood kindling or an electric starter. The electric starter is basically an electric element loop similar to those fitted in ovens. You need an electric outlet to use it, of course, and you should remove it once the charcoal has started to burn well. I have strong feelings against using lighter fluid, which imparts unpleasant flavors in the smoke and can taint the flavor of the food being grilled.

With briquettes or lump charcoal, stack the pieces in a pyramid over kindling or an electric starter. Let the coals burn down until they are covered by a uniform whitish-gray ash—about 20 to 30 minutes—then spread the coals out evenly inside the grill. Test the hotness of the grill by carefully holding your hand about 2 inches over the fire.

To impart an extra smoky flavor to your foods, add to the fire 6 to 8 hardwood chunks or chips of hickory, almond, cherry, apple, orange, pecan, or other flavor-enhancing wood that have first been soaked in water for 20 minutes.

For best results when grilling, scrub the metal bars of the grill with a wire brush and then oil them with a towel or rag before and after use. In addition, it helps to bring the meat or fish to room temperature before grilling so that the heat can penetrate to the center of the food more quickly without burning the outside.

While gas grills seem to be more prevalent today than those requiring charcoal or wood, they simply don't impart the same flavor to foods. If you're using a gas grill, the same timing and technique discussed here would generally apply. A gas grill turned to high radiates the same heat as a medium to medium-hot charcoal fire.

Roasting Garlic

Preheat the oven to 350°F. For about 1/3 cup roasted garlic purée, cut 3 heads of garlic in half, and place cut side up in a roasting pan. Pour 1 teaspoon of olive oil over each half. Sprinkle the pan with 2 to 3 tablespoons of water, cover tightly with foil, and bake for 30 to 40 minutes.

Uncover the pan and continue baking for 5 to 7 minutes longer or until the garlic is golden brown. Remove the halves from the pan and let cool. Squeeze the softened garlic into a blender, discarding the skin. Add just enough olive oil to make puréeing possible.

Alternatively, peel individual cloves from 3 heads of garlic with a paring knife. Place the cloves on a baking sheet or in a roasting pan, add 2 tablespoons of olive oil, and toss to coat thoroughly. Sprinkle with water, cover with foil, and roast in the oven at 350°F for 30 minutes. Remove the foil and roast for 5 to 7 minutes longer or until brown.

texas cooking

Roasting Corn

Preheat the oven to 400°F. Remove the outer layer of
husks from the ears of corn, leaving 1 or 2 layers
intact. Pull these remaining husks back, exposing
the kernels. Remove the corn silks, spread butter or
olive oil over the kernels, and sprinkle with a little
salt. Replace the husks over the kernels, place the
ears on a baking sheet, and bake for 30 minutes.

Oven-Drying Corn

Oven-drying corn concentrates the sweetness and full
flavor of the kernels. The dried corn can be used in
salads, salsas, and soups, or ground as cornmeal.
Preheat the oven to 175°F. With a sharp knife, remove
the corn kernels from the ears and spread evenly in
a single layer on a baking sheet. Place in the oven
and check every 30 minutes, turning the pan so the
heat is evenly distributed. Bake until the kernels
appear shriveled and almost dry, about 2 to 2 1/2 hours.
Continue to bake in the oven for an additional 1 1/2
hours, until the kernels are completely dry.
Remove from the oven and let cool.

Preparing Tomatoes

To blanch, peel, and seed tomatoes, prepare a large
bowl of ice water. With a sharp knife, make an "X"
1/4 inch deep into the bottom of each tomato.
Pour enough water into a large pan to come 4 inches up
the side; bring to a rapid boil. Plunge the tomatoes
into the water and cook for 20 seconds, making sure
they are covered with water. Remove the tomatoes
with a slotted spoon and place in the ice water.

Once cool, peel the tomatoes, cut in half, and squeeze
gently. Remove any remaining seeds with a blunt
knife or with your fingers, and discard.
For recipes that call for freshly chopped tomatoes,
simply remove the thick outer flesh with a paring
knife, as you would remove the peel from an orange.
Discard the pulp and seeds or use for sauces or
soups. Dice the tomato flesh into the desired-size
pieces (usually 1/8 inch).

Oven-Drying Cherry Tomatoes

As with corn, oven-drying cherry tomatoes accentuates
and intensifies their flavors and sweetness.
Preheat the oven to 200°F. For 2 cups of oven-dried
tomatoes, slice 8 pints of red cherry tomatoes (or a
combination of yellow and red) in half. Place cut side
up on a baking sheet, and season lightly with salt.
Place in the oven and check every 45 minutes, turning
the pan so the heat is evenly distributed. Bake until
the tomatoes are dry, about 4 to 5 hours. Remove from
the oven and let cool. If not using immediately, store
the tomatoes in vegetable or olive oil.

Toasting Seeds and Nuts

As with roasting peanuts or coffee, toasting seeds and
nuts brings out their full, rich flavor.
To toast seeds, place in a dry, hot skillet over medium-
high heat for 2 to 3 minutes; stir occasionally with a
wooden spoon until the seeds have lightly browned.
This is the more practical method as the seeds are easy
to watch. But alternatively, preheat the oven to 350°F.

Place the seeds in a single layer on a baking sheet, and toast in the oven for 15 to 20 minutes or until fragrant, stirring occasionally.

To toast nuts, place in a dry, hot skillet over medium-high heat for 5 to 7 minutes or until lightly browned; stir occasionally with a wooden spoon. Smaller nuts, such as pine nuts, will take 3 to 5 minutes. Alternatively, preheat the oven to 325°F. Place the nuts in a single layer on a baking sheet, and toast for 15 to 20 minutes or until lightly browned, stirring occasionally.

Preparing the Smoker

Smoking, like grilling, is one of the oldest cooking methods and was a favored means of preserving food before the advent of refrigeration. Now it is used mainly to impart flavorful dimensions to meats, poultry, fish, and vegetables.

Smoking on a large scale was brought to Texas in the 1800s by German immigrants who introduced the smokehouse for sausage making. The practice has remained an important part of the Texas culinary tradition and culture ever since. I started to experiment with smoking vegetables in the early 1980s and began a trend that is now widespread. I like to think this is my legacy, not only to the New Texas Cuisine, but to a far broader audience as well. Smoked tomato salsa, I have noticed, is now commonplace.

Home smokers are available from specialty hardware stores and mail-order sources. A relatively inexpensive piece of equipment, smokers are well worth the investment. You can also adapt a barbecue by adding a pan of water to the bottom, sealing all but one vent, and following the method described here:

Soak 6 to 8 chunks of aromatic hardwood, such as hickory, mesquite, or apple, in water for 20 minutes. Place a pan of water in the bottom of the smoker. Build a fire in the smoker with hardwood lump charcoal or charcoal briquettes and an electric starter (see Preparing the Grill, page 4, for notes on charcoal and starters). Let the charcoal burn down until covered by a uniform whitish-gray ash, about 20 to 30 minutes, and spread out the coals. Add the soaked hardwood chunks and let burn for 5 minutes. Place the ingredients to be smoked on the grill over the water pan, and cover with the top of the smoker. Keep the fire stoked every 30 minutes, adding more charcoal and soaked wood chunks as necessary.

As a general rule, an average 2½-pound chicken will smoke in 1½ to 2 hours at a temperature of 250°F; chicken or duck breasts will take 20 to 25 minutes; tomatoes will take 20 minutes; and chiles, bell peppers, and onions 20 to 25 minutes.

Preparing and Cooking Dried Beans

Historically, beans have always been an important element in the Southwestern diet. Black beans, pinto beans, and black-eyed peas are all used in the recipes in this book.

Always carefully sort through dried beans to remove imperfect beans and foreign particles such as twigs and small stones to avoid the dangerous surprise of a broken tooth.

Once cleaned, the beans should be rinsed thoroughly in a colander and soaked to "de-gas" them. Place the beans in a large pot, cover with enough water to come 2 inches above the beans, and soak overnight. The next day, drain and rinse the beans. Return them to the pot, cover with the same amount of water, and simmer until tender for 45 to 60 minutes. Never add salt until the last 15 minutes of cooking, as it will toughen the beans.

In addition to presoaking beans, cooking them with epazote also helps to minimize their legendary effect on the digestive system.

Preparing Citrus Fruit

To achieve optimum results from juicing citrus fruits, place the fruit on a flat surface. Press down firmly on the fruit with the palm of your hand, rolling backward and forward for about 20 seconds. Slice in half and juice as usual.

To cut citrus fruit into peeled slices, use a short paring knife to cut ½ inch off both ends of the fruit. Stand the fruit on the cut end, and remove the skin and all the white pith to reveal the flesh, cutting downward with the knife. Turn the fruit on its side and cut into slices of desired thickness.

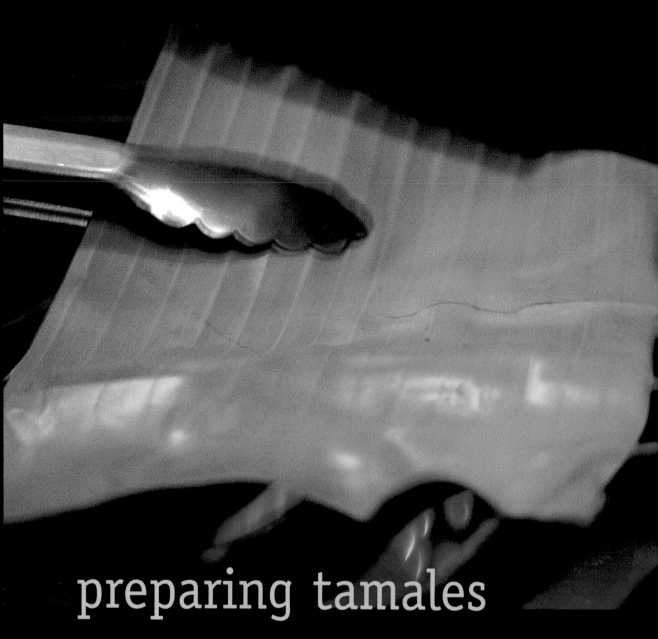

preparing tamales

Start with large banana leaves, about 12 by 36 inches each. Soften the banana leaves over an open flame for 10 seconds on each side, being careful not to burn them. Cut each leaf crosswise into 4 even pieces, about 8 by 10 inches each, and lay out on a flat work surface.

Divide the the masa dough into 8 even portions and place a portion in the center of each leaf. Spread into a 4-inch square, leaving at least a $1^1/_2$-inch border at the ends and a $^3/_4$-inch border on the long sides.

To fold the tamales, pick up the 2 long sides of the banana leaf and bring them together; the leaf will surround the filling. Tuck one side under the other and fold the flaps on each end underneath the tamale. Repeat for the remaining tamales.

Alternatively, you can tear $^1/_6$-inch-wide strips from an extra banana leaf and use them to tie one or both ends for a festive presentation.

Place the tamales in a steamer set over gently boiling water. Steam, covered tightly, for 20 to 25 minutes. Remove the tamales; cut or slice the banana leaf open at the top and peel back to expose the masa. Tuck the peeled-back leaf underneath the tamale or trim off to serve.

guide to fresh and dried chiles

Fresh chiles commonly used in Texas cooking include the Anaheim, a close relative of the New Mexico green chile; the fiery habanero; the jalapeño—a staple of Texas cuisine; the poblano; and the serrano. Most supermarkets carry a wide selection of fresh chiles now, but for those more hard-to-find ones, try your local Hispanic or Asian market. To facilitate identification, I recommend *The Great Chile Book* by Mark Miller (Ten Speed Press).

Buy chiles that have shiny, smooth skins and are heavy for their size. They should be dry and firm to the touch, and smell fresh and clean. They should be kept dry and stored in the crisper section of the refrigerator. Do not wrap them in plastic bags, as moisture could spoil them.

When handling fresh chiles, I recommend using rubber gloves to protect your hands against capsaicin, the potent chemical in chiles responsible for their heat. About 80 percent of the capsaicin in chiles is contained in the seeds and internal ribs, and these are often removed to modify the fiery effects of capsaicin. Another method of protecting your hands is to rub your fingers with vegetable oil; doing so helps prevent the capsaicin from penetrating the skin. In any event, be particularly careful not to touch your eyes or face when working with chiles, and always wash your hands thoroughly afterwards. You can neutralize capsaicin on your fingers by washing them in a mixture of 1 quart water and 1 tablespoon of bleach.

In preparing all fresh chiles, wash them under running water, pat dry, and—except for rellenos or stuffed chiles—remove the stem. In those recipes that call for raw chiles (salsas, for example), remove the seeds if called for. Where seeding the chiles is not specified, bear in mind that removing the seeds will reduce the heat by about one-half; you may wish to use additional seeded chiles. Conversely, when puréeing fresh chiles, you may retain the seeds, but you should use only half as many as the number of seeded chiles called for.

fresh chiles

jalapeño

Named after the region of Jalapa, this is the most popular and well-known chile in North America. Look for firm chiles that have white streaks down the side indicating their flavor has fully developed. They are very often found in pickled form and were the first chile to be taken into outer space.

serrano

Literally means "highland" or "mountain." Look for firm, shiny chiles that are not wrinkled. The serrano is very popular in Asian-influenced cuisines. This chile is similar in flavor to the jalapeño but is somewhat hotter and a little more acidic.

habanero

A close cousin of the Caribbean Scotch Bonnet, this is the hottest chile on the planet, registering some 450,000 units on the Scoville index. It comes in a variety of colors, including green, yellow, orange, and red.

poblano

A dark-green chile that tapers down to a point and is about 4 to 6 inches long. This chile is most often used for chile rellenos. It's relatively mild, about 3 to 4 on the heat scale, and is best when roasted and peeled.

anaheim

Named for the city of Anaheim, California, where it was grown as a variety of the New Mexico chile and renamed. This long (5 to 6 inches), relatively mild chile is also an excellent choice for rellenos.

cayenne

Almost always sold in its dried state, this chile is very popular as a powder. It's quite pungent, registering about an 8 on the heat scale. Cayenne is used extensively in Cajun and Creole cookery.

thai chile

A slightly less incendiary substitute for the habanero, this chile is becoming more popular in this country. One Thai chile is equal to approximately 3 serranos.

chilaca

This long, narrow, twisting chile is usually found in its dried state where it's known as the pasilla. Its colors range from a deep green to dark brown or purple.

dried chiles

The process of drying chiles concentrates their natural sugars and intensifies their flavors, giving sauces complex nuances of flavor as well as spiciness. The two most commonly used dried chiles in this book (and in Texas cooking in general) are the ancho (the dried poblano), which has mellow, sweet tones of chocolate, coffee, and raisin; and the chipotle (the dried smoked jalapeño), which has a smoky, earthy flavor of chocolate and tobacco tones. Other dried chiles include the cascabel, with a smoky and nutty flavor; the guajillo, with tones of greenness and berry; the pasilla (or chile negro), which has berry and herbaceous flavors; and the chile pequin, whose citrus and nut tones go particularly well in salsas.

Select dried chiles that are clean and not discolored; they should not be too brittle or broken. Freshly dried chiles will be relatively soft and supple, with a distinct aroma. Dried chiles are best used within a few months and should be stored in an airtight container in a dry, cool place.

Most dried chiles are roasted and rehydrated before processing into a chile purée.

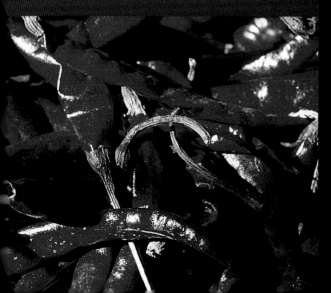

ancho

A ripe poblano chile that has been dried, this is the most commonly used dried chile in Texas and Mexico. It has an earthy, smoky flavor and is a preferred chile for purées and powder.

cascabel

Rounded, reddish-brown, and smooth, this chile looks like the harmless American cherry pepper. It's about a 4 to 5 on the heat scale, and its loose seeds make a rattling sound when shaken, hence its name—"rattler" in Spanish.

chipotle

A smoked dried jalapeño that is a favorite in Mexico, Texas, and the American Southwest. The smoky, earthy smell of the chipotle permeates the markets of Mexico with its unmistakable aroma. This chile is especially good as a purée or as a powder. Chipotles in adobo is one of the few canned products I recommend. They have a very complex flavor from being rehydrated with tomatoes and spices.

mora

A brownish, smoked and dried jalapeño, similar to the chipotle but smaller. An even smaller version is the morita, which is equal in heat, but orange-red to brown in color.

de arbol

Meaning "of the tree" or "treelike," this chile gets its name from the woody, treelike shape of its branches. It delivers quite a pungent heat and is closely related to the cayenne. I often infuse this chile with my cooking oils.

guajillo

This shiny, orange-red chile with some brown tones is a beautiful chile for making powder and purées. It's mild to moderately hot and has a bit of a tannic, yet sweet, finish.

pasilla

A dried chilaca, this chile's name means "little raisin." Long, dark, and wrinkled, this is an imperative ingredient in many moles. The pasilla is usually not too hot (about 3 to 4 on the heat scale) but is long on flavor with smoky, dried fruit overtones.

pequín

This is a small chile that delivers a fiery heat. It's about 1/2 inch long and 1/4 inch wide and has a beautiful shiny orange-red color.

roasting fresh chiles and bell peppers

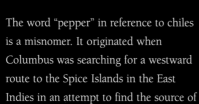

The word "pepper" in reference to chiles is a misnomer. It originated when Columbus was searching for a westward route to the Spice Islands in the East Indies in an attempt to find the source of the highly valued black pepper spice. Instead, he landed in the West Indies and discovered a plant bearing small red berries that resembled unripe black pepper berries. Columbus called these "peppers." He had actually encountered a type of chile that, like all others, is native to the New World. "Peppers" were brought back to Europe, and the botanically incorrect name has stuck ever since. Just remember, a pepper is a spice; a chile is a fruit.

Roasting chiles and bell peppers (which are actually chiles) concentrates their natural sugars and imparts a more intense, smoky flavor to these ingredients. Roasting also makes removing the skin of the chiles or bell peppers an easier task, as more than one grateful cook has noticed.

The process of roasting chiles or bell peppers blisters and blackens the skin on all sides without burning through the flesh. If being prepared whole, they should be roasted quickly and turned frequently. Several methods work well: They can be roasted on a grill, placed under a broiler, set on a wire rack over an open flame on top of the stove, or dipped in hot oil and then transferred to ice water. They can also be halved, seeded, and roasted on a baking sheet lined with parchment or wax paper in a 400°F oven for 20 minutes or until the skin blackens.

If the primary purpose is to peel the chiles or bell peppers rather than to provide flavor (preferable for preparing rellenos or stuffed chiles, for example), I recommend the hot oil method, as it allows the skin to be removed while keeping the texture intact for further use. Simply dip them in hot oil (about 375°F) until the skin blisters. Immediately place the blistered chiles in ice water.

For the other methods, place the charred chiles or bell peppers in a large paper bag and twist to secure, or place in a bowl covered with plastic wrap. Let them "steam" for 20 minutes or until cool, when they will be ready to peel with your fingers or sharp knife. Split open with a knife and remove the seeds and stem (unless preparing rellenos). For greater manageability of bell peppers, I recommend halving and seeding them *before* roasting. Roast them cut side down. Chiles and bell peppers can be roasted ahead of time and kept, chilled, up to 3 days.

puréeing dried chiles

A number of recipes in this book call for chile
purée, most often in sauces.

The first step in this process is to wash and
thoroughly dry the chiles. Cut off the stems
and slit open the dried chiles with a knife
and remove the seeds before roasting.

Heat the oven to 450°F, place the chiles in a
single layer on a baking sheet, and roast for
1 minute. Alternatively, dried chiles may be
dry-roasted over high heat in a skillet or on a
comal until they puff up, about 30 seconds to
2 minutes, depending on the heat of the skillet.

Transfer the chiles to a bowl, cover with warm
water, and submerge for 30 minutes to rehydrate.

Strain the chiles and reserve the liquid. Place the chiles in a blender and
purée to a thick paste, adding just enough of the soaking liquid to make
puréeing possible. Pass the purée through a medium or fine strainer and
strain directly into a sauce for a final product or reserve for later use.

selecting and preparing
pure chile powder

Many recipes in this book call for *pure chile powder*. I like to
differentiate between commercial chile powder, which contains
extraneous ingredients such as black pepper, salt, sugar, cumin,
garlic, and anti-caking agents, and the real thing, which is 100
percent ground dried chiles.

If you buy pure chile powder, look for a brick-red color, a slightly lumpy texture
(which shows that the natural oils are still present), and an intense, earthy smell.

To prepare your own chile powder, take a mixture (or single type) of dried chiles
such as anchos, chipotles, and guajillos. Preheat the oven to 300°F. Slit the chiles
open with a knife to remove the seeds before roasting. Place
the chiles in a single layer on a baking sheet and roast until
thoroughly dry and stiff, about 3 to 5 minutes.

Remove the dried chiles from the oven and crumble into a
bowl. Place in a spice grinder and grind them to a powder.
Store in an airtight container in a cool dry place for up to
1 month.

salsas,

condiments, and basics

tomatillo-habanero salsa

The combination of tomatillos and habaneros is one of my favorite flavor combinations. Here, the rich fatty avocado is counterbalanced by the acidulated, crunchy tomatillo.

4 garlic cloves, minced

4 scallions, chopped

16 medium tomatillos, husked and diced into $1/4$-inch pieces

1 tablespoon chopped fresh cilantro

1 habanero, seeded and minced

2 teaspoons fresh lime juice (about 1 lime)

Salt to taste

Purée the garlic, scallions, and half the tomatillos in a food processor. Combine the purée in a large bowl with the other half of the tomatillos and the cilantro, habanero, lime juice, and salt. Let stand for at least 30 minutes before serving. Serve at room temperature.

griddled salsa roja

It's essential that the tomatoes become deeply blackened to develop the smoky sweetness prevalent in this salsa.

6 medium-size ripe tomatoes, halved

2 tablespoons olive oil

1 cup sliced onions

6 medium jalapeños, seeded and sliced

4 garlic cloves, chopped

1 tablespoon chipotle purée (page 15) or 1 chipotle in adobo

$1/2$ cup chopped fresh cilantro

$1/2$ cup fresh lime juice (about 6 to 8 medium limes or 1 pound)

2 teaspoons salt

Heat a large cast-iron skillet on high for 3 minutes or until smoking. Place the tomatoes cut side down in the hot skillet; cook until charred and somewhat soft. Flip the tomatoes over and continue cooking 2 more minutes. Remove the tomatoes from the skillet and reduce the heat to medium; let the skillet stand on the medium heat for 2 minutes.

Add the olive oil, onion, jalapeños, and garlic to the hot skillet. Cook for 3 minutes or until the vegetables are soft, stirring occasionally.

Place the onion mixture, charred tomatoes, and chipotle purée in a food processor and blend well. Transfer to a serving bowl. Stir in the cilantro, lime juice, and salt. Serve at room temperature.

primo guacamole

Avocados, like tomatoes, are fruits. They are high in carotene, protein, and vitamins E and C—and their fat content is actually lower than most people think. Better yet, this native Mexican fruit has long had a reputation as an aphrodisiac. For best results, choose ripe, unblemished avocados and those that give gently when pressed.

$1/4$ cup finely diced onion

2 garlic cloves, minced

2 serranos, seeded and diced

1 teaspoon chopped fresh cilantro

Juice of 1 lime

$1/2$ teaspoon salt

2 large very ripe avocados, peeled, pitted, and chopped

1 large ripe tomato, blanched, peeled, seeded, and diced (page 5)

Combine the onion, garlic, serranos, cilantro, lime juice, and salt in a molcajete or mortar and pestle. Using the pestle of the molcajete, pulverize the mixture in the base. Add the avocados and tomato and continue to mash until thoroughly combined. Serve immediately.

pico de gallo

Literally meaning the "beak of a rooster," this simple but ubiquitous relish probably got its name in Mexico from the way it was eaten, with thumb and forefinger, mimicking the pecking action of a rooster. Pico de gallo varies from state to state in Mexico, even incorporating such diverse ingredients as jícama, orange, and pineapple. In Texas, however, this recipe is the "real deal."

5 medium-size ripe tomatoes, seeded and diced into $1/4$-inch pieces

1 tablespoon chopped fresh cilantro

1 garlic clove, minced

$1/2$ cup minced onion

Juice of $1/2$ lime

2 serranos, seeded and minced

Salt to taste

Combine all the ingredients in a medium bowl. Let stand for at least 30 minutes. Serve chilled or at room temperature.

morita salsita

The morita is a smoky, smaller cousin of the chipotle. I was first served a "salsita" in northern Vera Cruz, where my dear friend, the prolific author Patricia Quintana has a ranch. They were jam like in texture with a sweet, acidic, and fiery flavor that became addictive. Substitute chipotles if moritas are unavailable.

1 medium onion, coarsely chopped

4 garlic cloves

2 tablespoons water

1/2 cup sugar

1/3 cup fresh lime juice (4 to 6 limes)

1/2 cup morita purée (page 15)

2 tablespoons chopped fresh cilantro

Salt to taste

Purée the onion, garlic, and water in a food processor until fairly smooth, about 2 minutes. Transfer the mixture to a small saucepan. Add the sugar and bring the mixture to a gentle boil until it turns a deep blue-green color, about 12 minutes. Strain through a fine sieve and reserve both solids and liquid.

Combine the reserved solids with the lime juice and the remaining ingredients in a small bowl. Add the reserved liquid as needed for desired consistency. Serve chilled or at room temperature with Molasses Grilled Quail (page 134).

avocado-tomatillo salsa

This all-purpose salsa tastes fabulous with everything from taquitos to turkey, and the brilliant green color makes for a striking presentation.

2 large avocados, peeled, pitted, and diced

1 teaspoon diced red bell pepper

1 teaspoon diced green bell pepper

1 tablespoon diced scallion

4 medium tomatillos, husked and diced

1 garlic clove, minced

2 tablespoons chopped fresh cilantro

2 serranos, seeded and diced

2 teaspoons fresh lime juice (about 1 lime)

3 tablespoons olive oil

Salt to taste

Combine the avocados, bell peppers, scallion, and half the tomatillos in a large mixing bowl. Place the garlic, cilantro, serranos, lime juice, and remaining tomatillos in a blender and purée until smooth. Slowly drizzle in the olive oil. Add the purée to the avocado mixture; combine thoroughly and season with salt. Let stand for at least 30 minutes before serving. Serve chilled with Shrimp Taquitos (page 61) or Tuna Escabeche Tacos (page 138).

pinto-papaya relish

I love the combination of beans and fruit, especially fruit of the tropical variety. This dish works just as well as a side dish as it does a relish.

1 cup cooked pinto beans (page 7)

4 tablespoons diced papaya

2 tomatillos, husked and diced

1 small garlic clove, minced

2 scallions, thinly sliced (white parts only)

1 serrano, seeded and minced

2 teaspoons chopped fresh cilantro

$1/4$ cup roasted fresh corn kernels (page 5)

1 tablespoon fresh lime juice (about 1 lime)

2 tablespoons Texas Vinaigrette (page 36)

Combine all the ingredients in a large bowl; mix thoroughly. Let stand for at least 1 hour before serving. Serve chilled with Barbecued Duck and Wild Mushroom Tamales (page 154).

cucumber-jalapeño salsa

The sweet crunch of the cucumber makes the perfect foil to the spicy jalapeño and the acidic lime.

2 medium cucumbers, peeled, seeded, and diced

2 jalapeños, seeded and minced

1 tablespoon pure chile powder (page 15)

1 tablespoon sugar

Juice of 1 lime

1 tablespoon chopped fresh cilantro

Salt to taste

Combine all the ingredients in a medium bowl; mix well. Chill for at least 30 minutes before serving to allow the flavors to meld.

black bean-jícama salsa

Jícama lends that perfect crunch to an otherwise bland consistency. And the addition of black beans and mango makes this dish the perfect accompaniment to grilled fish or chicken.

1 cup cooked black beans (page 7)

$1/2$ cup peeled, diced ($1/4$-inch pieces) jícama

4 tablespoons diced mango

2 tomatillos, husked and diced

1 small garlic clove, minced

1 medium-size red bell pepper, seeded and finely diced

1 medium-size yellow bell pepper, seeded and finely diced

2 scallions, thinly sliced (white parts only)

2 serranos, seeded and minced

2 teaspoons chopped fresh cilantro

$1/4$ cup roasted fresh corn kernels (page 5)

2 teaspoons fresh lime juice (about 1 lime)

2 tablespoons Texas Vinaigrette (page 36)

Salt to taste

Combine all the ingredients in a large bowl; mix thoroughly. Let stand for at least 1 hour before serving. Serve at room temperature with Coriander Cured Beef Tenderloin (page 60).

green tomato chutney

This chutney is especially good with black-eyed peas stewed with ham hocks. Try it as a dressing on a ham sandwich, or for a new twist on an old favorite, how about a BL(Green)T?

6 medium-size green tomatoes (about 1 pound), chopped

2 small red bell peppers, seeded and diced

1 small green bell pepper, seeded and diced

8 scallions, thinly sliced

4 jalapeños, seeded and minced

$2/3$ cup red wine vinegar

$1/2$ cup roasted fresh corn kernels (1 small ear) (page 5)

$1/4$ cup firmly packed light brown sugar

1 tablespoon chopped fresh cilantro

1 teaspoon salt

1 garlic clove, minced

$1/4$ teaspoon cayenne powder

$1/4$ teaspoon ground cumin

Combine all the ingredients in a large saucepan; bring to a boil, stirring frequently. Reduce the heat and cook gently for 30 to 35 minutes or until thick, stirring occasionally. Cool completely. Chill, covered, until ready to serve with Pork Tenderloin (page 139).

pineapple-corn relish

I believe pineapple and corn have a real affinity for each other, and this relish is no exception. Try it with smoked dishes such as pork or chicken for a pleasing combination.

1 tablespoon olive oil

1 1/2 cups roasted fresh corn kernels (page 5)

1/2 small pineapple, peeled, cored, and diced

1 tablespoon minced onion

1 tablespoon roasted garlic purée (page 4)

2 tablespoons pasilla purée (page 15)

1 teaspoon chopped fresh cilantro

1 teaspoon chopped fresh basil

Combine all the ingredients in a medium bowl; mix well. Let stand for at least 1 hour before serving. Serve at room temperature with Sugar Cane–Skewered Shrimp (page 120).

cranberry-pecan relish

This relish brings the spirit of the autumn holidays to the table. The pecan—the state nut of Texas, no less—combined with cranberries and orange creates a holy "Lone Star trinity" of sorts, revered from one end of the state to the other.

1 cup cranberries

Juice of 1/2 orange

1/3 cup sugar

2 roasted red bell peppers, peeled, seeded, and diced (page 14)

3 tablespoons chopped fresh cilantro

2 tablespoons chopped pecans, toasted (page 5)

Zest of 1/2 lime

Zest of 1/2 orange

Salt to taste

Blend the cranberries, orange juice, and sugar in a food processor for 30 to 45 seconds. Transfer to a mixing bowl and add the roasted bell peppers, cilantro, pecans, citrus zests, and salt. Let stand for at least 30 minutes before serving. Serve chilled.

mole negro

"Mole" comes from the Nahautl mulli, meaning "sauce." Moles differ from region to region and even from cook to cook. The moles of Oaxaca are probably the best known; the most famous of these is the Mole Negro. Once a guest of a family in Oaxaca, I had the pleasure of observing the preparation of a traditional dark mole, with each ingredient being carefully ground on the metate. As is the case with many parts of rural Oaxaca, most of the food preparation is done not in the house itself, but in an adjacent outbuilding serving as la cocina. Serve this rich sauce with poultry or pork.

2 tablespoons coriander seeds

$1/2$ teaspoon cumin seeds

2 teaspoons corn oil

1 medium onion, peeled and chopped

1 medium carrot, peeled and chopped

1 stalk celery, chopped

4 garlic cloves, crushed

$1/2$ cup sherry

8 Roma tomatoes, charred

2 Granny Smith apples, cored and chopped

4 tablespoons vegetable shortening

1 bay leaf

$1/2$ cup pepitas

$1/2$ cup sliced almonds

$3/4$ cup raisins

2 pasillas, stemmed and seeded

2 anchos, stemmed and seeded

1 large ripe plantain, peeled and fried

$1/3$ cup black sesame seeds

1 canela stick

2 allspice berries

1 whole clove

$1/2$ teaspoon dried basil

$1/2$ teaspoon dried thyme

$1/2$ gallon chicken stock (page 33)

4 ounces Mexican chocolate

2 tablespoons roasted garlic purée (page 4)

Salt to taste

Toast the coriander and cumin seeds in a dry sauté pan until fragrant; remove from the heat. Heat the corn oil in a large saucepan until lightly smoking. Add the onion, carrot, and celery. Cook over high heat for 7 to 8 minutes or until the vegetables are well caramelized, stirring occasionally.

Add the garlic and cook for 1 more minute. Add the sherry to deglaze the pan, cooking until the mixture is reduced to a syrup. Add the charred tomatoes and apples; cook over low heat for about 20 minutes or until the tomatoes and apples are thick and pasty.

Heat the vegetable shortening in a frying pan until lightly smoking. Fry the bay leaf, pepitas, almonds, raisins, pasillas, anchos, plantain, sesame seeds, canela, allspice, and clove in small batches to a golden or dark brown; place on paper towels to drain. Reserve the shortening for refrying the sauce.

Add the fried foods, toasted seeds, basil, thyme, chicken stock, chocolate, and garlic purée to the sauce; simmer for 10 minutes. Blend the sauce in batches in a food processor or blender until very smooth. Pass through a fine sieve or chinois.

Place the reserved shortening in a large saucepan with high sides; heat until lightly smoking. Slowly pour the sauce into the pan, being careful of the hot grease. The sauce will slowly come to a simmer. Reduce the heat and continue to simmer for 10 to 12 minutes or until the sauce reaches a consistency of heavy cream. Season with salt to taste.

pineapple mole

Redolent of spices and fruit, this time-consuming dish is well worth the effort. I serve this mole with foie gras tamales at Star Canyon. A mole should be prepared in large portions. Fortunately, this one freezes well.

1 quart chicken stock (page 33)

6 ounces dried pineapple

1 yellow tomato, chopped

1/2 fresh pineapple, peeled and chopped

1/2 cup sherry

1 cinnamon or canela stick

3 tablespoons golden raisins

1/2 teaspoon cumin

1 teaspoon pure chile powder (page 15)

1 small onion, peeled and chopped

3 garlic cloves, chopped

1 serrano, seeded and chopped

2 anchos, stemmed and seeded

1/3 cup sliced almonds

1/4 cup sesame seeds

3 fried corn tortillas

1 pinch ground cloves

1/4 teaspoon ground allspice

1 ounce white chocolate chips or chopped white chocolate bar

2 tablespoons vegetable shortening

Salt to taste

Preheat the oven to 350°F.

Combine the chicken stock, dried pineapple, tomato, fresh pineapple, sherry, cinnamon, raisins, cumin, and chile powder in a large saucepan; bring to a boil. Reduce the heat and simmer for 10 minutes.

Combine the onion, garlic, serrano, anchos, almonds, sesame seeds, and tortillas on a baking sheet; toast in the oven until the tortillas are dark, about 10 minutes. Remove from the oven and crumble the tortillas. Add the toasted ingredients to the saucepan.

Add the cloves, allspice, and chocolate to the saucepan; stir well. Transfer the mixture in batches to a blender. Purée each batch on high speed for about 2 minutes or until smooth.

Heat the shortening in a large saucepan until lightly smoking. Add the puréed sauce to the pan and reduce the heat. Fry for 15 minutes or until thickened, being careful of spattering grease. Remove from the heat and strain through a fine sieve or chinois. Season with salt to taste. Serve warm.

mayonnaise

Absolutely, positively no comparison to store-bought. This French classic is an easy and necessary component to every good cook's repertoire.

2 large egg yolks, at room temperature

2 teaspoons fresh lemon juice

$3/_4$ teaspoon salt

Freshly ground black pepper to taste

1 teaspoon Dijon mustard

$1/_2$ cup peanut, canola, or safflower oil

$1/_2$ cup extra-virgin olive oil, at room temperature

Whisk together the yolks, lemon juice, salt, pepper, and mustard in a medium bowl. Combine the oils separately and drizzle them into the yolks, whisking continuously. Continue to whisk until thoroughly incorporated. Season to taste with additional salt and pepper.

lemon-horseradish mayonnaise

The combination of lemon and horseradish makes a condiment that works equally well with fish or beef. Try it on your favorite barbecue sandwich.

2 large egg yolks, at room temperature

$3/_4$ teaspoon salt

1 tablespoon prepared horseradish

1 tablespoon lemon zest

2 tablespoons fresh lemon juice (about 1 small lemon)

1 teaspoon Dijon mustard

$1/_2$ cup canola or other vegetable oil

$1/_2$ cup extra-virgin olive oil, at room temperature

Salt (optional)

Combine the egg yolks, salt, horseradish, lemon zest, lemon juice, and mustard in a food processor; blend for 15 seconds. Combine the oils in a measuring cup. Drizzle $3/_4$ cup of the oil mixture into the food processor through the feed tube, making sure all the oil gets incorporated. Stop the machine and check the consistency. If it is too thick, add a small amount of water; if too thin, add more oil. Check the flavor and add more lemon juice and salt if necessary.

chipotle chile aïoli

Chipotles are finally getting the widespread recognition they deserve. These smoked jalapeños add a zip to this otherwise classic garlic mayonnaise.

2 large egg yolks, at room temperature

1 tablespoon red wine vinegar

$1/2$ cup corn oil, at room temperature

$1/4$ cup olive oil, at room temperature

$1/4$ teaspoon chipotle purée (page 15)

$1/4$ teaspoon paprika

$1/4$ teaspoon pure chile powder (page 15)

$1/4$ teaspoon cayenne powder

$1/2$ teaspoon salt

$1/2$ shallot, minced

1 small garlic clove, minced

1 teaspoon fresh lime juice (about $1/2$ lime)

Whisk together the egg yolks and vinegar in a mixing bowl. Combine the oils in a measuring cup. Drizzle the oil into the yolks while continuing to whisk the mixture.

Add the remaining ingredients and whisk just long enough to combine thoroughly. Serve chilled with Gulf Coast Seafood Chowder (page 122).

saffron aïoli

16 threads saffron

2 tablespoons hot water

3 tablespoons minced garlic

2 large egg yolks, at room temperature

2 tablespoons fresh lemon juice

$1/2$ teaspoon salt

$1 1/4$ cups extra-virgin olive oil, at room temperature

Combine the saffron with the hot water in a small bowl and let steep for 15 minutes. Combine the garlic with the egg yolks, lemon juice, and salt in a medium bowl. Slowly drizzle in the oil, whisking continuously until thickened. Add the saffron water, and stir until incorporated. Serve with Fried Oyster Tostadas (page 95).

master tamale dough

This is the basic dough that I use as the foundation for many of my tamales.

1³/₄ cups masa harina

1¹/₄ cups hot water

10 tablespoons vegetable shortening, chilled

1¹/₂ teaspoons salt

1 teaspoon baking powder

¹/₄ cup chicken stock, chilled (page 33)

Place the masa harina in the bowl of an electric mixer fitted with a paddle attachment. Add the water in a slow, steady stream with the mixer on low speed until the dough forms a ball. Continue mixing on medium speed for 5 minutes. Transfer the dough to a clean bowl and chill for 1 hour.

Return the chilled dough to the bowl of the electric mixer. Beat for 5 minutes on high speed. With the machine still running, slowly add the shortening in 2-tablespoon increments. Continue mixing, scraping the sides of the bowl occasionally, until the dough is smooth and light, about 5 minutes.

Combine the salt, baking powder, and chicken stock in a small bowl. Slowly pour the stock mixture into the masa in a steady stream, mixing until thoroughly combined. Mix for 5 minutes more on high speed.

veal demi-glace

6 pounds veal bones

1 large onion, halved

¹/₂ garlic head

1 cup chopped carrots

1 cup chopped celery

6 to 8 sprigs fresh thyme or 1 teaspoon dried

6 bay leaves

1 cup chopped fresh parsley

¹/₂ teaspoon black peppercorns

6 large tomatoes, chopped

6 ounces canned tomato paste

2 quarts red wine (8 cups)

6 quarts water or chicken stock

Preheat the oven to 450°F. Place the bones in a roasting pan and bake until well browned on all sides, about 2 hours. Add the onion, garlic, carrots, and celery for the last 30 minutes of cooking.

Remove the pan from the oven and place the ingredients in a large stockpot. Stir in the thyme, bay leaves, parsley, peppercorns, tomatoes, and tomato paste. Place the roasting pan on the stove over high heat and deglaze with the red wine, cooking for 2 minutes while scraping to dissolve any hardened or browned particles. Pour the pan liquids into the stockpot and add enough water to cover. Bring to a boil, reduce the heat, and simmer strongly for at least 6 hours. Reduce the heat further and simmer gently for an additional 4 hours. Add more water as necessary and let simmer for at least 1 hour after the last addition of liquid.

Remove from the heat and let cool. Skim off any fat and strain the stock into a clean pan. Reduce the stock by half over medium heat to enhance and intensify the flavor, skimming and stirring occasionally. Reduce by half again for a demi-glace. The stock will keep up to 1 week in the refrigerator, and up to 2 months frozen.

chicken stock

A must-have for every kitchen. No exceptions.

1/2 large, unpeeled onion

3 unpeeled garlic cloves

5 pounds raw chicken wings, backs, or necks (or a combination)

1 cup chopped carrots

1 cup chopped celery

6 to 8 sprigs fresh thyme or 1 teaspoon dried

3 bay leaves

1/2 teaspoon black peppercorns

Heat a nonstick skillet over high heat until extremely hot, about 7 minutes. Place the onion in the skillet, cut side down, and cook for 15 minutes or until completely charred. Add the garlic and cook until charred on both sides, about 5 minutes.

Place the onion and garlic in a large stockpot and add the chicken, carrots, celery, thyme, bay leaves, and peppercorns. Pour in enough water to cover. Bring to a boil, reduce the heat, and let simmer for at least 2 hours, or up to 6 hours. Add water as necessary and let simmer for 20 minutes after the last addition. Remove from the heat and let cool. Skim off any fat and strain the stock. For an even richer flavor, reduce the stock by half.

The stock will keep for 3 to 4 days chilled, and up to 2 months frozen.

brown chicken stock

This richer, more flavorful version of standard chicken stock works particularly well for hearty dishes.

5 pounds raw chicken wings, backs, or necks (or a combination)

1/2 large onion, chopped

3 garlic cloves, chopped

1 cup chopped carrots

1 cup chopped celery

6 to 8 sprigs fresh thyme or 1 teaspoon dried

3 bay leaves

2 teaspoons black peppercorns

2 quarts water, plus additional to cover

Preheat the oven to 450°F. Place the chicken pieces in a roasting pan and bake until deeply browned on all sides, about 1 hour. Add the onion, garlic, carrots, and celery for the last 30 minutes of baking.

Remove the pan from the oven and transfer the baked ingredients to a large stockpot. Add the thyme, bay leaves, and peppercorns. Place the roasting pan over high heat on the stove; deglaze with 2 quarts of water by scraping to dissolve any hardened, browned particles for about 2 minutes. Pour the liquid into the stockpot and add enough water to cover.

Bring to a boil, reduce the heat, and simmer strongly for 3 hours. Reduce the heat further and simmer gently for an additional 2 hours. Add more water as necessary and let simmer for 1 hour after the last addition.

Remove from the heat and let cool. Skim off any fat and strain the stock into a clean pan. Reduce the stock by three quarters over medium heat, skimming and stirring occasionally, until the stock is very brown and rich.

The stock will keep for up to 1 week chilled, and up to 2 months frozen.

honey-garlic marinade

Don't limit this marinade to poultry—try it on your favorite vegetables, too. The honey caramelizes particularly nicely when it's grilled or sautéed.

1/2 cup soy sauce

1/4 cup dark beer

2 tablespoons honey

Zest of 1 lemon, blanched

Zest of 1 orange, blanched

1 tablespoon chopped lemon verbena

4 tablespoons peeled, minced ginger

2 garlic cloves, minced

Combine all the ingredients in a medium bowl; mix well. Use as a marinade for fish or poultry.

habanero-orange marinade

I love the combination of orange and habanero. One habanero, measuring an incredible 450,000 units on the Scoville scale, goes a long way to adding fire to your food.

1 cup fresh orange juice (about 1 pound oranges)

1/2 cup fresh lemon juice (about 1/2 pound lemons)

1/2 cup olive oil

4 garlic cloves, minced

2 teaspoons black peppercorns, cracked

3 bay leaves, crushed

3 tablespoons chopped fresh cilantro

1 habanero, stemmed, seeded, and minced

Combine all the ingredients in a medium bowl; mix well. Let stand at room temperature for at least 30 minutes to develop the flavors. Use as a marinade for fish, poultry, or fajitas.

molasses-balsamic glaze

Molasses is the brownish-black liquid that is left over from the refining process of sugar cane or sugar beets. It is more healthful than sugar and has a rich caramel flavor. Although this simple reduction was created for a salad, it can also be used to enliven fish or chicken.

1 cup balsamic vinegar

1 cup molasses

Bring the vinegar and molasses to a boil in a small saucepan. Reduce by half to a glaze and remove from the heat. Use to garnish salads. In particular, serve with Vine-Ripened Tomato Salad (page 57).

texas vinaigrette

I call this a Texas vinaigrette because I've given it a dose of cumin and cilantro. It's a good dressing to have on hand and is useful for just about any salad or relish. I even simply sprinkle it over a piece of grilled fish when I'm eating on the run.

$2^1/_2$ tablespoons balsamic vinegar

$2^1/_2$ tablespoons red wine vinegar

1 cup olive oil

1 cup vegetable oil

1 small serrano, seeded and minced

1 teaspoon chopped fresh cilantro

1 teaspoon chopped fresh thyme

1 teaspoon chopped fresh basil

$^1/_2$ teaspoon cumin

2 teaspoons Dijon mustard

$1^1/_2$ tablespoons roasted garlic purée (page 4)

$^1/_2$ teaspoon salt

Freshly ground black pepper to taste

Combine the vinegars in a mixing bowl. Combine the oils in a measuring cup. Drizzle the oils into the vinegars while whisking continuously. Whisk in the remaining ingredients. Toss with your favorite salad.

coriander cure

Cures such as this recipe date back centuries before the advent of refrigeration. The salt preserved the meat, which was most usually smoked. We use this cure on beef tenderloin, but it tastes just as delicious on pork, lamb, and game.

4 tablespoons coriander seeds

4 tablespoons black peppercorns

4 shallots

6 garlic cloves

3/4 cup kosher salt

6 tablespoons light brown sugar

Pulsate the coriander and black peppercorns in a food processor for about 1 minute or until coarsely ground. Add the shallots, garlic, kosher salt, and sugar, and process to a thick paste. Marinate the meat of your choice in the mixture for at least 3 hours, turning occasionally, or use with Coriander Cured Beef Tenderloin (page 60).

brisket rub

1/4 cup salt

2 tablespoons freshly ground black pepper

2 tablespoons paprika

1 tablespoon cayenne powder

Combine all the ingredients together in a small bowl. Store in a dry, cool place in an airtight container until ready to use with the Sourdough Chicken Fried Steak (page 76) or other meat of your choice.

texas tapas and cocktails

smoked chicken nachos
with avocados, black beans, and monterey jack cheese

These nachos make a great prelude to a Mexican or Texican feast, and work just as well as snacks for watching the game on TV. I served so many of these at one of my restaurants, the chef asked if we could build a Smoked Chicken Nacho annex for preparation.

NACHOS

1 chicken (about 3 pounds)

1 gallon Brine

Vegetable or canola oil for frying

16 corn tortillas, cut into quarters

Salt to taste

1 1/2 cups diced avocado

1 cup cooked black beans (page 7)

4 cups grated Monterey Jack or Asiago cheese

3 cups Pico de Gallo (page 20)

Sour cream for garnish

BRINE

4 quarts water (1 gallon)

1 cup kosher salt

1/2 cup dark brown sugar, tightly packed

1 bay leaf

1 tablespoon chopped fresh thyme

1/2 teaspoon black peppercorns

2 cloves

1 garlic clove, crushed

1 teaspoon cayenne powder

NACHOS (YIELDS 6 TO 8 SERVINGS)

Marinate the chicken in brine overnight in the refrigerator.

Prepare the smoker (page 7). Remove the chicken from the brine, pat dry, and smoke for 1 1/2 hours or until the breast meat is firm but springs back when squeezed. If necessary, finish cooking in a 350°F oven until done.

Preheat the oven to 350°F.

Heat enough oil in a large skillet to come 1/2 inch up the side. Fry the tortilla quarters until crisp. Drain thoroughly on paper towels and lightly salt.

Remove the meat from the chicken and dice into 1/4-inch pieces. Combine the avocado, beans, and chicken in a medium bowl. Spread the tortilla chips on a baking sheet, cover with the diced chicken mixture, and sprinkle with the cheese. Bake for 15 minutes or until the cheese has completely melted.

To serve, spoon Pico de Gallo on top of the nachos and garnish with sour cream.

BRINE

Combine all the ingredients in a large stockpot and bring to a boil over medium heat, stirring often. Reduce the heat and simmer for 5 minutes. Remove from the heat and let cool before using.

jalapeños stuffed with chorizo and goat cheese

These stuffed chiles were a staple of our holiday table growing up. We called them jalapeño poppers because we always had a contest to see who could pop the most in their mouths without bringing out the fire extinguisher.

1 tablespoon vegetable oil

1 tablespoon finely minced onion

1 garlic clove, finely minced

3 ounces chorizo sausage

3 ounces goat cheese

1 tablespoon sour cream

Salt to taste

12 fresh or pickled jalapeños, halved, seeded, and deribbed

(YIELDS 24 STUFFED JALAPEÑO HALVES)

Heat the oil in a skillet; add the onion and garlic and sauté over medium heat for 2 to 3 minutes or until translucent. Add the chorizo and cook for 5 minutes or until done, breaking up the meat with a fork as it cooks. Remove the skillet from the heat and cool slightly. Stir in the goat cheese and sour cream; season with salt. Spoon the mixture into the jalapeño halves and serve.

shrimp flautas
with mango–red pepper relish

These little shrimp "flutes" are like crisp taquitos and make great cocktail hors d'oeuvres. They can also be served as a garnish for a fish dish. The tropical sweetness from the mango provides a nice complement to the savory shrimp and the tart tomatillo. Crunchy on the outside and soft and chewy in the center, they always stimulate my taste buds. Once you make this Mango–Red Pepper Relish, you'll see that these ingredients not only make a good gustatory combination, but are visually striking as well.

FLAUTAS

1 tablespoon vegetable oil

$^1/_2$ cup finely diced onion

2 garlic cloves, minced

1 jalapeño, seeded and minced

2 tomatillos, husked and minced

1 poblano, roasted, peeled, seeded, and diced (page 14)

$^1/_2$ cup chicken stock (page 33)

1 cup finely diced cooked shrimp

1 tablespoon chopped fresh cilantro

Salt and freshly ground black pepper to taste

2 tablespoons sour cream

Vegetable or canola oil for softening and deep-frying tortillas

12 corn tortillas

Mango–Red Pepper Relish

MANGO–RED PEPPER RELISH

1 mango, peeled, pitted, and julienned

1 red bell pepper, roasted, peeled, seeded, and julienned (page 14)

1 poblano, roasted, peeled, seeded, and julienned (page 14)

1 tablespoon diced scallion

1 teaspoon fresh lime juice (about $^1/_2$ lime)

3 tablespoons olive oil

1 teaspoon chopped fresh cilantro

1 serrano, seeded and diced

Salt to taste

FLAUTAS (YIELDS 12 FLAUTAS)

Heat the oil in a large skillet over high heat. Add the onion, garlic, and jalapeño, and sauté until the onion is translucent, about 2 minutes. Add the tomatillos and poblano, and cook for 30 seconds more. Add the stock and shrimp, and continue cooking until the stock is reduced to a glaze. Add the cilantro and season with salt and pepper. Stir in the sour cream. Remove from the heat and cool slightly.

Pour enough oil into another skillet to come $^1/_2$ inch up the side. Heat on medium to 350°F or until just smoking. Submerge each of the tortillas in the oil for 5 seconds to soften. Drain each tortilla on paper towels and keep warm; do not stack the tortillas.

Divide the shrimp mixture among the tortillas. Roll each tortilla, securing the ends with toothpicks to ensure they won't unroll when fried. Add more oil to the skillet to deep-fry the flautas and reheat until just smoking. Deep-fry in batches until crisp, about 30 seconds. Drain the flautas on paper towels, being careful to remove all the toothpicks before serving. Cut them in half, if desired, and serve with Mango-Red Pepper Relish.

MANGO–RED PEPPER RELISH

Combine half the mango, red pepper, poblano, and scallions in a large bowl. Place the other half of the mango, red pepper, poblano, and scallions in a blender. Add the lime juice and remaining ingredients to the blender, and process until smooth. Add the puréed ingredients to the bowl and marinate for 30 minutes before serving.

smoked salmon and apple quesadillas
with horseradish crema

Just about any combination of savory tastes will mix beautifully for a quesadilla. And the combination of apples, smoked salmon, and horseradish is no exception. As for the Horseradish Crema, don't just reserve it for your quesadillas. Try it with prime rib or a good steak.

QUESADILLAS

8 ounces thinly sliced smoked salmon, julienned

1 Granny Smith apple, cored and julienned

8 ounces Monterey Jack cheese, shredded

$1/4$ cup grated Asiago

1 tablespoon chopped fresh tarragon

3 tablespoons finely diced red onion

1 teaspoon fresh lime juice (about $1/2$ lime)

4 flour tortillas, at room temperature

2 tablespoons unsalted butter ($1/4$ stick), melted

Horseradish Crema

HORSERADISH CREMA

2 tablespoons prepared horseradish

2 tablespoons chopped chives

$1/2$ cup sour cream

$1/2$ cup mayonnaise (page 30)

3 tablespoons heavy cream

1 tablespoon fresh lemon juice (about $1/2$ lemon)

1 teaspoon salt

QUESADILLAS (YIELDS 4 QUESADILLAS)

Combine the salmon, apple, cheeses, tarragon, onion, and lime juice in a large bowl, mixing well. Spread one-fourth of the mixture over half of each tortilla and fold over.

Heat a large nonstick pan. Brush each tortilla with melted butter; cook at medium heat for 3 to 4 minutes on each side or until golden brown. Cut each quesadilla into 3 triangles and serve with Horseradish Crema.

HORSERADISH CREMA

Whisk all the ingredients together in a large bowl.

sweet and spicy pecans

sweet and spicy pecans

These are always a hit at a cocktail party, as they go particularly well with mixed drinks, beer, and wine. Or, for something more sophisticated, try them as a garnish for your favorite salad, or serve with ripe pears or apples for a classic dessert.

2 tablespoons unsalted butter
($^1/_4$ stick)

3 cups pecan halves

$^1/_2$ cup firmly packed light
brown sugar

1 teaspoon paprika

2 teaspoons pure chile powder
(page 15)

1 tablespoon cumin

$^1/_4$ cup apple cider vinegar

Salt to taste

(YIELDS ENOUGH TO GARNISH 6 SALADS OR SERVE 1 TAILGATE PARTY)

Preheat the oven to 350°F.

Melt the butter in a large skillet over medium heat. Add the pecans and sauté until lightly browned, about 3 minutes. Add the brown sugar and cook until lightly caramelized. Stir in the paprika, chile powder, and cumin. Add the vinegar and reduce until all the liquid has evaporated. Season with salt.

Spread the pecans on a cookie sheet. Bake until crisp, about 3 to 5 minutes. Cool and then store in an airtight container until ready to serve.

crab and queso fresco sopes
with cascabel chile aïoli

This dish is just one of the many corn masa snacks found throughout Mexico and Texas known as antojitos, or "little whimsies." These little "masa boats" are stuffed and then fried until just crunchy on the outside, hot and moist on the inside. The cascabel chile, Spanish for "rattle," gets its name from the sound it makes when shaken. At 20,000 Scoville units, it rates about a 6 or 7 on a heat scale of 1 to 10. You can substitute ancho purée (page 15) for a milder but equally visually appealing aïoli.

SOPES

2 cups masa harina

$1^{1}/_{4}$ cups hot water

2 tablespoons lard or shortening

$1/_{3}$ cup all-purpose flour

$1/_{2}$ teaspoon salt

1 teaspoon baking powder

8 ounces queso fresco or feta cheese, crumbled

8 ounces crabmeat, shell and cartilage removed

Vegetable oil for frying

Cascabel Chile Aïoli

CASCABEL CHILE AÏOLI

2 cups mayonnaise (page 30)

4 tablespoons roasted garlic purée (page 4)

1 teaspoon cascabel purée (page 15)

1 teaspoon paprika

$1/_{2}$ teaspoon pure chile powder (page 15)

$1/_{4}$ teaspoon cayenne powder

SOPES (YIELDS ABOUT 48 SOPES)

Combine the masa harina with the hot water in a large bowl; cover and let stand for 30 minutes. Add the lard, flour, salt, and baking powder to the masa harina mixture and mix thoroughly.

Divide the dough into 12 balls. Divide the 12 balls into 24, then the 24 into 48. Place the masa balls (sopes) on a cookie sheet and cover with a damp towel or plastic wrap.

Lightly oil your fingers and flatten one of the sopes by patting it between the fingers of one hand and the palm of your other hand. Place about 1 teaspoon of the cheese and 1 teaspoon of the crabmeat in the middle and enclose it with the masa dough, forming a boat or diamond shape. Repeat the process for the remaining sopes.

Pour enough oil in a large skillet to come $1/_{4}$ inch up the side; heat until lightly smoking. Fry the sopes over medium-high heat for 2 minutes per side or until golden brown. Drain on paper towels and serve warm with Cascabel Chile Aïoli for dipping.

CASCABEL CHILE AÏOLI

Place the mayonnaise in a medium bowl; add the roasted garlic and whisk until thoroughly combined. Whisk in the cascabel purée, paprika, chile powder, and cayenne.

tres bebidas

Mezcal is quickly becoming as popular in America as tequila. The centuries-old process of making mezcal remains as pure and simple as ever, using little or no modern equipment. The result is an earthy, smoky, mysterious flavor that lends itself to these three creative but familiar cocktails.

piña diablo

1 pineapple, peeled, cored, and sliced

1 vanilla bean, split in half lengthwise and scraped

2 serranos, sliced

3 canela sticks

Zest of 1 orange

$1/2$ cup fresh mint

1 quart mezcal

$1/2$ cup brown sugar

(YIELDS 12 SERVINGS)

Layer the pineapple with the vanilla bean, serranos, canela sticks, orange zest, and mint in a half-gallon, lidded jar.

Whisk the mezcal and brown sugar together in a medium mixing bowl. Heat very slightly over warm water to dissolve the sugar. Pour the mezcal over the fruit and screw the lid on tightly. Refrigerate for a couple of weeks, or longer for a stronger flavor. Ladle the mezcal over ice and serve.

infused mezcal champagne cocktail

1 cup champagne, chilled

$1/4$ cup Piña Diablo

(YIELDS 2 SERVINGS)

Combine the champagne and Piña Diablo. Serve straight in champagne flutes.

mezcolada

$1/8$ cup sugar

$1/8$ cup water

$1/4$ cup mezcal, preferably Oaxacan

$1/4$ cup coconut milk

$1/4$ cup pineapple juice

1 slice pineapple for garnish

(YIELDS 1 STIFF DRINK)

Make a simple syrup by combining the sugar and water in a small saucepan over high heat. Bring to a boil, and then immediately remove from the heat. Stir to completely dissolve the sugar; let cool completely before using.

Pour the cooled sugar water, mezcal, coconut milk, and pineapple juice into a bar shaker with ice. Shake, shake, shake. Strain into a martini glass and garnish with the pineapple slice. Serve immediately.

tres margaritas

Margaritas have long been associated with Texas and, by most accounts, were invented in Juárez, the twin city of El Paso. Exotic fruit purées or juices make good additions to the standard margarita, but don't take the shortcut of using that terrible sweet-and-sour mix. Fresh lime juice is an absolute must!

mango margarita

$^1/_2$ cup fresh lime juice (4 to 6 limes)

5 tablespoons superfine sugar

2 ripe mangos, peeled, pitted, and chopped

$^3/_4$ cup good-quality tequila (4 jiggers)

$1^1/_2$ ounces Triple Sec (1 jigger)

Crushed ice

(YIELDS 4 COCKTAILS)

Combine the lime juice and sugar in a large bowl. Let stand, stirring occasionally, until the sugar dissolves completely. Purée the chopped mangos in a blender; add the tequila, Triple Sec, and lime and sugar mixture and blend until smooth, about 30 seconds. Serve in margarita glasses over crushed ice.

cactus margarita

$^1/_2$ cup fresh lime juice (4 to 6 limes)

5 tablespoons superfine sugar

1 cup cactus pear purée

$^3/_4$ cup good quality tequila (4 jiggers)

$1^1/_2$ ounces Triple Sec (1 jigger)

Crushed ice

(YIELDS 4 COCKTAILS)

Combine the lime juice and sugar in a large bowl. Let stand, stirring occasionally, until the sugar dissolves completely. Add the cactus pear purée, tequila, and Triple Sec, combining thoroughly. Serve in margarita glasses over crushed ice.

star canyon high-hog margarita

1 cup fresh lime juice (10 to 12 limes)

5 tablespoons superfine sugar

$^3/_4$ cup Herradura Gold tequila (5 jiggers)

$1^1/_2$ ounces Grand Marnier (1 jigger)

Ice cubes

Kosher salt

(YIELDS 4 COCKTAILS)

Combine the lime juice and sugar in a large bowl. Let stand, stirring occasionally, until the sugar dissolves completely. Add the tequila, Grand Marnier, and ice cubes. Stir vigorously and strain immediately into salt-rimmed margarita glasses.

star canyon high-hog margarita

border sangrita

border sangrita

Tequila comes from the heart of a mature maguey cactus that has been roasted, shredded, and fermented. For a nice diversion, serve these at your next Sunday brunch instead of the more traditional Bloody Mary.

3 cups tomato juice

1/4 cup cocktail onions

1 small garlic clove, minced

2 teaspoons Worcestershire sauce

1 teaspoon salt

2 serranos, seeded and chopped

1/2 teaspoon dill seed

1/2 teaspoon celery seed

1 teaspoon prepared horseradish

Juice of 2 limes, plus lime wedges
    for garnish

6 ounces gold tequila (4 jiggers)

6 to 8 drops Tabasco

(YIELDS 4 COCKTAILS)

Combine all the ingredients except the lime wedges in a blender. Purée until completely smooth, about 1 minute. Strain and pour into tall, ice-filled glasses. Garnish with lime wedges.

canela-spiked pineapple daiquiris

This is a cocktail with Brazilian inspiration. The longer it sits and ferments, the more mellow and delicious (if not lethal) it becomes.

3 cups dark rum

2 cups light rum

2 cups coconut rum

2 vanilla beans, split in half lengthwise
    and scraped

2 large ripe pineapples, peeled, cored,
    and diced into 1-inch pieces

1 cup firmly packed dark brown sugar

4 jalapeños, split

5 canela sticks

3/4 cup crushed fresh mint

(YIELDS 12 TO 14 COCKTAILS)

Place all the ingredients in a large glass jar with a tight-fitting lid and stir to dissolve the sugar. Place the jar in a warm place and let stand for 1 week. Store in the refrigerator and strain into chilled martini glasses when ready to serve.

pisco sour

silver shaker of pisco sours

Pisco is a 90-proof grape liqueur from Peru that is aged in paraffin-lined containers—as opposed to wood barrels—to keep it from absorbing flavor and color. This drink takes me back to sunsets over Machu Picchu, high in the Peruvian Andes.

3/4 cup pisco

4 large egg whites

1 tablespoon superfine sugar

1/4 cup fresh lime juice (about 3 limes)

1 cup crushed ice

Angostura bitters

Lime wedges for garnish

(YIELDS 4 COCKTAILS)

Place the pisco, egg whites, sugar, lime juice, and ice in a martini shaker; shake vigorously. Strain into martini glasses and add one dash bitters to each. Garnish with lime wedges.

urban cowboy chic

Urban Cowboy Chic is a phrase I coined
to describe a certain style of cooking, and
living, for that matter. Put simply, Urban
Cowboy Chic is creative Southwestern
big-city cooking using classic techniques
in a sleek ranch setting. It seems to
effectively describe the experience we
hope our guests have at Star Canyon.
As a fifth-generation Texan, I was raised on
most of the ingredients that I cook with
today, with a few obvious additions such
as foie gras. After working in my father's
Truck Stop Cafe, I studied music in college,
then took a trip to France that would change
my life. Back in Dallas, I opened Routh
Street Cafe to much acclaim, where
I prepared food that would come to be
known as Southwestern cuisine. Ten years
later, I opened Star Canyon, where I now
practice what I call New Texas Cuisine,
the latest evolution in my Southwestern
style of cooking.

vine-ripened tomato salad

vine-ripened tomato salad
with texas mozzarella and garlic-chile croutons

This salad's roots rest deep in Italy where fresh mozzarella is abundant. My friend Paula Lambert, having lived in Umbria for many years, returned to Dallas with withdrawals from fresh Italian cheeses. In 1982, with lots of spunk and more than a little naïveté, she launched the Mozzarella Company, which now produces some of the best Italian-style cheeses in America. I keep this simple-but-delicious vinaigrette on hand at all times. It's a foolproof, all-purpose staple that no kitchen should go without.

SALAD

1 cup arugula, washed

1 medium-size red tomato, diced into 1-inch pieces

1 medium-size yellow tomato, diced into 1-inch pieces

1 small red onion, diced and blanched in boiling water for 30 seconds

1 1/2 cups Garlic-Chile Croutons

1 1/2 cups 1-inch cubed fresh mozzarella cheese

Vinaigrette

Salt to taste

3 tablespoons Molasses-Balsamic Glaze (page 36)

Freshly ground black pepper

GARLIC-CHILE CROUTONS

4 slices French or sourdough bread, crusts removed

3 tablespoons olive oil

Salt to taste

1 tablespoon roasted garlic purée (page 4)

2 teaspoons pure chile powder (page 15)

VINAIGRETTE

1/3 cup balsamic vinegar

1/4 cup red wine

3 tablespoons chopped fresh basil

1 cup olive oil

Salt to taste

SALAD (YIELDS 4 SERVINGS)

Combine the arugula, tomatoes, onion, croutons, and mozzarella in a medium bowl and toss with the Vinaigrette. Season the salad with salt.

Place one-fourth of the salad in the center of each plate. Spoon the Molasses-Balsamic Glaze around the outside of the salad, sprinkle the plate lightly with the ground pepper, and serve immediately.

GARLIC-CHILE CROUTONS

Preheat the oven to 350°F.

Slice the bread into 1-inch strips, then again into 1-inch cubes. Combine the olive oil, salt, and roasted garlic in a large bowl. Add the bread cubes, mixing thoroughly to season well. Place the bread cubes on a cookie sheet and bake until the croutons are golden brown, about 5 to 7 minutes.

Place the croutons in a bowl, sprinkle with the chile powder, and toss until thoroughly coated.

VINAIGRETTE

Whisk together the vinegar, red wine, and basil in a small bowl. Slowly drizzle in the olive oil while whisking. Season with salt.

achiote lamb chops
with wild mushroom–golden raisin empanadas

Achiote is the paste made from the seeds of the annatto tree, which grows in tropical and subtropical climates around the world. The seeds and paste are a bright orange-red; achiote is the component that is used to give American cheddar cheese its color. Although achiote imparts more color than taste, it nonetheless has a subtle earthy flavor. This empanada's ingredients give it an almost Mediterranean flavor.

LAMB CHOPS

8 rib lamb chops, about 1 inch thick

1 cup Achiote Oil

Salt to taste

ACHIOTE OIL

$^1/_4$ cup achiote seeds

1 cup olive oil

LAMB CHOPS (YIELDS 4 TO 6 SERVINGS)

Combine the chops with the Achiote Oil in a large bowl and let marinate for 2 to 8 hours.

Prepare the grill (page 4). Remove the chops from the oil, shaking off as much of the excess oil as possible. Season the chops with salt and grill to desired doneness. Serve with Wild Mushroom–Golden Raisin Empanadas.

ACHIOTE OIL

Heat the achiote seeds and oil in a small skillet on medium-high until very hot. Remove from the heat and let infuse for 3 hours. Carefully skim off the colored oil, leaving the bottom layer undisturbed. Store, chilled and covered, up to 3 months.

WILD MUSHROOM–GOLDEN RAISIN EMPANADAS

1 1/3 cups all-purpose flour

1 tablespoon chopped fresh cilantro

6 tablespoons vegetable shortening

4 tablespoons cold water

1/4 teaspoon salt

6 medium portobello mushrooms, cleaned and stemmed

1 1/2 tablespoons soy sauce

1 tablespoon balsamic vinegar

5 tablespoons olive oil, divided

2 tablespoons diced yellow onion

2 garlic cloves, minced

1 tablespoon diced yellow bell pepper

1 tablespoon diced red bell pepper

2 tablespoons pitted and diced kalamata olives

2 tablespoons golden raisins, soaked in 1/2 cup Marsala wine

1 teaspoon orange zest

1 teaspoon chopped fresh marjoram

1 teaspoon chopped fresh chives

1/4 teaspoon chopped fresh rosemary

2 tablespoons goat cheese, plus additional for garnish

Salt to taste

1 large egg

1/4 cup water

WILD MUSHROOM–GOLDEN RAISIN EMPANADAS

Combine the flour and cilantro in the bowl of an electric mixer. Using the paddle attachment, add the shortening on low speed until the mixture resembles oatmeal.

Combine 4 tablespoons water and the salt in a small bowl. Drizzle the salt mixture into the flour with the mixer on low speed and combine until the water is fully incorporated. Wrap the dough in plastic and chill for 30 minutes.

Preheat the oven to 400°F.

Place the mushrooms in a small roasting pan and drizzle with the soy sauce, balsamic vinegar, and 4 tablespoons of the olive oil. Cover the pan with foil and roast for 20 to 30 minutes. Remove from the oven and, when cool enough to handle, cut the mushrooms into 1/4-inch slices.

Heat the remaining tablespoon of olive oil in a small sauté pan until lightly smoking. Sauté the onion, garlic, and bell peppers for 1 minute. Add the olives, raisins, and Marsala, and cook until the Marsala has evaporated. Stir in the orange zest, herbs, mushrooms, and 2 tablespoons of the goat cheese, combining thoroughly. Remove from heat; taste the mixture and season with salt. Let the mixture cool while rolling out the dough.

Cut the chilled dough into 16 equal pieces and roll out each piece to a 1/8-inch-thick circle. Whisk together the egg and 1/4 cup water. Divide the filling evenly among the circles, placing the filling in the center of each piece of dough. Brush the exposed edges of the dough with the egg mixture using a small pastry brush. Gently fold each circle in half to completely enclose the filling and crimp the edges with a fork to seal tightly.

Make a small slit in each empanada with a paring knife to allow steam to escape and brush the tops with the remaining egg mixture. Place the empanadas on a lightly greased cookie sheet and bake for 25 minutes or until golden brown. Garnish with crumbled goat cheese.

coriander cured beef tenderloin

In Texas, coriander refers to the seeds of the plant and cilantro refers to the aromatic leaves; they are not interchangeable. In many cultures, coriander is used as a spice for baking. This cure works particularly well for game such as venison.

CORIANDER CURED BEEF TENDERLOIN

4 teaspoons coriander seeds

4 teaspoons black peppercorns

4 shallots, peeled and minced

6 garlic cloves, peeled and minced

³/₄ cup kosher salt

6 teaspoons dark brown sugar

1 beef tenderloin (about
   2³/₄ pounds), trimmed

1 teaspoon vegetable oil

Black Bean–Jícama Salsa (page 24)

Sweet Potato Tamales

SWEET POTATO TAMALES

1 sweet potato (about 12 ounces)

1³/₄ cups masa harina

1¹/₄ cups very hot water

¹/₂ cup plus 2 tablespoons vegetable
   shortening, chilled

1¹/₂ teaspoons salt, plus additional
   to taste

1 teaspoon baking powder

¹/₄ cup chicken stock, chilled (page 33)

1 tablespoon maple syrup

1 teaspoon cayenne powder

1 teaspoon pure chile powder
   (page 15)

10 corn husks, soaked in water

CORIANDER CURED BEEF TENDERLOIN (YIELDS 4 SERVINGS)

Preheat the oven to 400°F.

Pulse the coriander seeds and peppercorns in a food processor for about 1 minute or until coarsely ground. Add the shallots, garlic, salt, and sugar; continue to process to a thick paste. Place the mixture in a large bowl; add the beef tenderloin and let cure for at least 3 hours, turning occasionally.

Heat the vegetable oil in a large sauté pan until lightly smoking. Sear the tenderloin on all sides, then place in a small baking dish. Bake for about 8 minutes or until medium-rare. Serve with Black Bean–Jícama Salsa and Sweet Potato Tamales.

SWEET POTATO TAMALES

Preheat the oven to 350°F. Bake the sweet potato for about 50 minutes, until completely soft.

Place the masa harina in the bowl of an electric mixer fitted with a paddle attachment. On low speed, slowly add the water in a constant stream until the dough forms a ball. Continue to mix on high speed for 5 minutes. Remove the dough from the bowl and allow to cool completely in the refrigerator for about 30 minutes. Return the masa to the bowl and beat for 5 minutes on high speed. Slowly add the shortening in tablespoon additions while beating. Continue beating until smooth and light, about 5 minutes. Stop the mixer to scrape the sides of the bowl, then reduce to low speed and continue to beat.

Combine the salt, baking powder, and chicken stock in a small bowl. Slowly drizzle the chicken stock mixture into the masa, combining thoroughly. Whip on high speed for 5 minutes longer.

(continued)

coriander cured beef tenderloin

coriander cured beef tenderloin *(continued)*

Peel the potato and combine it with the maple syrup, cayenne, chile powder, and salt to taste in a mixing bowl. Mash the potato with a fork and combine thoroughly with the other ingredients. Add half of the sweet potato mash to the master masa mix and combine thoroughly.

Drain the corn husks and pat dry. Tear 16 ($^1/_6$-inch-wide) strips from 2 of the husks for tying the tamales. Place about 2 tablespoons of the tamale dough on top of each husk, then add about 2 tablespoons of the sweet potato mash on top of the dough, leaving 1 inch uncovered at each end. Roll the corn husks so that the dough is completely enclosed. Twist and tie each end with the reserved strips. Repeat the procedure for remaining tamales.

Steam the tamales in a conventional steamer or in a strainer set in a saucepan and covered with a tightly fitting lid that allows little or no steam to escape while cooking. Steam for 30 to 35 minutes; the water should always be lightly boiling. The tamales are done when the dough comes away easily from the husk.

tamale tart
with red pepper custard, artichokes, and wild mushrooms

I created my first tamale tart about 14 years ago. Made with venison chili, it was sort of a takeoff on another childhood favorite, Frito Chili Pie. It's not uncommon to see tamale tarts today on menus around the country that feature Southwestern cuisine. They can be made with everything from crabmeat to rabbit, and it's a flavor you'll never forget.

4 red bell peppers, roasted, peeled, seeded, and puréed (page 14)

3 cups heavy cream

1 tablespoon roasted garlic purée (page 4)

4 large egg yolks

Salt and freshly ground black pepper to taste

4 cups masa harina

1/2 cup yellow cornmeal

1/2 teaspoon cayenne powder

3 teaspoons ground cumin

1 tablespoon salt

12 tablespoons vegetable shortening, room temperature

12 tablespoons ancho purée (page 15)

2 cups water

2 tablespoons olive oil

1/2 small onion, finely diced

1 poblano, seeded and diced

1 pound assorted wild mushrooms, cleaned and julienned

1/4 cup seeded and diced red tomato (outside flesh only)

1/4 cup seeded and diced yellow tomato (outside flesh only)

8 artichoke hearts, quartered

2 tablespoons chopped fresh oregano

2 tablespoons lime juice (about 1 lime)

Salt and pepper to taste

(YIELDS 4 TO 6 SERVINGS)

Heat three-fourths of the red bell pepper purée in a small saucepan over high heat, stirring constantly until very thick, about 5 minutes. Reduce the cream to 1 cup plus 2 tablespoons in a small saucepan over medium heat. Whisk in the garlic.

Whisk the egg yolks lightly in a medium bowl while drizzling in the cream mixture. Add the reduced bell pepper purée to the cream sauce. Season with salt and pepper. Cover and set aside to cool.

Combine the masa harina, cornmeal, cayenne, cumin, and 1 tablespoon salt in a medium bowl. Whip the shortening in the bowl of an electric mixer until light and fluffy. Gradually beat in the dry ingredients until smooth. Beat in the ancho purée and the reserved red bell pepper purée.

Form the dough into a disk and pat evenly over the bottom and sides of a 9-inch tart pan with removable bottom. (In lieu of 1 large tart, 6 to 8 individual portions can be made.) Fill with the reserved pepper custard and cover with plastic wrap.

Place a round metal cooking rack inside a wok. Fill with 2 cups water, with the rack positioned about 3 inches above the water. Bring the water to a boil over high heat, then reduce to a simmer. Place the wrapped tart on the rack and cover the wok. Steam until the custard is set but trembles slightly, about 25 to 30 minutes. Using 2 pot holders, carefully lift the tart off the rack; remove the plastic wrap and the sides of the tart ring. Place on a serving platter.

Heat the olive oil in a large skillet until lightly smoking. Add the onion and poblano and sauté for 1 minute, stirring continuously. Add the mushrooms and sauté for 3 more minutes until the mushrooms are fully cooked and tender. Add the tomatoes, artichokes, oregano, and lime juice. Heat for 2 minutes longer. Add salt and pepper to taste.

Cover the top of the tart with the artichoke mixture and cut into wedges to serve.

cranberry pudding tamales

cranberry pudding tamales
with tequila-orange curd

These delicious little packets are the perfect Christmas dessert. The pudding can be made in a traditional steamed pudding mold, but the banana leaves are a much more festive presentation. (Banana leaves are available at Hispanic and Asian markets.) The Tequila-Orange Curd, although extremely complementary to the tamales, is a good accompaniment to just about any dessert.

TAMALES

$3^3/_4$ cups picked-over cranberries

1 cup ground pecans

$1^3/_4$ cups sugar, divided

3 tablespoons all-purpose flour

$^3/_4$ teaspoon cinnamon

$^1/_4$ teaspoon ground allspice

$^1/_4$ teaspoon ground ginger

$1^1/_2$ cups finely ground bread crumbs

1 cup ground gingersnap cookies

$^3/_4$ cup unsalted butter ($1^1/_2$ sticks), melted and cooled

$^2/_3$ cup milk

3 eggs, lightly beaten

1 tablespoon baking powder

$^1/_2$ teaspoon salt

2 large banana leaves, about 12 by 36 inches each

Tequila-Orange Curd

Cranberry Glaze

TAMALES (YIELDS 8 SERVINGS)

Coarsely chop the cranberries in a food processor. Place the chopped cranberries in a medium bowl and stir in the pecans. Add 1 cup of the sugar, flour, cinnamon, allspice, and ginger; combine thoroughly. Combine the bread crumbs, cookies, butter, milk, eggs, baking powder, salt, and the remaining $^3/_4$ cup sugar in another bowl. Stir this mixture into the cranberry mixture and combine thoroughly. Chill for at least 30 minutes to make forming the tamales easier.

Soften the banana leaves over an open flame for 10 seconds on each side, being careful not to burn them. Cut each leaf crosswise into 4 even pieces, about 8 by 10 inches each, and lay out on a flat work surface.

Divide the the cranberry masa dough into 16 even portions and place a portion in the center of each leaf. Spread into a 4-inch square, leaving at least a $1^1/_2$-inch border at the ends and a $^3/_4$-inch border on the long sides.

To fold the tamales, pick up the 2 long sides of the banana leaf and bring them together; the leaf will surround the filling. Tuck one side under the other and fold the flaps on each end underneath the tamale. Repeat for the remaining tamales.

Place the tamales in a steamer set over gently boiling water. Steam, covered tightly, for 20 to 25 minutes. Remove the tamales; slice the banana leaf open to expose the cranberry pudding.

Pour some Tequila-Orange Curd on each of 8 plates. Place 2 tamales on each plate and spoon with Cranberry Glaze.

(continued)

cranberry pudding tamales *(continued)*

TEQUILA-ORANGE CURD

$3/4$ cup fresh orange juice (about $3/4$ pound oranges)

2 cups milk

1 vanilla bean, split in half lengthwise and scraped

6 egg yolks

$2/3$ cup sugar

1 tablespoon gold tequila

1 teaspoon grated orange zest

$3/4$ cup heavy cream or crème fraîche, chilled

CRANBERRY GLAZE

1 cup cranberry juice

1 cup sugar

1 cup picked-over cranberries

TEQUILA-ORANGE CURD

Reduce the orange juice to $1/4$ cup (4 tablespoons) in a saucepan over high heat. Bring the milk to a boil in a small saucepan with the vanilla bean. Remove from the heat, cover, and let infuse for 15 minutes. Place the yolks in a medium bowl and whisk in the sugar until the yolks have lightened in color. Bring the milk back to a boil. Stirring constantly, slowly pour the milk through a strainer into the yolks. Discard the vanilla bean.

Pour the strained mixture back into the saucepan; cook over low heat, stirring constantly with a wooden spoon. Scrape down the sides and bottom of the pan, and continue to cook until the mixture registers 185°F on a candy thermometer and has thickened considerably, about 5 to 10 minutes. Immediately remove from the heat and place the pan over ice. Stir in the reduced orange juice, tequila, zest, and chilled cream. Let chill thoroughly in the refrigerator before serving.

CRANBERRY GLAZE

Cook the cranberry juice and sugar over moderate heat in a deep, heavy saucepan, stirring frequently. Dip a brush in cold water and wash down any sugar crystals that cling to the side of the pan. Cook until the sugar is dissolved.

Bring the mixture to a boil, gently swirling the pan until a candy thermometer registers 250°F. Add the cranberries, remove the pan from the heat, and let the glaze cool. Place in a small bowl and chill, covered, until ready to serve.

grilled veal chops
with red flannel hash and bacon-scallion crema

Though hash seems utterly American, it actually is derived from the French word hacher, *meaning "to chop." Red Flannel Hash, getting its name and color from beets, is a New England specialty that made its way westward during the late nineteenth century. Traditional recipes stated that 85 percent of the volume of the recipe should come from beets. Try the Bacon-Scallion Crema simply on a piece of grilled fish, meat, or chicken.*

VEAL CHOPS

6 to 8 7-ounce veal chops

Olive oil

Salt to taste

Red Flannel Hash

Bacon-Scallion Crema

RED FLANNEL HASH

4 medium beets

1 cup water

1 cup cream

Vegetable oil for frying

1 medium-size baking potato, peeled, julienned, and reserved in water

1 tablespoon olive oil

12 Brussels sprouts, quartered and blanched

1/4 cup pecans, toasted (page 5)

Salt to taste

BACON-SCALLION CREMA

1 cup sour cream

4 slices bacon, cooked until crispy and diced

4 scallions, thinly sliced

2 tablespoons milk

VEAL CHOPS

Rub each veal chop with olive oil and season to taste. Place each chop on the grill, grilling each side for 5 minutes or until desired doneness.

Place some Red Flannel Hash on each plate, place a chop on the bed of hash, and top the chops with a dollop of Bacon-Scallion Crema.

RED FLANNEL HASH

Prepare a medium-hot charcoal grill and preheat the oven to 350°F.

Combine the beets and water in an ovenproof casserole. Cover tightly and bake for 30 minutes or until the beets are tender when poked with a paring knife. Remove from the oven and allow to cool. Once cool, the skins should slide off easily. Remove the skins and stem; julienne the remainder.

Bring the cream to a boil in a small saucepan over medium-high heat and reduce to 1/3 cup; set aside. Pour enough vegetable oil in a medium saucepan to come 1 inch up the side. Heat the oil to 350°F or until lightly smoking. Drain the potatoes very thoroughly, then slowly add the potatoes to the hot oil, being careful of spattering grease. Cook the potatoes until golden brown and crispy, about 3 minutes, and drain on a paper towel–lined cookie sheet. Set aside.

Heat the olive oil in a large skillet until lightly smoking. Add the reserved beets, Brussels sprouts, pecans, and cream, and heat through. Season with salt to taste. Keep warm while preparing the Bacon-Scallion Crema and grilling the chops. Before serving, add the reserved potatoes to the warm hash.

BACON-SCALLION CREMA

Combine the sour cream, bacon, scallions, and milk in a medium bowl, stirring well to combine.

stacked banana–crème brûlée tostada

stacked banana–crème brûlée tostada

with cajeta and candied pecans

This dessert combines some of my favorite taste sensations: The crisp tortilla is a fantastic foil for the creamy brûlée, the rum-infused bananas (a Texas delicacy by way of New Orleans: Bananas Foster with a Western drawl), and the tangy caramelized sweetness of the goat milk cajeta. (I became addicted to this caramel the first time I tasted it in Mexico. It reminded me of a childhood theater favorite—Sugar Babies.) Top it off with some candied pecans, and you're in Texas heaven.

CRÈME BRÛLÉE

4 egg yolks

4 tablespoons sugar

1$^1/_2$ cups heavy cream

$^1/_4$ vanilla bean, split in half lengthwise and scraped

2 tablespoons dark rum

CAJETA

1$^1/_2$ cups sugar, divided

2 cups goat's milk

2 cups cow's milk

1 teaspoon cornstarch

Pinch of baking soda

(YIELDS 4 TOSTADAS)

Whisk the egg yolks and the sugar vigorously in a large, heatproof bowl set over gently simmering water until the mixture thickens, forms a ribbon, and resembles a thick hollandaise sauce. (Briefly remove the bowl from the heat if the mixture begins to cook too rapidly around the edges.) Heat the yolks until warmed through.

Combine the cream, vanilla bean, and rum in a small saucepan and bring to a boil. Slowly strain into the yolks, stirring continuously. Cook over barely simmering water for 40 to 45 minutes, stirring occasionally, until the custard is slightly thickened and heavily coats the back of a spoon. The heat should be very low and the custard should never be too hot to the touch. Strain through a fine sieve into a bowl set over ice; let the custard cool while preparing the Cajeta and Tostadas.

CAJETA

Place $^3/_4$ cup of the sugar in a small skillet and melt over medium heat for about 7 minutes, stirring continuously until golden brown and free of lumps. Remove from the heat.

Combine both milks in a medium bowl. Pour 1 cup of the mixture into a small bowl; stir in the cornstarch and baking soda. Add the remaining $^3/_4$ cup of sugar to the 3 cups of milk. Heat in a saucepan over medium heat, stirring occasionally. Bring just to the boiling point, then add the caramelized sugar all at once while stirring vigorously. Add the reserved milk and cornstarch, and stir well.

Reduce the heat to low and simmer for 30 to 40 minutes, stirring occasionally. During the last 15 minutes of cooking, stir the thickened Cajeta more frequently to prevent sticking.

(continued)

stacked banana–crème brûlée tostada *(continued)*

CARAMELIZED BANANAS

3 medium bananas, slightly underripe

4 tablespoons brown sugar

4 tablespoons butter

2 tablespoons dark rum

TOSTADAS

4 large flour tortillas, each cut into
  three 3-inch circles

Vegetable oil for frying

4 tablespoons granulated sugar

2 tablespoons cinnamon

Confectioners' sugar for dusting

CANDIED PECANS

1 cup pecan pieces

1 egg white

2 tablespoons sugar

CARAMELIZED BANANAS

Peel and slice the bananas on the bias into $1/4$-inch slices.

Combine the sugar and butter in a medium sauté pan. Cook over high heat to a thick, dark brown, extremely bubbly mixture, about 10 minutes. Add the bananas and cook for 10 seconds. Add the rum to flambé, then remove from the heat and spread evenly onto a lightly oiled cookie sheet. Allow to cool while preparing the Tostadas.

TOSTADAS

Preheat the oven to broil.

Pour enough vegetable oil to come 2 inches up the side of a medium saucepan. Heat the oil to 350°F or until lightly smoking. In a small mixing bowl, combine the granulated sugar and the cinnamon. Fry the tortillas in the oil, turning often, until crisp and golden, about 2 minutes. Drain on paper towels. Sprinkle with the cinnamon-sugar mixture and dust with the confectioners' sugar. Caramelize the sugar under a broiler, being careful not to burn.

CANDIED PECANS

Preheat oven to 350°F.

Place the pecans in a small mixing bowl. Add enough egg white to coat and moisten the nuts. Add the sugar and combine thoroughly. Spread the pecans on a cookie sheet and toast in the oven for 10 minutes or until the coating is dry.

Allow the pecans to cool to room temperature, then separate to keep from sticking.

ASSEMBLY

Place 1 Tostada in the center of each plate. Place 3 slices of the Caramelized Bananas on each Tostada. Spoon 1 tablespoon of the Crème Brûlée over the bananas, followed by some of the Candied Pecans. Repeat the procedure for a second layer, then top with a caramelized Tostada. Spoon the Cajeta around the plate and garnish with more Candied Pecans.

heaven and hell cake™

This has become our signature dessert at Star Canyon. It's labor intensive, but worth every second spent concocting it. Growing up, my two favorite cakes were angel food and devil's food. My favorite candy bar was a Reese's Peanut Butter Cup. If the angel food symbolizes heaven and the devil's food hell, does that make the rich filling and icing a chocolate-and-peanut-butter purgatory?

ANGEL FOOD CAKE

1⅓ cups cake flour

2 cups confectioners' sugar

2 cups egg whites (about 14 to 16 large eggs)

2 teaspoons cream of tartar

Pinch of salt

1⅓ cups sugar

2 teaspoons vanilla

1 teaspoon almond extract

DEVIL'S FOOD CAKE

½ cup cocoa powder

1 cup strong coffee

½ cup shortening

1½ cups sugar

1 teaspoon vanilla

2 large eggs

1½ cups cake flour

¾ teaspoon salt

¼ teaspoon baking powder

1 teaspoon baking soda

ANGEL FOOD CAKE (YIELDS ONE 10-INCH CAKE)

Cut a circle of parchment paper or waxed paper to fit the bottom of a 10-inch cake pan. Do not grease the pan or paper. Preheat oven to 375°F.

Sift together the flour and confectioners' sugar. Place the egg whites in the bowl of a heavy-duty mixer. Beat slowly while adding the cream of tartar and salt. Continue beating for 2 minutes. Increase the speed to medium and pour the sugar into the whites by tablespoons until all is incorporated. Continue beating about 3 minutes longer. When the egg whites form stiff peaks, add the vanilla and almond extract.

Remove the bowl from the mixer. Sprinkle half of the powdered sugar-flour mixture over the top of the egg whites and fold in with a rubber spatula. Sprinkle in the remaining sugar-flour mixture and fold in again, using a minimum number of strokes so that the egg whites do not deflate. Gently spoon the mixture into the pan and bake for 1 hour.

Remove from the oven and let cool. Once cool, carefully slice the cake in half horizontally with a serrated knife to make 2 layers.

DEVIL'S FOOD CAKE

Preheat the oven to 350°F. Oil and flour a 10-inch cake pan.

Sift the cocoa powder into a small mixing bowl; drizzle in the coffee while whisking to make a smooth paste. Combine the shortening, sugar, vanilla, and eggs in the bowl of an electric mixer and beat with a paddle attachment for 2 minutes on medium speed.

Sift together the flour, salt, baking powder, and baking soda in a large bowl. Alternately add the cocoa-coffee mixture and the dry ingredients to the sugar-egg mixture; continue beating until incorporated. Pour the batter into the cake pan and bake for 30 minutes.

Remove from the oven and let cool. Once cool, carefully slice the cake in half with a serrated knife to make 2 layers.

(continued)

heaven and hell cake™ *(continued)*

PEANUT BUTTER MOUSSE

12 ounces cream cheese

1³/₄ cups confectioners' sugar

2 cups peanut butter, at
room temperature

³/₄ cup heavy cream,
whipped stiff

GANACHE

2 cups cream

2 pounds milk chocolate, chopped

PEANUT BUTTER MOUSSE

Whip the cream cheese in the bowl of an electric mixer until light
and creamy. Gradually beat in the confectioners' sugar. Add the
peanut butter; continue beating until thoroughly incorporated and
fluffy. Transfer the mixture to another bowl.

Place the heavy cream in the electric mixer bowl and whip until stiff.
Fold the whipped cream into the peanut butter mixture.

GANACHE

Bring the cream to a boil in a medium saucepan. Stir in the
chocolate. Cover the pan for the chocolate to melt quickly.
Once melted, whisk the mixture to combine thoroughly. Let
cool to room temperature before frosting the cake.

ASSEMBLY

Place one layer of Devil's Food Cake on a cake plate and spoon
one-third of the Peanut Butter Mousse on top. Place a layer
of the Angel Food Cake on top of the mousse, then spread with
another third of the Peanut Butter Mousse. Continue layering
until you have four layers of cake and three layers of mousse.

Whisk the Ganache and spread with a spatula over the top and
sides of the cake to frost generously. Chill for at least two hours
before serving.

heaven and hell cake™

From the days of the Spanish settlers and early Anglo-
American pioneers, Texans have lived as ranchers and
cattlemen. By the latter part of the nineteenth century,
the major cattle drives had made their mark on the lore of
the Lone Star State. With the invention of barbed wire,
large enclosed ranches transformed not only the cattle
industry, but also the topography of Texas, giving birth
to the idyllic vision of the American Cowboy.

Two dishes that were born of this era are chili, that fiery
"bowl of red," and chicken fried steak.

Chili was most likely created on a trail drive by a chuck wagon
cook who ran out of black pepper and substituted chiles,
forever changing the profile of his common beef stew.
In San Antonio, washerwomen prepared their version of
chili for the Republic of Texas Army in the nineteenth
century, earning them the nickname "Chili Queens."

Chicken fried steak was created from limited resources on the
cattle drive, where beef—but not that much else—was a
given. When left with the less tender hindquarter, the cook
had to make his steaks palatable. He achieved this by
pounding them, seasoning with salt and pepper, dredging
in flour, and pan-frying in hot oil. Milk was also in vast
supply, so cream gravy was created to smother the steak.

home on the range

sourdough chicken fried steak
with black pepper gravy

Sourdough cookery was a staple technique of the open range in the late nineteenth century. On the move between camps, they usually carried the crocks under cover in the wagon box. These sourdough cooks considered themselves artists, never revealing their secret formulas.

CHICKEN FRIED STEAK AND GRAVY

1 to 1 1/2 pounds round or chuck steak, about 1/2 inch thick and divided into 4 portions

1 cup Sourdough Starter

1 cup plus 2 tablespoons all-purpose flour

1 tablespoon Brisket Rub (page 37)

Vegetable oil for frying

1 cup milk

1/2 cup cream

Salt to taste

1/2 teaspoon Tabasco

1 tablespoon freshly ground black pepper

SOURDOUGH STARTER

2 cups water

2 1/2 teaspoons active dry yeast

2 teaspoons sugar

2 cups unbleached flour

CHICKEN FRIED STEAK AND GRAVY (YIELDS 4 SERVINGS)

Preheat the oven to 200°F.

Using a metal meat pounder, pound the steaks to a 1/8-inch thickness. Place the Sourdough Starter in a medium bowl. Place 1 cup of the flour on a plate. Season both sides of the steaks with the dry rub. Dip each steak in the starter and coat with flour, shaking to remove excess.

Pour enough oil in a medium cast-iron skillet to come 1/4 inch up the side; heat over medium heat. Add the steak and cook for 5 minutes on each side until golden brown. Drain on a paper towel–lined cookie sheet and place in a warm oven while cooking the remaining steaks.

Discard all but 2 tablespoons of the oil and decrease the heat to low. Whisk in the remaining 2 tablespoons flour and cook for 2 minutes without letting the flour brown. Whisk in the milk and cream; bring to a simmer and cook for 2 minutes or until thickened. Stir in the salt, Tabasco, and black pepper; serve over the steaks.

SOURDOUGH STARTER

Whisk together the water, yeast, and sugar in a medium bowl; let stand for 5 minutes. Beat in the flour. Cover with plastic wrap and let stand at room temperature for 48 hours, stirring once a day. Rinse a 1-quart jar with a tight-fitting lid. Place the starter in the jar and seal the lid; chill for up to three days. If a brown liquid—the alcohol by-product of yeast—rises to the top, simply stir to incorporate.

To use the starter, combine 1/2 cup flour and 1/2 cup water for every 1 cup of starter removed. Repeat this process every two weeks whether you need to use the starter or not, and it will keep in the refrigerator indefinitely.

southwestern caesar salad
with jalapeño-polenta croutons and parmesan-anchovy wafer

This salad has been on one of my menus since 1984. This version represents the evolution of the recipe that brings it into 1998. The wafers are a wonderful addition to any salad (or soup for that matter), and you'll find the croutons addictive.

SALAD

4 romaine hearts, split, cleaned, and dried

Dressing

Parmesan-Anchovy Wafers

Jalapeño-Polenta Croutons

$^1/_2$ cup grated Asiago cheese for garnish

DRESSING

4 anchovy fillets

1 small shallot, minced

2 tablespoons roasted garlic purée (page 4)

1 teaspoon ground cumin

4 teaspoons Dijon mustard

1 teaspoon tamarind paste

2 tablespoons chipotle purée (page 15)

1 tablespoon balsamic vinegar

1 tablespoon fresh lemon juice (about $^1/_2$ lemon)

1 teaspoon pure chile powder (page 15)

1 egg

$^1/_2$ cup extra-virgin olive oil

$^1/_2$ cup vegetable oil

Salt and cayenne powder to taste

PARMESAN-ANCHOVY WAFERS

1 cup grated Parmesan cheese

8 anchovy fillets, thoroughly chopped

JALAPEÑO-POLENTA CROUTONS

1 jalapeño, seeded and minced

$^1/_2$ teaspoon cayenne powder

$1^1/_2$ teaspoons salt

$2^3/_4$ cups milk

$1^1/_2$ cups yellow cornmeal, divided

6 cups peanut oil

SALAD (YIELDS 4 SERVINGS)

Place the romaine hearts in a large bowl. Drizzle with the dressing and toss to coat thoroughly. Place 2 pieces of the romaine on each serving plate in the shape of an X. Slide a Parmesan-Anchovy Wafer in between the 2 pieces and place Jalapeño-Polenta Croutons around the plate. Sprinkle with Asiago and serve.

DRESSING

Place the anchovies in a large wooden bowl and mash thoroughly with a wooden spoon. Add the shallot and garlic purée, continuing to mash and stir. Add the cumin, Dijon, tamarind, chipotle purée, vinegar, lemon juice, and chile powder. Place the egg in very hot water for 1 minute. Whisk the egg into the mixture, and drizzle in the oils in a steady stream, continuing to whisk. Season to taste and set aside.

PARMESAN-ANCHOVY WAFERS

Preheat the oven to 350°F.

Combine the anchovies and cheese in a mixing bowl. Pat the mixture into thin circles, about 3 inches in diameter each. Place the circles on an oiled cookie sheet and bake until golden brown all the way through. Cool and remove from the pan.

JALAPEÑO-POLENTA CROUTONS

Combine the jalapeño, cayenne, salt, and milk in a medium saucepan and bring to a rapid boil. Slowly add 1 cup of the cornmeal while stirring constantly. Cook over medium heat for 3 to 5 minutes or until the mixture pulls away from the sides of the pan and forms a ball. Press the mixture into a 9-inch pie pan lined with plastic wrap. Chill, uncovered, to cool. Remove from the pan and dice into $^1/_2$-inch cubes.

Heat the peanut oil to 350°F in a medium saucepan. Dredge the polenta cubes in the remaining $^1/_2$ cup cornmeal. Fry the croutons until crisp, about 1 to 2 minutes. Remove from the oil with a slotted spoon, drain on paper towels, and keep warm until ready to serve.

bone-in cowboy rib-eye
with pinto–wild mushroom ragout and
red chile onion rings

This has become our best-selling dish at Star Canyon, and I would probably receive hate mail if I took
it off the menu. It's about as representative a dish as I can think of when I try to explain New Texas Cuisine,
my trademark style of cooking.

COWBOY RIB-EYE

$1/2$ cup kosher salt

1 cup ground assorted dried chiles
(such as guajillo, pasilla,
and chipotle)

1 cup paprika

$1/3$ cup sugar

4 bone-in rib-eye steaks, 14 to 16
ounces each

Pinto–Wild Mushroom Ragout

Red Chile Onion Rings

PINTO–WILD MUSHROOM RAGOUT

$1/2$ cup pinto beans, soaked overnight
and drained

1 quart ham hock broth or water

Salt and freshly ground black pepper
to taste

1 tablespoon clarified butter or
vegetable oil

2 tablespoons minced shallots

2 garlic cloves, minced

$1 1/2$ cups cleaned and sliced assorted
fresh wild mushrooms

$1/2$ cup fresh corn kernels (about
1 small ear)

$1/2$ cup dry red wine

$1 1/2$ cups Veal Demi-Glace (page 32)

1 teaspoon chipotle purée (page 15)

1 teaspoon chopped fresh sage

1 medium-size ripe tomato, blanched,
peeled, seeded, and diced (page 5)

1 tablespoon unsalted butter, at
room temperature

COWBOY RIB-EYE AND RAGOUT (YIELDS 4 SERVINGS)

Combine the kosher salt, dried chiles, paprika, and sugar in
a large bowl; mix thoroughly. Dredge the steaks in the
mixture, coating evenly. Let marinate in the refrigerator for
12 hours or overnight.

Prepare a medium-hot fire in a grill with charcoal briquettes.
Grill steaks to desired doneness, about 5 to 7 minutes per side
for medium rare. Serve with Pinto–Wild Mushroom Ragout
and Red Chile Onion Rings.

PINTO–WILD MUSHROOM RAGOUT

Place the beans in a saucepan with the broth or water. Bring to a
boil, reduce the heat to a simmer, and cook for 45 to 60 minutes
or until tender, checking every 20 minutes or so. Add more liquid
as needed to keep the beans covered. When the beans are tender,
season with salt and pepper and set aside. Heat the clarified
butter in a large skillet over medium heat until lightly smoking.
Add the shallots, garlic, wild mushrooms, and corn; cook for
1 minute. Deglaze the pan with red wine, scraping the pan with
a spatula to dissolve any solidified juices; reduce the liquid by
three-quarters over high heat. Add the Veal Demi-Glace, chipotle
purée, sage, tomato, and cooked, drained beans. Reduce the
liquid by one-third. Whisk in the 1 tablespoon butter and
season with salt.

(continued)

bone-in cowboy rib-eye

bone-in cowboy rib-eye *(continued)*

RED CHILE ONION RINGS

Canola oil for frying

3 onions, cut into very thin rings

Milk for soaking

1 cup all-purpose flour

$1/2$ cup paprika

$1/2$ cup pure chile powder (page 15)

2 tablespoons ground cumin seeds

Salt to taste

Cayenne powder to taste

Pour enough canola oil in a large frying pan to come 3 to 4 inches up the side. Heat the oil to 350°F or until lightly smoking.

Place the onions in a large bowl and cover with milk; let soak for 20 minutes.

Combine the flour, paprika, chile powder, and cumin in a medium bowl; mix thoroughly. Shake the excess milk off the onions and toss in the flour mixture until well coated. Fry in the hot canola oil until golden. Drain the rings on paper towels and season with salt and cayenne to taste.

blue corn skillet stars

I first created this recipe at Routh Street Cafe in 1984. I've since had them on menus at five different restaurants in some form or another. They're also delicious when spread with a mixture of one part jalapeño jelly and three parts cream cheese whipped together. They're also best served warm.

$^1/_4$ pound unsalted butter (1 stick)

8 tablespoons shortening

4 serranos, seeded and minced

3 garlic cloves, minced

1 cup all-purpose flour

$1^1/_4$ cups blue cornmeal

2 tablespoons sugar

1 teaspoon baking powder

$1^1/_2$ teaspoons salt

3 large eggs

$1^1/_4$ cups milk, at room temperature

3 tablespoons chopped fresh cilantro

Olive oil for brushing

(YIELDS ABOUT 50 STARS)

Preheat the oven to 400°F.

Place a well-seasoned cast-iron star mold in the oven to warm for at least 5 minutes. (A cast-iron skillet or muffin pan will work as well.)

Gently melt the butter and shortening in a small saucepan over low heat. Add the serranos and garlic, and sauté for 10 minutes. Sift together the flour, cornmeal, sugar, baking powder, and salt in a large bowl. Beat the eggs lightly in a medium bowl. Add the serrano mixture and stir in the milk. Pour the liquid ingredients into the dry ingredients; beat just until smooth. Add the cilantro.

Remove the cast-iron cornbread mold from the oven and brush generously with the oil. Reheat the mold for about 2 minutes, then fill with the batter.

Bake in the center of the oven for 20 to 25 minutes or until the cornbread is lightly browned but still blue and springy to the touch.

venison–black bean chili
with goat cheese crema and slang jang

We have a saying in Texas: If you know beans about Texas chili, you know Texas chili has no beans. But this is, after all, New Tastes from Texas, *and the combination of black beans and venison tastes great. As for the Slang Jang—or as I like to call it, Southern Salsa—it has always had a spot on the table for New Year's Day right next to the black-eyed peas, a staple for any superstitious Southerner.*

CHILI

4 tablespoons olive oil

1 pound venison leg, well trimmed of fat and finely chopped

6 garlic cloves, finely chopped

1 onion, chopped

1 jalapeño, seeded and chopped

4 tablespoons ancho purée (page 15)

2 chipotles in adobo, chopped

4 medium tomatoes, blanched, peeled, seeded, and diced (page 5)

2 teaspoons ground cumin

1 quart chicken stock (page 33) or vegetable stock, or more as needed to cover in cooking process

1 12-ounce bottle dark beer, such as Shiner Bock

1 cup black beans, soaked overnight and drained

1 teaspoon epazote

2 tablespoons masa harina

1 tablespoon chopped fresh cilantro

Salt and freshly ground black pepper to taste

Goat Cheese Crema

Slang Jang

CHILI (YIELDS 4 TO 6 SERVINGS)

Heat the oil in a heavy stockpot or casserole until lightly smoking. Add the venison, garlic, onion, and jalapeño; cook over medium heat until the meat has browned, about 15 minutes. Add the ancho purée, chipotles, tomatoes, and cumin; cook for 10 minutes longer.

Add the stock and beer; bring to a boil. Add the black beans and epazote. Reduce the heat and let simmer for $1^{1}/_{2}$ to 2 hours or until the meat and beans are perfectly tender, stirring occasionally. Add more stock throughout the cooking process, if necessary, to keep meat and beans covered. Whisk in the masa harina and cilantro. Season with salt and pepper to taste and garnish with Goat Cheese Crema and Slang Jang.

(continued)

venison-black bean chili

venison–black bean chili *(continued)*

GOAT CHEESE CREMA

1 cup heavy cream

6 ounces fresh goat cheese, crumbled

2 tablespoons roasted garlic purée
(page 4)

SLANG JANG

1 ear of corn, in husk

2 ripe tomatoes, seeded and diced
into $1/4$-inch pieces

1 medium-size green bell pepper,
seeded and diced into $1/4$-inch pieces

1 small onion, minced

2 stalks celery, peeled and diced into
$1/4$-inch pieces

1 jalapeño, seeded and minced

2 teaspoons sugar

$1/2$ cup cider vinegar

2 tablespoons olive oil

Salt and freshly ground black pepper
to taste

GOAT CHEESE CREMA

Heat the cream in a small saucepan until just boiling. Place in a blender and slowly add the goat cheese and garlic, blending 2 to 3 minutes or until smooth. Serve at room temperature.

SLANG JANG

Preheat the oven to 325°F.

Roast the ear of corn in its husk for 20 minutes. Let cool to room temperature and cut the kernels off the cob.

Combine the corn and the remaining ingredients in a medium bowl; chill for 2 to 3 hours before serving. Serve chilled or at room temperature.

campfire buttermilk biscuits

Growing up, we had these biscuits at least three times a week. My mother and grandmother swore by self-rising flour. This recipe simulates "campfire" biscuits that were cooked in a Dutch oven with heated lids, making them "toasty" on top. Edna Lewis, the doyenne of classic Southern cooking, makes some of the best biscuits on the planet. Hopefully, she would approve of these.

8 teaspoons unsalted butter

10 tablespoons vegetable shortening

3 cups self-rising flour

$1^1/_3$ cups buttermilk

(YIELDS 8 TO 10 BISCUITS)

Preheat the oven to 400°F. Place the butter in a $9^1/_2$-inch skillet and warm in the oven for 5 minutes to heat the pan and melt the butter.

Using your fingertips, crumble the shortening in a medium bowl with the flour until a crumbly consistency the size of small peas. Add the buttermilk in 3 or 4 additions, stirring continuously with a wooden spoon or spatula until the buttermilk is thoroughly incorporated. Do not overbeat; the dough should be quite sticky and hold together.

Turn the dough out onto a floured surface and lightly flour the top. Using a rolling pin, roll out the dough into a circle about $1/_2$ inch thick. Cut the biscuits into $2^1/_2$-inch circles. Dip each biscuit in the melted butter, coating thoroughly, and arrange the biscuits in the skillet.

Bake in the oven on the middle rack for 8 to 10 minutes, or until the biscuits have risen and are lightly browned on the bottom. Turn on the broiler, transfer the skillet to the upper rack of the oven, and broil the biscuits for 4 to 5 minutes or until browned. Turn out onto a rack to cool.

canela-pecan coffee cake

Once you've discovered the taste of canela, you might never go back to the harder stick cinnamon. While cinnamon can certainly be substituted for this recipe, I urge you to seek out the canela, even if by mail order.

CAKE

2/3 cup unsalted butter, at room temperature

1 cup sugar

3 large eggs

2 cups all-purpose flour

1 teaspoon baking powder

1 teaspoon baking soda

1 teaspoon ground canela

1 pinch salt

1 1/2 cups buttermilk

Topping

2/3 cup pecan pieces, toasted (page 5)

TOPPING

1 cup firmly packed light brown sugar

1/4 cup all-purpose flour

4 tablespoons unsalted butter (1/2 stick), chilled

CAKE (YIELDS ONE 9X12-INCH CAKE)

Preheat the oven to 350°F. Lightly grease a 9x12-inch baking dish.

Cream the butter and sugar together in the bowl of an electric mixer for 2 minutes on medium speed or until smooth and light. Add the eggs, one at a time, incorporating each before adding the next. Sift together the flour, baking powder, baking soda, ground canela, and salt in a medium bowl. Slowly add one-third of the dry ingredients into the mixer bowl with the machine on low speed. Alternately add the buttermilk and dry ingredients until both are completely incorporated without any lumps.

Pour the batter into the baking dish. Sprinkle the batter with the topping; sprinkle the topping with the pecan pieces. Bake for 25 to 30 minutes or until a toothpick inserted in the center comes out clean.

Allow to cool slightly, cut into squares, and serve.

TOPPING

Combine the brown sugar, flour, and butter with a pastry cutter in a small bowl.

biscuit–dried apple pudding
with lemon curd

Many cultures have a version of this homey but oh-so-delectable dessert, from the British Bread and Butter Pudding to the Cajun Bread Pudding with Whiskey Sauce. This biscuit-based rendition evolved from necessity out on the range: The chuck wagon cook had to do something with the stockpile of biscuits he often ended up with. A real treat for the cowpokes was the occasional sweet ending around the campfire. Although the addition of dried apples is mine, they were certainly a staple in the "cookies" pantry and probably found their way into a Dutch oven on occasion.

PUDDING

$3/4$ cup firmly packed brown sugar

3 large eggs

$1/2$ teaspoon ground cinnamon

1 tablespoon vanilla extract

3 tablespoons bourbon

$1^1/2$ cups milk

6 stale Campfire Buttermilk Biscuits, cut in quarters (page 85)

$1/4$ cup chopped dried apple pieces

3 tablespoons unsalted butter, cut into pieces

1 cup pecan pieces, toasted (page 5)

Lemon Curd

LEMON CURD

$3/4$ cup fresh lemon juice (about $3/4$ pound lemons)

2 cups milk

6 egg yolks

$2/3$ cup sugar

1 tablespoon Grand Marnier

1 teaspoon grated lemon zest

$3/4$ cup heavy cream or crème fraîche, chilled

PUDDING (YIELDS 4 TO 6 SERVINGS)

Whip the brown sugar and eggs together in a large bowl until smooth. Add the cinnamon, vanilla, and bourbon; whisk in the milk. Place the biscuit quarters in the egg mixture and chill overnight.

Preheat the oven to 350°F.

Lightly butter a 10-inch round cake pan. Place the apples in the bottom of the pan. Pour the soaked biscuit mixture over the apples, dot with butter pieces, and sprinkle with pecans.

Bake for 50 minutes or until a toothpick inserted in the center comes out clean. Remove from the oven and allow to cool slightly. Serve with Lemon Curd spooned on top.

LEMON CURD

Place the lemon juice in a small saucepan and reduce to $1/2$ cup over high heat. Remove from heat and let cool. Bring the milk to a boil in a medium saucepan.

Place the yolks in a medium bowl and whisk in the sugar, continuing to whisk until slightly thickened and paler yellow. Pour the boiling milk slowly into the yolks, stirring continuously.

Pour the mixture back into the saucepan and cook over low heat, stirring continuously with a wooden spatula. Scrape down the sides and bottom of the pan, and continue to cook until the mixture registers 185°F on a candy thermometer and has thickened considerably, about 5 to 10 minutes. Immediately remove from the heat and place the pan on a bed of ice. Stir in the reduced lemon juice, Grand Marnier, lemon zest, and chilled cream; chill thoroughly in the refrigerator before serving.

chocolate-pecan cheesecake brownie
with ruby grapefruit crème anglaise

This dessert combines two of my favorites: brownies and cheesecake. The addition of pecans and Ruby Red grapefruit make it thoroughly Texan. At Star Canyon, I use Hawaiian Vintage Chocolate, the only chocolate being grown and processed in the United States. The beans are grown on the various islands of Hawaii and then blended, giving each year a slightly different flavor than the year before.

BROWNIE

1 1/2 cups all-purpose flour

1/2 teaspoon baking powder

1/4 teaspoon salt

3/4 cup unsalted butter (1 1/2 sticks)

3/4 cup sugar

1 large egg

4 ounces bittersweet chocolate, finely chopped

1 cup pecan pieces, toasted (page 5)

Filling

Ruby Grapefruit Crème Anglaise

1 Ruby Red grapefruit, peeled with a knife and sectioned with the membrane removed

FILLING

8 ounces cream cheese

7 ounces confectioners' sugar

2 teaspoons minced grapefruit zest

1 teaspoon lemon zest

2 large eggs

RUBY GRAPEFRUIT CRÈME ANGLAISE

1 cup milk

1/2 vanilla bean, split in half lengthwise and scraped

3 egg yolks

1/4 cup fresh squeezed grapefruit juice (about 1/4 grapefruit)

1/3 cup heavy cream or crème fraîche, chilled

BROWNIE (YIELDS ONE 8-INCH CAKE)

Preheat the oven to 325°F. Lightly oil an 8-inch square baking pan. Sift together the flour, baking powder, and salt in a medium bowl; set aside. Place the butter and sugar in the bowl of an electric mixer and beat until creamy. Add the egg and beat until incorporated. Gradually add the flour mixture, beating until just combined. Fold in the bittersweet chocolate with a spatula. Spread the brownie mixture evenly in the oiled pan and sprinkle with pecans. Pour the Filling over the pecans. Bake for 40 to 45 minutes or until a skewer inserted in the center comes out clean. Cool to room temperature and cut into squares. Drizzle with Ruby Grapefruit Crème Anglaise and garnish with grapefruit sections.

FILLING

Place the cream cheese in the bowl of an electric mixer and beat until creamy. Sift the confectioners' sugar into the mixing bowl and continue to beat until completely smooth, about 3 minutes. Add the zests and eggs, beating until thoroughly incorporated.

RUBY GRAPEFRUIT CRÈME ANGLAISE

Bring the milk to a boil with the vanilla bean in a medium saucepan. Remove from the heat; let infuse for 15 minutes. Place the yolks in a medium bowl and whisk in the sugar until the yolks have lightened in color. Bring the milk back to a boil. Stirring constantly, slowly pour the milk through a strainer into the yolks. Discard the vanilla bean.

Pour the strained mixture back into the saucepan; cook over low heat, stirring constantly with a wooden spoon. Scrape the sides and bottom of the pan, and continue to cook until the mixture registers 185°F on a candy thermometer and has thickened considerably, about 5 to 10 minutes. Immediately remove from the heat and place the pan over ice. Stir in the grapefruit juice and chilled cream. Let chill thoroughly before serving.

chocolate-pecan cheesecake brownie

from texas cajun

country

One only has to remember that France once laid claim to Texas in the late seventeenth century to understand there is an influence from that culture. While most of the impact can be seen in neighboring Louisiana with its Cajun-Creole cookery, there is, nonetheless, a certain French style seen in Texas cuisine.

The French influence can be seen on two levels in Texas cookery. In south Texas, especially around the Louisiana border, it's not difficult to find the Cajun influence with festivals featuring dishes such as jambalaya, shrimp creole, and spicy gumbo while folks dance all night to Zydeco music.

The second level of French influence is much more recent and can be seen in current upscale restaurant cooking. A handful of chefs, myself included, have taken classic French techniques and applied them to Texas recipes using indigenous ingredients to reinterpret regional dishes.

grillades and green chile grits

Grillades probably originated in the country butcher shops of Louisiana bayous. Initially, pork was used for grillades, but today veal is used more often. Grillades and grits have become a staple on many Sunday brunch menus in New Orleans. Just remember, grits are nothing more than Southern polenta!

GRILLADES

6 veal round steaks, 6 inches square and $1/2$ inch thick

$1/2$ cup all-purpose flour

$1/2$ teaspoon cayenne powder

1 teaspoon freshly ground black pepper

2 tablespoons olive oil

1 small onion, finely diced

$1/2$ cup finely diced celery

$1/2$ cup finely diced green bell pepper

2 jalapeños, chopped with seeds

8 garlic cloves, minced

1 cup diced tomatoes, seeded

1 cup fresh mushrooms, preferably wild

1 tablespoon chopped fresh thyme

2 bay leaves

2 cups chicken stock (page 33)

4 tablespoons chopped fresh parsley

Salt to taste

Green Chile Grits

GREEN CHILE GRITS

3 cups chicken stock (page 33)

$1^1/2$ cups milk

1 cup stone-ground white grits

3 tablespoons unsalted butter

1 poblano, roasted, peeled, seeded, and diced (page 14)

$3/4$ cup grated pecorino cheese or other hard-grating cheese

Salt to taste

GRILLADES (YIELDS 4 TO 6 SERVINGS)

Cut each steak into 4 equal pieces. Combine the flour, cayenne, and black pepper in a medium bowl. Toss the meat in the flour mixture, coating thoroughly. Discard the remaining flour. Heat the olive oil in a large, heavy-bottom saucepan until lightly smoking. Brown the meat in batches, being careful not to overcrowd the pan. Reserve the browned meat on a plate.

Add the onion, celery, bell pepper, jalapeños, and garlic to the pan. Cook for 5 minutes or until the vegetables are lightly browned and wilted. Add the tomatoes, mushrooms, thyme, and bay leaves; simmer until the mushrooms are wilted. Add the reserved meat. Stir in the stock and bring to a boil. Reduce to a simmer, cover, and allow to cook for 25 minutes. Remove the bay leaves, add the parsley, and season to taste with salt. Serve with Green Chile Grits.

GREEN CHILE GRITS

Bring the stock and milk to a boil in a medium saucepan. Slowly add the grits, stirring constantly. Cover and simmer, stirring occasionally, for 18 to 20 minutes or until the stock and milk have been absorbed. Remove from the heat. Stir in the butter, poblano, and cheese. Season with salt and serve hot.

eggplant stuffed with oyster pan roast

I prepared a version of this dish for the opening of my first restaurant, Routh Street Cafe, in 1983.
While stuffed eggplant is Cajun in influence, the pan roast is an inspiration from a New York institution,
The Oyster Bar at Grand Central Station.

EGGPLANT

3 large eggs

2 cups milk

3 cups all-purpose flour

2 teaspoons salt

1 teaspoon cayenne powder

1 teaspoon freshly ground
    black pepper

$1/2$ teaspoon ground cumin

4 small eggplants

Vegetable oil for frying

Oyster Pan Roast

Chopped fresh parsley or basil
    for garnish

OYSTER PAN ROAST

3 tablespoons unsalted butter

2 tablespoons chili sauce or ketchup

1 teaspoon Tabasco

$1 1/2$ tablespoons Worcestershire sauce

Dash of celery salt

$3/4$ cup heavy cream

1 teaspoon chopped fresh thyme

12 fresh oysters, shucked and in
    their liquor

Salt to taste

$1/2$ teaspoon paprika

EGGPLANT (YIELDS 4 TO 6 SERVINGS)

Preheat the oven to 200°F.

Combine the eggs, milk, and beer in a medium bowl and whisk together. Place the flour in a medium bowl. Stir in the salt, cayenne, black pepper, and cumin. Peel the eggplants; cut $3/4$ inch off the top and bottom of each so they will sit flat. Cut each eggplant in half widthwise. Scoop out the flesh with a spoon and discard, leaving $1/2$ inch of flesh.

Pour enough vegetable oil in a large, deep saucepan to come 4 inches up the side. Heat to 350°F or until lightly smoking. Dip each eggplant "bowl" in the milk mixture, coating thoroughly inside and out. Dredge thoroughly in the flour mixture, shaking off the excess. Carefully drop as many "bowls" into the oil as will fit, and fry for 2 to 3 minutes or until golden brown. Drain on a paper towel–lined cookie sheet and keep warm in the oven while frying the remaining eggplants.

To serve, place the eggplants on a serving dish. Ladle some Oyster Pan Roast into each eggplant. Garnish with chopped parsley or basil.

OYSTER PAN ROAST

Combine the butter, chili sauce, Tabasco, Worcestershire, celery salt, cream, and thyme in the top of a double boiler set over gently simmering water. Whisk until the mixture is smooth and slightly thickened, about 2 to 3 minutes. Stir in the oysters and cook until they just start to curl. Season with salt and stir in the paprika. Keep warm until ready to assemble.

fried oyster tostadas

fried oyster tostadas
with andouille

This recipe has become a favorite appetizer at Star Canyon. Andouille is a French sausage that made its way to Louisiana with the Arcadian migration centuries ago. Fried oysters, breaded in cornmeal and stacked with tortillas, offer a great example of Mexican-Cajun fusion.

1 cup cornmeal

$1/2$ cup all-purpose flour

1 teaspoon salt

$1/2$ teaspoon paprika

$1/2$ teaspoon cayenne powder

1 tablespoon olive oil

1 small yellow onion, diced

4 scallions, sliced

3 garlic cloves, minced

1 pound andouille, diced

$1/2$ cup heavy cream

1 tablespoon Tabasco

Vegetable oil for frying

8 blue corn tortillas, cut into 4-inch circles

32 fresh oysters, shucked and in their liquor

2 bunches spinach (about 1 cup), cleaned, stemmed, and thinly sliced

6 medium radishes, cut into thin slices

$3/4$ cup Saffron Aïoli (page 31), divided

(YIELDS 4 SERVINGS)

Combine the cornmeal, flour, salt, paprika, and cayenne in a small bowl; mix thoroughly. Heat the olive oil in a medium skillet until lightly smoking. Add the onion, scallions, and garlic, and sauté until the onions are translucent, about 3 minutes. Add the andouille and cook for 3 minutes longer. Stir in the cream and Tabasco; reduce the cream by half, about 2 minutes. Remove from the heat.

Pour enough oil in a medium saucepan to come $1/2$ inch up the side; heat to 350°F or until lightly smoking. Fry the blue corn tortillas one at a time until crispy, about 1 minute, and drain on paper towels.

Dredge the oysters in batches of 4 to 6 in the cornmeal mixture. Carefully place in the hot oil and fry each batch for 2 minutes or until golden brown; drain on paper towels.

Place the spinach and radish slices in a mixing bowl and dress with half of the Saffron Aïoli. Place one tostada on each serving plate and spoon on the andouille mixture. Place 4 oysters on top of the andouille, and top with another tostada. Place some of the spinach mixture on top of the tostada. Top with 4 more oysters. Drizzle the remaining Saffron Aïoli around plates.

cajun sweet potato and sausage casserole

I originally developed this dish for a Thanksgiving class at my cooking school at Star Canyon three years ago. It has been a staple on my table for that most-American-of-holidays ever since.

3 medium sweet potatoes

1 tablespoon olive oil

1 small onion, peeled and diced

1 cup diced andouille

1 tablespoon maple syrup

2 tablespoons unsalted butter ($1/_4$ stick)

$1/_4$ teaspoon cayenne powder

1 tablespoon chopped fresh basil

Salt to taste

1 cup chopped pecans, toasted (page 5)

1 orange, peeled and sliced

(YIELDS 4 TO 6 SERVINGS)

Preheat the oven to 350°F. Place the sweet potatoes in a baking pan in the oven. After 20 minutes, remove 1 potato; peel and cut into $1/_2$-inch-thick slices. Roast the remaining sweet potatoes for an additional 25 minutes or until completely soft.

Heat the olive oil in a saucepan over medium-high heat until lightly smoking. Add the diced onion and cook for 3 minutes or until translucent. Add the andouille and continue to cook for 2 minutes longer.

When the potatoes have finished roasting, remove from oven. Peel and place in a food processor. Add the maple syrup, butter, cayenne, basil, and salt to taste; purée.

Lightly oil a 9x5-inch baking pan. Line the sliced sweet potatoes on the bottom of the pan and lightly season with salt. Sprinkle the pecan pieces over the sweet potatoes; top the pecans with the sausage mixture. Spoon the sweet potato purée evenly over the casserole; top with the orange slices. Cover the casserole with foil and bake for 15 minutes. Uncover and bake an additional 10 minutes.

red beans and rice
in tortilla cups

This dish gets its inspiration from several cultures, one of which is the Caribbean. I recently spent a week in Haiti with an anti-poverty delegation, and I was most interested to see the depth of Creole cookery there. Beans and rice were served with many of the Haitians' preparations. Serving them in the fried tortilla cup gives this dish a new texture and flavor.

3 slices bacon, diced

$1/2$ cup finely diced onion

$1/4$ cup finely diced celery

1 green bell pepper, seeded and diced

2 pickled jalapeños, chopped

6 garlic cloves, minced

1 pound andouille sausage, cut into $1/4$-inch semicircles

5 cups chicken stock (page 33)

1 cup red beans, soaked overnight and drained

$3/4$ cup rice

Vegetable oil for frying

6 corn tortillas

Salt and freshly ground black pepper to taste

4 green onions, chopped

3 tablespoons chopped fresh cilantro

(YIELDS 4 TO 6 SERVINGS)

Cook the bacon in a large saucepan over medium heat until crispy and lightly browned, about 5 minutes. Add the onion, celery, bell pepper, jalapeños, and garlic; cook for 5 minutes or until the onion is translucent. Add the sausage and cook for 2 minutes more. Add the chicken stock and beans and bring to a boil. Reduce the heat to a simmer and allow to cook for 1 hour or until the beans are al dente. Stir in the rice. Cover and allow to simmer for 20 minutes more or until the rice and beans are tender.

Pour enough oil in a large saucepan to come 3 inches up the side. Using two metal ladles, one a little larger than the other, shape the tortillas into cups in the hot oil and leave submerged in the oil for 2 minutes or until crispy. Drain the tortilla cups on paper towels.

Season the rice and beans to taste; stir in the green onions and cilantro. Serve the beans in the tortilla cups.

texas gulf coast jambalaya

A rustic and complex dish, jambalaya is relatively easy to execute and can be prepared in one dish. It relies on seafood from the Gulf Coast of Texas and Mexico, but can be prepared with whatever fish is available to you. After all, jambalaya is merely a variation on the classic Spanish dish, paella.

1/4 cup olive oil

3/4 cup chorizo sausage (about 6 ounces)

2/3 cup tasso ham

2 cups finely chopped onion

6 scallions, chopped

6 garlic cloves, minced

1 large green bell pepper, seeded and finely chopped

1 large red bell pepper, seeded and finely chopped

6 stalks celery, finely chopped

8 ripe tomatoes (about 2 pounds), blanched, peeled, seeded, and chopped (page 5)

1 tablespoon chopped fresh oregano

2 teaspoons chopped fresh basil

1 tablespoon chopped fresh cilantro

1 teaspoon chopped fresh thyme

3 bay leaves

1 teaspoon ground cumin

2 teaspoons cayenne powder

3 cups chicken stock (page 33)

3 cups uncooked rice

24 medium-size raw shrimp, peeled and deveined

24 fresh Gulf Coast oysters (about 1 pound), shucked and in their liquor

8 ounces fresh Gulf Coast crabmeat, shell and cartilage removed

Salt to taste

(YIELDS 4 TO 6 SERVINGS)

Preheat the oven to 350°F.

Heat the olive oil in a large, ovenproof saucepan or casserole until lightly smoking. Add the chorizo and tasso and sauté over medium heat until crisp, 6 to 8 minutes. Add the onion, scallions, garlic, bell peppers, and celery, and sauté for 5 minutes more.

Add the tomatoes and seasonings, stir thoroughly, and cook for 5 minutes. Stir in the stock and bring to a boil. Add the rice, stir well. Remove from the heat. Cover the pan with foil, place in the oven, and bake until the rice is just tender, about 15 minutes.

Stir in the shrimp, oysters, and crabmeat. Cover and bake for 15 minutes more. Remove the bay leaves. Season with salt to taste and serve immediately.

texas gulf coast jambalaya

pumpkin-pecan pie
with whiskey butter sauce

This dessert was inspired by my good friend and great Cajun chef Paul Prudhomme. He prepares his with sweet potatoes, which are available year-round and, hence, give his version a longer seasonal shelf life than mine. If there's anything better than pumpkin pie or pecan pie, it's the two of them together. The whiskey butter adds a thoroughly Cajun twist to this sweet ending.

PIE CRUST

1 1/2 cups all-purpose flour

1/4 teaspoon salt

1/2 cup butter (1 stick)

3 to 4 tablespoons cold water

PUMPKIN FILLING

1 cup cooked pumpkin purée

1/4 cup firmly packed light brown sugar

2 tablespoons sugar

1 large egg, beaten until frothy

1 tablespoon heavy cream

1 tablespoon unsalted butter, softened

1 tablespoon vanilla extract

1/4 teaspoon salt

1/4 teaspoon ground cinnamon

Pinch of ground allspice

Pinch of ground nutmeg

PIE CRUST (YIELDS ONE 8-INCH PIE)

Combine the flour and salt in a mixing bowl. Add the butter and incorporate with your fingertips until the mixture resembles very coarse cornmeal. Sprinkle the water over the flour mixture in tablespoon increments, stirring continuously with a fork. Form the dough into a ball and chill in the refrigerator for 1 hour.

PUMPKIN FILLING

Combine all the ingredients thoroughly in a medium bowl; set aside.

PECAN SYRUP

3/4 cup sugar

3/4 cup dark corn syrup

2 small eggs

1 1/2 tablespoons unsalted
    butter, melted

2 teaspoons vanilla extract

1 pinch salt

1 pinch ground cinnamon

3/4 cup pecan pieces

WHISKEY BUTTER SAUCE

4 tablespoons unsalted butter (1/2 stick)

1/3 cup sugar

1 large egg

1/2 tablespoon very hot water

1/4 cup heavy cream

1/4 cup bourbon whiskey

PECAN SYRUP

Combine all the ingredients thoroughly in a medium bowl; set aside.

ASSEMBLY

Preheat the oven to 325°F. Grease an 8-inch springform cake pan.

Roll out the dough on a lightly floured work surface to 3/16 inch.
   Very lightly flour the top of the dough and fold it into quarters.
   Carefully place the dough in the greased cake pan. Press firmly in
   place and trim the edges. Chill for 15 minutes.

Spoon the Pumpkin Filling into the pan, spreading evenly to
   distribute. Gently pour the Pecan Syrup on top. Bake until a
   knife inserted in the center comes out clean, about 1 hour and
   45 minutes. Cool and serve with Whiskey Butter Sauce.

WHISKEY BUTTER SAUCE

Melt the butter in the top of a double boiler set over gently
   simmering water.

Beat the sugar and egg in a small bowl until blended. Stir the egg
   mixture into the butter. Add the hot water and stir until the
   mixture coats the back of a spoon, about 7 minutes. Remove from
   the double boiler and let cool to room temperature. Stir in the
   cream and whiskey.

praline ice cream
with sambuca–hot fudge sauce

Pralines, that great Cajun sweet, turn an ordinary vanilla ice cream into a multi-textured dessert. The Sambuca–Hot Fudge Sauce, while a bit indulgent, makes this a dessert worth skipping the main course for.

ICE CREAM

3 cups heavy cream

1 cup milk

3/4 cup sugar

1/2 vanilla bean, split in half lengthwise and scraped

4 large egg yolks

1 cup chopped Pecan Pralines

Sambuca–Hot Fudge Sauce

ICE CREAM (YIELDS 4 TO 6 SERVINGS)

Prepare 1 large bowl filled with ice and 1 smaller clean bowl.

Heat the cream, milk, sugar, and vanilla bean in a medium saucepan, stirring occasionally, until the sugar is dissolved and the mixture is hot. Remove from the heat. Cover and let infuse for 15 minutes.

Whisk the egg yolks for about 30 seconds in a medium bowl. Gradually pour about 1 cup of the cream mixture through a strainer into the yolks, stirring with a spatula.

Pour the egg yolk mixture into a clean saucepan together with the remaining cream mixture. Cook over low heat, stirring frequently and scraping the sides and bottom of the pan. Continue cooking until the custard thickens, reaches 185°F on a candy thermometer, and coats the back of a spoon, about 5 to 10 minutes. Do not let the mixture boil.

Once the custard thickens, remove the pan immediately from the heat; strain the mixture into the clean bowl. Set the mixture over the bowl of ice, stirring occasionally. Pour into an ice cream machine and freeze according to the manufacturer's directions. When almost frozen, fold in the chopped Pecan Pralines and continue to churn for 3 to 5 minutes. Top with Sambuca–Hot Fudge Sauce before serving.

PECAN PRALINES

6 tablespoons unsalted butter ($3/4$ stick)

$1/2$ cup sugar

$1/2$ cup firmly packed light brown sugar

2 tablespoons corn syrup

$3/4$ cup cream

$1^1/_2$ cups pecan pieces

1 teaspoon vanilla extract

1 teaspoon orange zest

SAMBUCA–HOT FUDGE SAUCE

$3/4$ pound milk chocolate, chopped

6 tablespoons strong coffee

3 tablespoons sambuca

$1/4$ cup light corn syrup

1 cup heavy cream

PECAN PRALINES

Melt the butter in a large, heavy saucepan over high heat. Add the sugars, corn syrup, and cream. Cook for 1 minute, whisking constantly. Add the pecan pieces and cook 4 minutes more, whisking constantly. Reduce the heat to medium and continue whisking 5 minutes longer. Add the vanilla and orange zest and continue whisking until a candy thermometer registers 240°F, about 15 to 20 minutes longer.

Remove the pan from the heat. Quickly and carefully drop the batter by heaping spoonfuls onto a cookie sheet, using a second spoon to scoop the batter out of the first. The pralines should be about 2 inches wide and $1/2$ inch thick. Cool and store in an airtight container.

SAMBUCA–HOT FUDGE SAUCE

Combine all of the ingredients in the top of a double boiler set over gently simmering water. Stir frequently until the chocolate has melted and all the ingredients are completely blended. Remove from the heat when the sauce is smooth. Serve warm.

the southern influence on

east texas

Southern cooking was developed by black Africans who were brought to the South. The chronicle of Africans in America doesn't follow the typical pattern of settlers who left their homelands to seek better conditions, whether economically or politically. Instead, they were a people uprooted from their native country and brought to the New World as slaves. When the female slaves cooked for themselves, they often used ingredients their masters didn't want, such as lesser cuts of meats: hog jowls, pig's feet, and internal organs. Their diets were supplemented with ingredients they had brought from Africa such as okra and black-eyed peas. They also consumed the greens of such root vegetables as turnips, collards, and beets.

The first Anglo-American settlers in East Texas came from other Southern states. Attracted by rich farmland, they began arriving in the early 1800s. They brought with them the same genteel way of life they had known on the plantations. Texas was part of the Confederacy, and the South is an integral part of the Texas culture.

fried green tomato and okra salad
with roasted corn vinaigrette and capers

The notion for this recipe obviously came from someone who loved tomatoes so much they couldn't wait for the summer harvest of ripe, red tomatoes. Green tomatoes hold up remarkably well to the pan-frying process and are the perfect accompaniment to the flavors of corn and capers. Slaves brought the okra from Africa to America, where it became a staple of Southern cooking, especially when fried.

2 large ears corn, in husks

$1/2$ large shallot, minced

1 garlic clove, minced

1 tablespoon white wine vinegar

$1/2$ cup chicken stock (page 33)

$1/4$ cup olive oil

$1/4$ cup corn oil, plus more for frying

Salt to taste

1 large egg

$1/4$ cup milk

1 cup cornmeal

3 teaspoons salt

4 small green tomatoes, sliced into $1/2$-inch-thick rounds

12 large okra spears (about 6 ounces), cut into $1/3$-inch rounds

6 ounces assorted salad greens, rinsed and dried

1 medium tomato, blanched, peeled, seeded, and diced (page 5)

2 tablespoons capers, drained

$1/2$ cup grated pecorino cheese

(YIELDS 6 SERVINGS)

Preheat the oven to 400°F. Roast the corn for 15 minutes on a large, heavy baking sheet. Remove the corn from the oven and let cool slightly. Remove the husks and silks; cut the corn kernels off the cobs using a sharp knife.

Combine the cooled corn kernels with the shallot, garlic, vinegar, and chicken stock in a blender or food processor; process until the corn is puréed. With the machine running, slowly drizzle in the olive oil and $1/4$ cup corn oil. When thoroughly incorporated, strain the vinaigrette into a bowl and season with salt to taste. Thin with a little chicken stock or water if necessary. Cover.

Pour enough corn oil in a large cast-iron skillet to come $1/4$ inch up the side. Heat over medium-high until lightly smoking.

Beat the egg and milk together in a small bowl. Combine the cornmeal and 3 teaspoons salt in a medium bowl. Working in batches, dip the tomato slices and okra in the egg wash, then dredge in the cornmeal to coat thoroughly.

Fry the tomatoes in the hot oil until golden brown, about 1 minute per side. Remove with a slotted spoon or spatula and drain on a paper towel–lined cookie sheet. Add the okra to the pan and fry, stirring occasionally, until golden brown and crisp, about 2 minutes. Using a slotted spoon, transfer the okra to the cookie sheet with the tomatoes.

Place the salad greens in a large mixing bowl and drizzle with the corn vinaigrette; toss thoroughly. Arrange the greens on serving plates, then place the fried tomatoes and okra on the greens. Garnish the salads with the diced tomato, capers, and pecorino. Drizzle the fried tomatoes with a little of the vinaigrette, if desired.

fried green tomato and okra

spicy fried chicken
with thyme cream gravy and wilted southern greens

Sometimes I think I would choose fried chicken as my last meal on earth. The art of frying chicken is most often passed from generation to generation, and my family is no exception. My execution of this Southern classic is based on the technique my great-grandmother used. The Wilted Southern Greens, while the perfect accompaniment to the chicken, also makes a terrific first course.

SPICY FRIED CHICKEN

2 cups buttermilk

5 garlic cloves, smashed

$2^1/_4$ teaspoon salt, divided

$1^1/_2$ teaspoons freshly ground black pepper, divided

1 3-pound fryer, cut into eighths

1 cup all-purpose flour

2 teaspoons cayenne powder

Vegetable oil for frying

Thyme Cream Gravy

Wilted Southern Greens

SPICY FRIED CHICKEN (YIELDS 4 SERVINGS)

Combine the buttermilk, garlic, $1/_4$ teaspoon of the salt, and $1/_2$ teaspoon of the pepper in a shallow nonreactive dish. Place the chicken pieces in the mixture and chill overnight, turning once or twice.

Combine the flour, remaining 2 teaspoons of salt, remaining 1 teaspoon of pepper, and cayenne in a medium bowl; set aside.

Preheat the oven to 200°F.

Pour enough vegetable oil in a large cast-iron skillet to come $1/_2$ inch up the side. Heat the oil to 360°F. Remove the dark meat from the buttermilk mixture, shaking to remove any excess. Dredge in the flour mixture. Carefully add the dark pieces of chicken to the skillet one by one, adjusting the heat to maintain an oil temperature of 315°F. Cook the dark pieces for 12 to 15 minutes per side or until the juices run clear when the thickest part is pierced with a knife. Remove the dark pieces to a paper towel–lined cookie sheet and hold warm in the oven until ready to serve.

Allow the oil to climb back to 360°F and repeat the previous steps with the white pieces of chicken, but reduce the cooking time to 10 to 12 minutes per side or until the juices run clear when the thickest part is pierced with a knife. Add the white pieces to the cookie sheet and reserve in the oven while preparing the Thyme Cream Gravy and Wilted Southern Greens.

THYME CREAM GRAVY

$1/2$ cup dry white wine

$1/2$ cup chicken stock (page 33)

$11/2$ cups heavy cream

2 tablespoons chopped fresh thyme

1 teaspoon minced lemon zest

1 tablespoon raspberry vinegar

1 tablespoon honey

Salt to taste

WILTED SOUTHERN GREENS

$3/4$ cup fresh cranberries, coarsely chopped

$1/4$ cup sugar

4 ounces bacon, diced

2 shallots, minced

2 garlic cloves, minced

$1/4$ cup corn oil

$1/4$ cup olive oil

2 tablespoons balsamic vinegar

2 tablespoons red wine vinegar

2 sprigs fresh rosemary, chopped

$1/2$ cup chopped pecans, toasted (page 5)

2 green apples, cored and coarsely chopped

8 ounces assorted greens (turnip, collard, or mustard greens), rinsed and dried

Salt and freshly ground black pepper to taste

THYME CREAM GRAVY

Discard all the oil from the cast-iron skillet. Heat the skillet and deglaze with the wine to dissolve any particles from the bottom of the pan. Add the chicken stock and reduce by half, about 3 to 4 minutes. Stir in the cream, thyme, lemon zest, and vinegar; continue to reduce until the sauce is thick enough to coat the back of a spoon, about 5 to 6 minutes. Add the honey and season with salt to taste.

WILTED SOUTHERN GREENS

Place the cranberries and sugar in a blender on medium speed for 30 seconds.

Cook the bacon in a large skillet until all the fat is rendered. Remove the bacon from the pan with a slotted spoon and set aside. Sauté the shallots and garlic in the bacon fat until soft. Whisk the oils and vinegars into the skillet. Stir in the rosemary, pecans, apples, and macerated cranberries, and cook for 1 minute.

Add the greens and toss until just wilted, about 20 to 30 seconds, and season with salt and pepper to taste. Garnish with the reserved bacon.

honey-glazed apple-stuffed pork chops
on black-eyed pea–sweet potato hash

Stuffed pork chops have always been a favorite dish of mine, and the combination of apples, honey, and pork makes an incomparable threesome. This dish is the epitome of the Southern influence in Texas cookery. Pork, sweet potatoes, and black-eyed peas are all genre-defining ingredients associated with the Lone Star State. The Black-eyed Pea–Sweet Potato Hash makes a great accompaniment for any number of meats, such as lamb, beef, and poultry—particularly if they are roasted.

PORK CHOPS

8 center-cut pork chops, about 8 ounces each

4 tablespoons olive oil, divided

6 ounces country sausage

1/2 small onion, diced

1 stalk celery, diced

1 garlic clove, minced

1/2 red bell pepper, seeded and diced

1 serrano, seeded and minced

2 green apples, cored and diced into 1/8-inch pieces

2 fresh sage leaves, chopped

1 sprig fresh rosemary, chopped

1/2 cup crumbled cornbread

1/4 cup sour cream

1/2 cup chopped pecans

Salt and freshly ground black pepper to taste

1 cup Honey Glaze

Black-eyed Pea–Sweet Potato Hash

PORK CHOPS (YIELDS 4 TO 6 SERVINGS)

Preheat the oven to 160°F.

Place a pork chop flat on a work surface. Hold it down with one hand; slice it through the middle with the point of the knife to form a pocket. Cut deeply to the bone, open the chop, and flatten each half with a meat pounder to make it a little larger for stuffing. Repeat these steps for the remaining pork chops.

Heat 2 tablespoons of the olive oil in a large skillet over medium heat until lightly smoking. Add the sausage and sauté, breaking it up with a fork as it cooks. Add the onion, celery, garlic, bell pepper, and serrano; cook for 2 to 3 minutes longer. Add the apples, herbs, and cornbread crumbs, tossing to heat through.

Remove the skillet from the heat and stir in the sour cream and pecans. Season with salt and pepper. When the stuffing has cooled, divide among the pork chops. Push the stuffing into the pockets and close securely. Do not overstuff, and make sure the meat is pressed together around the opening. Secure with toothpicks if desired. Season the chops with salt and pepper.

Heat the remaining 2 tablespoons of olive oil in a clean, large skillet over medium heat until lightly smoking. Add the chops and cook on one side for 3 to 4 minutes or until browned. Turn the chops over, cover, and reduce heat. Cook for an additional 6 to 7 minutes. Remove the chops from the skillet, brush generously with the glaze, and keep warm in the oven until ready to serve with Sweet Potato Hash.

HONEY GLAZE

1 cup honey

1 cup chicken stock (page 33)

2 tablespoons balsamic vinegar

2 tablespoons sherry vinegar

2 tablespoons pure chile powder (page 15)

1 tablespoon kosher salt

1 teaspoon chopped fresh sage

1 teaspoon chopped fresh thyme

1 teaspoon chopped fresh marjoram

BLACK-EYED PEA–SWEET POTATO HASH

1 medium sweet potato (about 1 pound), peeled and diced into $1/4$-inch pieces

2 tablespoons olive oil

1 small onion, peeled and thinly sliced

4 garlic cloves, minced

1 red bell pepper, seeded and diced

2 serranos, seeded and minced

2 cups cooked black-eyed peas

$1^1/_2$ teaspoons salt

Freshly ground black pepper to taste

1 teaspoon chopped fresh cilantro

$1/2$ teaspoon chopped fresh thyme

HONEY GLAZE

Place all the ingredients in a medium saucepan and bring to a boil. Reduce the heat and let simmer until the mixture is reduced to 1 cup. Remove from the heat and allow to cool to room temperature.

BLACK-EYED PEA–SWEET POTATO HASH

Cook the diced sweet potato in boiling salted water for 1 minute or until barely tender. Drain and place in cold water.

Heat the oil in a large skillet over medium-high heat until lightly smoking and sauté the onion until caramelized, about 3 minutes. Add the garlic, bell pepper, and serranos; sauté for another 2 minutes. Gently stir in the black-eyed peas, sweet potatoes, salt, pepper, cilantro, and thyme; heat through and serve.

baked maple grits
with wild mushrooms and country ham

While some people think of grits as Southern polenta, I think of polenta as Italian grits. After all, corn was consumed in the Americas thousands of years before it was brought to Europe. The wild mushrooms and ham give this casserole a complex flavor profile that makes it a great main-course dish, but also a nice dish with just about any meat or poultry, especially duck.

1³/₄ cups chicken stock (page 33)

³/₄ cup milk

³/₄ cup stone-ground grits

3 tablespoons unsalted butter

¹/₄ cup grated Parmesan cheese

Salt to taste

1 tablespoon olive oil

12 ounces wild mushrooms (cremini, shiitake, or portobello), sliced

1 garlic clove, minced

2 tablespoons white wine

¹/₂ teaspoon fresh thyme

6 ounces thinly sliced honey-baked ham, cut into thin strips

1 tablespoon unsalted butter, melted

¹/₄ cup maple syrup

¹/₄ teaspoon red chile flakes

(YIELDS 4 TO 6 SERVINGS)

Preheat the oven to 325°F. Butter a 9x12-inch baking dish.

Bring the stock and milk to a boil in a medium saucepan. Slowly pour in the grits, stirring constantly. Cover and simmer, stirring occasionally, for 18 to 20 minutes or until the stock and milk have been absorbed. Stir in the butter and Parmesan. Season to taste with salt and pour into the buttered dish.

Heat a medium sauté pan and pour in the olive oil. Add the mushrooms and garlic, sautéing until the mushrooms are wilted. Pour in the white wine and thyme, and simmer until the liquid is evaporated.

Spread the mushrooms over the grits. Layer the ham evenly over the mushrooms. Combine the melted butter, maple syrup, and red chile flakes in a small bowl; pour over the ham.

Bake in the oven for 20 to 25 minutes or until the ham is crispy.

warm minted strawberry shortcake

warm minted strawberry shortcake
with lemon verbena ice cream

A true Southern shortcake is nothing more than a sweet biscuit and bears no resemblance to the sponge cake–like grocery store concoction mistakenly called shortcake. Lemon verbena, the key ingredient for this ice cream, is a native South American herb introduced to Europe by the Spanish. Its highly lemon-flavored taste makes it a good substitute for lemongrass, lemon zest, or even lemon thyme.

STRAWBERRY SHORTCAKE

3 cups cake flour

2$^1/_4$ cups sugar, divided

1$^1/_2$ tablespoons baking powder

1 teaspoon salt

$^3/_4$ cup vegetable shortening, chilled

2 large eggs

$^1/_2$ cup milk

1 teaspoon vanilla extract

7 cups strawberries, cleaned
and stemmed

2 tablespoons Grand Marnier

Lemon Verbena Ice Cream

Mint sprigs for garnish

STRAWBERRY SHORTCAKE (YIELDS 6 TO 8 SERVINGS)

Combine the flour, 1 cup of the sugar, baking powder, and salt in a large bowl. Cut in the shortening with a fork. Whip together the eggs, milk, and vanilla in a separate bowl, blending until smooth. Add to the dry ingredients and incorporate thoroughly. The dough should be thinner and more sticky than regular shortcake or biscuit dough. Chill for 30 minutes.

Slice 5 cups of the strawberries. Purée the remaining 2 cups of strawberries, 1 cup of sugar, and the Grand Marnier in a blender. Fold the purée into the sliced berries.

Preheat the oven to 325°F. Grease a cookie sheet.

When shortcake dough has chilled, lay it out onto a well-floured surface and lightly sprinkle the top with flour. Roll out to a $^3/_4$-inch thickness. Cut the dough with a biscuit cutter into 6 to 8 shortcakes. Place on the greased cookie sheet, sprinkle with the remaining $^1/_4$ cup of sugar, and return to the refrigerator to chill for 30 minutes more.

Bake the shortcakes for 20 to 25 minutes or until golden brown. Slice the shortcakes in half while they are still hot. Place a scoop of Lemon Verbena Ice Cream on the bottom, and top with some of the strawberry mixture. Place the top of the shortcake on the ice cream and berries. Garnish with a mint sprig.

(continued)

warm minted strawberry shortcake *(continued)*

LEMON VERBENA ICE CREAM

3 teaspoons lemon zest, blanched for 30 seconds and drained well

1/3 cup fresh lemon verbena

1 cup milk

1 cup cream

1 vanilla bean, split in half lengthwise and scraped

4 large egg yolks

1/4 cup sugar

1/2 cup sour cream

Prepare 1 large bowl filled with ice and a smaller clean bowl.

Combine the lemon zest, lemon verbena, milk, cream, and vanilla bean in a small saucepan; bring to a boil. Remove from the heat, cover, and let infuse for 30 minutes.

Place the yolks in a medium bowl. Whisk in the sugar until the yolks lighten in color and form a ribbon. Bring the milk mixture back to a boil and gradually pour through a strainer into the yolks, stirring with a spatula. Discard the verbena and vanilla bean.

Pour the mixture into a clean saucepan and cook over low heat, continuing to stir. Scrape the sides and bottom of the pan, and continue cooking until the mixture thickens and reaches 185°F on a candy thermometer and coats the back of a spoon, about 5 to 10 minutes. Do not let the mixture boil.

Immediately remove the pan from the heat and strain the mixture into the clean bowl set over ice. Stir in the sour cream and let chill thoroughly. Place into an ice cream machine and freeze according to the manufacturer's directions.

peach crunch
with cinnamon-buttermilk ice cream

It wouldn't be summer in Texas without a warm peach dessert topped with ice cream. A crunch is a derivative of the cobbler and has many cousins including buckles, slumps, crisps, grunts, and betties, to name a few. The acidity of the Cinnamon-Buttermilk Ice Cream brings a nice balance to the sweetness of the crunch.

PEACH CRUNCH

8 medium-size ripe peaches, peeled and sliced

2 teaspoons fresh lemon juice (about $^1/_2$ lemon)

3 teaspoons granulated sugar

$^1/_2$ teaspoon ground ginger

4 tablespoons unsalted butter ($^1/_2$ stick)

$^1/_4$ cup oats

$^1/_2$ cup all-purpose flour

$^3/_4$ cup firmly packed light brown sugar

$^1/_2$ cup chopped pecans

1 teaspoon ground cinnamon

$^1/_2$ teaspoon grated nutmeg

1 pint Cinnamon-Buttermilk Ice Cream

CINNAMON-BUTTERMILK ICE CREAM

1 cup heavy cream

1 vanilla bean, split in half lengthwise and scraped

3 cinnamon sticks

1 large egg

2 large egg yolks

$^1/_3$ cup sugar

2 cups buttermilk

PEACH CRUNCH (YIELDS 4 TO 6 SERVINGS)

Preheat the oven to 350°F. Butter a 9- or 10-inch baking dish.

For the fruit filling, toss the peaches in a large bowl with the lemon juice, sugar, and ginger. Lay the fruit in the buttered baking dish.

For the topping, place the butter, oats, flour, brown sugar, chopped pecans, cinnamon, and nutmeg in a mixing bowl. Combine with your fingertips until crumbly and thoroughly mixed. Cover the fruit filling with the topping. Bake for 30 to 35 minutes or until the topping is browned. Serve with Cinnamon-Buttermilk Ice Cream.

CINNAMON-BUTTERMILK ICE CREAM

Prepare 1 large bowl filled with ice and a smaller clean bowl.

Bring the cream to a boil with the vanilla bean and cinnamon sticks in a medium saucepan. Remove from the heat, cover, and let infuse for 30 minutes.

Place the egg and yolks in a large bowl. Add the sugar, whisking continuously until the eggs lighten in color and form a ribbon. Bring the cream mixture back to a boil and gradually pour through a strainer into the yolks, stirring with a spatula. Discard the vanilla and cinnamon sticks.

Pour the mixture into a clean saucepan and cook over low heat, continuing to stir. Scrape the sides and bottom of the pan, and continue cooking until the custard thickens, reaches 185°F on a candy thermometer, and coats the back of a spoon, about 5 to 10 minutes. Do not let the mixture boil.

Immediately remove the pan from the heat, strain the mixture into the clean bowl, and set over the bowl of ice. Stir in the buttermilk and let chill thoroughly. Place into an ice cream machine and freeze according to the manufacturer's directions.

When most of the rest of the country thinks of Texas cooking, seafood preparation rarely comes to mind. But it should: with 372 miles of shoreline, Texas has more coast than any other state, except Florida, California, and Alaska. Padre Island alone has 80 miles, which are part of the National Park Service, making it one of the longest undeveloped beaches in North America. The Gulf Coast is rich with such shellfish as shrimp, blue crabs, and oysters and such finfish as red snapper, black sea bass, grouper, cobia, mackerel, and marlin.

It's easier to select fresh fish when they are whole. Always start with the eyes, which should be clear, bright, and shiny—never dull and cloudy. Check the gills, lifting up the gill cover behind the cheek. They should be clear red as well as moist and shiny.

If your shop only has fillets, make sure they are firm and springy to the touch; the indentation where you pressed should spring back. The fillets should be shiny and never dark or discolored. The most important aspect of any fish is its smell: It should always be almost odorless, never fishy and, if anything, redolent of the sea.

of the texas gulf coast

sugar cane–skewered shrimp
with pineapple-corn relish

In this Asian- and Caribbean-influenced dish, the sugar cane not only flavors the shrimp, but also tenderizes it slightly. And it's always an added pleasure to chew on the flavored cane after the shrimp are eaten. Don't limit the Pineapple-Corn Relish to this dish—try it with grilled chicken or fish for a nice complement.

1 habanero, seeded and diced

$1/4$ cup peeled and diced ginger

2 kaffir lime leaves

2 tablespoons soy sauce

3 tablespoons honey

1 tablespoon chopped fresh basil

1 lemongrass stalk, thinly sliced

16 shrimp (U-10 count), peeled (except for the tail section) and deveined

12 inches sugar cane, $1^1/_2$ to 2 inches in diameter

Pineapple-Corn Relish (page 27)

(YIELDS 4 SERVINGS)

Combine the habanero, ginger, lime leaves, soy sauce, honey, basil, and lemongrass in a large bowl. Add the shrimp; mix well and chill for 1 to 2 hours in the marinade. Prepare an outdoor grill or preheat the broiler. Cut the sugar cane in eighths lengthwise to produce 8 skewers.

Remove the shrimp from the marinade. Thread 4 pieces of shrimp onto 2 skewers, with 1 skewer going through the heads, the other going through the tails. The shrimp should be as straight as possible to prevent curling while cooking. Repeat with the remaining shrimp and skewers. You will have 4 double skewers, each holding 4 shrimp. Grill the shrimp about 6 inches from the heat source until very charred and just cooked through, about 3 minutes per side. Alternatively, you can broil the shrimp about 10 inches from the heat source for 3 minutes per side. Remove the shrimp to plates and serve with Pineapple-Corn Relish.

tuna escabeche tacos

Escabeche is a cooking process brought to the New World from Spain that is similar to ceviche.
Both processes use acidity such as lime juice or vinegar to "cook" the product. But while the product for
ceviche goes straight into an acidic marinade, an escabeche calls for searing or lightly grilling the food before
being "pickled," usually in a vinegar-based mixture.

2 tablespoons ground cumin

1 tablespoon pure chile powder (page 15)

1 teaspoon paprika

1 teaspoon salt

2 tablespoons ancho purée (page 15)

2 tablespoons olive oil

8 ounces tuna (preferably yellow fin), $^1/_2$-inch-thick, center-cut fillets

2 ripe tomatoes, blanched, peeled, seeded, and diced (page 5)

1 small onion, chopped

2 tablespoons roasted garlic purée (page 4)

$^1/_2$ cup fish or chicken stock (page 33)

Juice of 2 limes

3 tablespoons chile-infused white wine vinegar

Vegetable oil, for softening and frying the tortillas

8 corn tortillas

$^1/_2$ cup Avocado-Tomatillo Salsa (page 22)

$^1/_2$ cup shredded romaine lettuce for garnish

(YIELDS 4 SERVINGS)

Combine the cumin, chile powder, paprika, and salt in a medium bowl. Spread the ancho purée on the tuna, then coat in the spice mixture.

Heat the olive oil in a skillet over medium heat until lightly smoking. Sear the tuna for 30 to 45 seconds per side; it should be very dark on the outside, but rare in the center. Place the seared tuna in a nonreactive pan or ceramic dish just large enough to hold the fillet.

Purée the tomatoes, onion, garlic, stock, lime juice, and vinegar in a blender. Pour the purée over the tuna and marinate, chilled, for 6 to 8 hours, turning the fish occasionally if it is not completely covered with the marinade. Remove the tuna from the marinade, cut into 4 strips lengthwise, then finely slice each strip. Discard the marinade.

Pour enough vegetable oil in a medium skillet to come $^1/_2$ inch up the side. Heat the oil to 350°F or until just smoking. Submerge the tortillas in the oil one by one for 5 seconds each to soften. Holding the tortillas with tongs, fold in half and fry in a U-shape until crisp. Drain on paper towels and keep warm.

Divide the tuna evenly among the tacos. Top each taco with 1 tablespoon Avocado-Tomatillo Salsa and garnish with romaine lettuce.

gulf coast seafood chowder
with chipotle chile aïoli

The great bouillabaisse from the south of France created the inspiration for this dish. I like it not only because it tastes delicious, but also because it is healthful—high in nutritious vitamins and minerals. I particularly like to prepare this one at home because it's made in only one pot. One important note: if you're like me, you'll want extra aïoli; I recommend passing some separately in a sauceboat.

CHOWDER

1 tablespoon unsalted butter

2 ounces bacon, diced

$1/4$ cup diced red bell pepper

$1/4$ cup diced yellow bell pepper

$1/4$ cup diced green bell pepper

1 serrano, seeded and minced

$1/2$ cup diced onion

$1/2$ cup diced celery

$1/4$ cup bourbon

1 cup dry white wine

1 quart chicken stock (page 33)

1 small sweet potato, peeled and diced into $1/2$-inch pieces

$1/2$ cup fresh corn kernels

8 live crawfish

6 ounces redfish or red snapper fillets, diced into 1-inch pieces

2 ripe tomatoes, blanched, peeled, seeded, and diced (page 5)

24 Gulf Coast oysters, shucked

2 teaspoons salt

2 teaspoons fresh lime juice (about 1 lime)

2 tablespoons chopped fresh cilantro

$1/2$ cup jícama, diced into $1/2$-inch pieces

2 to 3 tablespoons Chipotle Chile Aïoli (page 31)

4 to 6 slices French bread, about 3 inches in diameter

CHOWDER (YIELDS 4 TO 6 SERVINGS)

Melt the butter and sauté the bacon over high heat in a medium saucepan for 1 minute. Add the bell peppers, serrano, onion, and celery; continue cooking for 3 minutes, stirring constantly. Deglaze with the bourbon. Add the wine and reduce the liquid by one-third.

Add the stock and bring to a boil. Add the sweet potato and corn, simmering for 3 minutes. Stir in the crawfish, redfish, and tomatoes. Cover and simmer for another $1^{1}/_{2}$ minutes. Add the oysters and simmer for 1 minute more. Season with salt and stir in the lime juice, cilantro, and jícama. Spread the aïoli on the bread and float one in each bowl of chowder.

gulf coast seafood chowder

barbecued gulf shrimp
with jícama cole slaw

This very rich but very satisfying dish is pure Southern. Served with the Jícama Cole Slaw, it's a complete meal.

SHRIMP

3 tablespoons olive oil

$1/3$ cup diced onion

4 teaspoons garlic, minced

16 to 18 large shrimp, peeled and deveined

Seasoning Mix

$1/4$ cup heavy cream

$1/2$ cup blanched, peeled, seeded, and diced tomatoes (page 5)

2 tablespoons fresh lemon juice (about 1 lemon)

2 tablespoons Worcestershire sauce

4 tablespoons scallions, finely sliced

6 tablespoons unsalted butter ($3/4$ stick)

Salt to taste

Jícama Cole Slaw

SEASONING MIX

$1/2$ teaspoon cayenne powder

$1/2$ teaspoon freshly ground black pepper

1 teaspoon paprika

$1/4$ teaspoon ground cumin

2 teaspoons chopped fresh thyme

2 teaspoons chopped fresh oregano

SHRIMP (YIELDS 4 TO 6 SERVINGS)

Heat the oil in a large skillet until lightly smoking. Add the onion, garlic, and shrimp; continue cooking until the shrimp are half-cooked. Increase the heat to high and stir in the Seasoning Mix, cream, tomatoes, lemon juice, and Worcestershire sauce; reduce the mixture by half. Add the scallions. Whisk in the butter by tablespoonfuls. Incorporate well and season with salt. Serve with Jícama Cole Slaw.

SEASONING MIX

Combine all the ingredients thoroughly in a small bowl; set aside.

JÍCAMA COLE SLAW

2 cups shredded red cabbage

$1/2$ cup grated carrots

1 medium jícama, peeled and julienned

1 medium-size red bell pepper, seeded and finely diced

1 medium-size yellow bell pepper, seeded and finely diced

1 small onion, peeled and grated

2 jalapeños, seeded and finely diced

$1/2$ cup mayonnaise (page 30)

2 tablespoons honey

1 tablespoon raspberry vinegar

1 tablespoon fresh lemon juice (about $1/2$ lemon)

Salt and freshly ground black pepper to taste

JÍCAMA COLE SLAW

Combine the cabbage, carrots, jícama, bell peppers, onion, jalapeños, mayonnaise, honey, vinegar, and lemon juice in a large bowl; mix thoroughly. Season with salt and pepper to taste. Chill well before serving.

grilled red snapper

grilled red snapper

with black bean–roast banana mash, coconut-serrano broth, and mango-tortilla salad

The combination of black beans and bananas is common in certain Central America countries and even in the Caribbean. Starting as an idea in Guatemala, this dish became fully developed once I returned from a culinary journey through Asia. Palm trees and coconuts are to Asia what corn is to the Americas. This sauce has all the complexities that are intrinsic in Asian cuisine, and I am particularly fond of the combination of sherry and coconut milk.

RED SNAPPER

6 6-ounce red snapper fillets

Salt to taste

Olive oil to coat

Black Bean–Roast Banana Mash

Coconut-Serrano Broth

Mango-Tortilla Salad

BLACK BEAN–ROAST BANANA MASH

1 cup black beans, soaked overnight and drained

4 cups chicken stock (page 33)

2 bananas

2 tablespoons olive oil

1/2 small onion, finely diced

1 tablespoon tomato paste

1/2 tablespoon pure chile powder (page 15)

1 garlic clove, chopped

1 tablespoon unsalted butter, divided

2 teaspoons fresh lime juice (about 1 lime), divided

Salt and freshly ground black pepper to taste

RED SNAPPER (YIELDS 6 SERVINGS)

Prepare the grill (page 4).

Salt the fillets, then lightly coat with oil. Grill fillets for 2 minutes. Carefully turn the fillets 45° with a spatula to make attractive grill marks. Cook 2 more minutes. Turn the fish over and repeat the process. Remove the fish from the grill and serve with Black Bean–Roast Banana Mash, Coconut-Serrano Broth, and Mango-Tortilla Salad.

BLACK BEAN–ROAST BANANA MASH

Preheat the oven to 350°F.

Combine the black beans and stock in a stockpot. Cook over high heat until the beans are very soft and the stock is almost completely reduced.

Roast the bananas (in the skin) until the fruit is soft and the skins are black, about 15 minutes.

Heat the olive oil in a small sauté pan until lightly smoking. Add the onion and sauté for 1 minute or until translucent. Add the tomato paste, chile powder, and garlic; continue cooking for 2 minutes. Remove from the heat.

Take half of each mixture and blend in a food processor with half the butter and half the lime juice. Repeat this process with the remaining half. Season with salt and pepper to taste.

(continued)

grilled red snapper *(continued)*

COCONUT-SERRANO BROTH

1 tablespoon olive oil

1/2 medium carrot, peeled and
  roughly chopped

1 celery stalk, chopped

1/2 medium onion, chopped

3 serranos, seeded and chopped

1/2 teaspoon ground cumin

2 lemongrass stalks, chopped

2 kaffir lime leaves

1 cup sherry

1 14-ounce can coconut milk

1 cup chicken stock (page 33)

1 cup cilantro leaves

1/2 cup basil leaves

Salt to taste

MANGO-TORTILLA SALAD

3 cups vegetable oil

2 yellow corn tortillas, julienned

1 red corn tortilla, julienned

1 blue corn tortilla, julienned

Juice of 4 limes

1/2 cup olive oil

Salt to taste

1 jícama, peeled and julienned

1/2 mango, peeled, pitted,
  and julienned

1/2 red bell pepper, julienned

1/4 cup cilantro leaves

COCONUT-SERRANO BROTH

Heat the olive oil in a large saucepan over high heat. Sauté the carrot, celery, and onion for 3 minutes or until the onion is translucent. Add the serranos, cumin, lemongrass, and lime leaves; continue to sauté for 1 minute more.

Deglaze the pan with the sherry and reduce to a glaze. Add the coconut milk and stock; bring to a boil. Reduce the heat and simmer for 5 minutes. Place in a blender and purée until smooth, about 1 minute. Strain the broth through a fine sieve. Tie the cilantro and basil together and steep them in the broth. Season with salt to taste.

MANGO-TORTILLA SALAD

Heat the vegetable oil in a medium sauté pan until lightly smoking. Fry the tortillas until crisp. Remove from the oil and drain on paper towels.

Pour the lime juice in a medium bowl. Slowly drizzle in the olive oil while whisking until an emulsion forms. Season with salt to taste. Combine the jícama, mango, bell pepper, and cilantro in a large bowl. Toss with the vinaigrette and use to garnish the dish.

pineapple–macadamia nut upside-down skillet cake

with orange-caramel sauce

Upside-down cakes were one of my mother's real specialties, and this cake was on the opening dessert menu at Baby Routh in 1986. I myself never saw a macadamia nut until I was grown, but they're the natural partner for pineapples in this cake. The caramel sauce is obviously a good accompaniment with any number of other desserts. Try it on top of your favorite ice cream sometime.

UPSIDE-DOWN CAKE

- 3/4 cup firmly packed light brown sugar
- 4 tablespoons unsalted butter (1/2 stick), melted
- 1 golden ripe pineapple, peeled, cored, and chopped into 1-inch chunks
- 1/2 cup roughly chopped macadamia nuts
- 1 1/2 cups all-purpose flour
- 2 teaspoons baking powder
- 1/4 teaspoon ground canela or ground cinnamon
- 1/4 teaspoon salt
- 4 tablespoons unsalted butter (1/2 stick)
- 1 cup sugar
- 2 large eggs
- 1 teaspoon vanilla extract
- 1/2 cup milk
- Orange-Caramel Sauce

ORANGE-CARAMEL SAUCE

- 1 cup sugar
- 1/3 cup fresh orange juice (about 1 orange)
- 1/4 cup water
- 2 tablespoons unsalted butter (1/4 stick)
- Juice of 1/2 lemon

UPSIDE-DOWN CAKE (YIELDS ONE 9-INCH CAKE)

Preheat oven to 350°F.

Spread the brown sugar over the bottom of a 9-inch cast-iron skillet. Pour the melted butter evenly over the sugar. Spread the pineapple chunks and macadamia nuts over the sugar-butter mixture; set aside.

Sift together the flour, baking powder, ground canela, and salt in a large bowl.

Cream together the butter and sugar in the bowl of an electric mixer until light and fluffy. While the mixer is running, add the eggs one at a time, beating until fully incorporated between additions. Beat in the vanilla extract.

Turn the mixer on low speed, and add the sifted ingredients and the milk alternately in three additions. Mix until just blended.

Pour the batter over the pineapple in the cake pan. Bake for 50 to 60 minutes or until a cake tester comes out clean. Remove the skillet from the oven and let the cake rest for 5 minutes. Run a pairing knife around the side to release the cake and, using hot pads, invert the skillet onto a large plate. Serve with Orange-Caramel Sauce.

ORANGE-CARAMEL SAUCE

Heat the sugar in a medium-size heavy saucepan; stir until completely melted and golden brown. Remove from the heat and stir in the orange juice and water until smooth, being careful of the hot caramel. Whisk in the butter and lemon juice, and serve warm or at room temperature.

brown butter–mango custard tart

If there's anything better than a simple, perfectly ripe mango, it's this mango tart. It's best served with some lightly sweetened whipped cream or even a nut-flavored ice cream.

CRUST

1³/₄ cups all-purpose flour

5 tablespoons sugar

5 tablespoons unsalted butter, cut into pieces

1 large egg yolk

1 tablespoon heavy cream, chilled

2 tablespoons cold water

MANGO CUSTARD

Pinch of cinnamon

6 large egg yolks

¹/₃ cup sugar

1¹/₂ tablespoons all-purpose flour

1 cup milk

1 cup mango purée

¹/₂ vanilla bean, split in half lengthwise and scraped

CRUST (YIELDS ONE 12-INCH TART)

Combine the flour and sugar in a medium bowl. Add the butter and cut in with a fork or pastry cutter until the mixture resembles cornmeal. Do not overwork. Combine the egg yolk, cream, and water in a small bowl. Slowly add the egg mixture to the flour mixture, mixing with a fork until the dough forms a ball. Wrap in plastic and chill for 1 hour.

Preheat the oven to 425°F. Lightly oil a removable-bottom, 12-inch tart pan.

Roll the dough out to a ¹/₈-inch thickness on a lightly floured work surface. Place the sheet of dough into the tart pan, making sure to tuck the dough into the corners. Cut off the excess dough from the edges and discard. Prick the bottom of the dough with a fork at ¹/₂-inch intervals. Place a sheet of aluminum foil on top of the crust and push into the surface of the dough, making sure it fits snugly. Top the foil with dry beans to fill and chill for 20 to 30 minutes. Bake for 12 to 15 minutes. Reduce the oven heat to 300°F, remove the beans and foil, and bake for an additional 6 minutes, or until golden brown. Allow to cool.

MANGO CUSTARD

Combine the cinnamon, egg yolks, sugar, and flour in a medium bowl; whisk until the yolks have lightened in color. Place the milk, mango purée, and vanilla bean in a medium saucepan and bring to a boil.

BROWN BUTTER FILLING

4 large eggs

1 cup sugar

$1/2$ cup all-purpose flour

$2/3$ cup unsalted butter

$1/4$ teaspoon nutmeg

$1/2$ vanilla bean, split in half lengthwise and scraped

ASSEMBLY

2 ripe mangos, peeled, pitted, and diced

Stir $1/4$ cup of the milk mixture into the egg mixture through a strainer. Gradually add the remaining milk mixture while stirring constantly. Return the mixture to the saucepan and cook over medium heat, stirring constantly while scraping the bottom and sides with a flat-bottomed wooden spoon until the mixture has thickened considerably and reaches 180°F to 185°F on a candy thermometer. Pour the mixture back through the strainer into the medium bowl. Cover with plastic wrap with the plastic touching the surface of the custard to keep it from forming a skin. Chill until needed.

BROWN BUTTER FILLING

Combine the eggs, sugar, and flour in a medium bowl. Whip until the mixture is lemon-colored and frothy. Combine the butter, nutmeg, and vanilla bean in a small saucepan over medium heat and cook until the butter browns and has a pleasant nutty smell, about 4 minutes. Pour the butter mixture into the egg mixture, stirring continuously. Remove the vanilla bean. Set aside the filling until ready to assemble.

ASSEMBLY

Preheat the oven to 350°F.

Place the diced mango evenly over the crust. Top the mango with the reserved brown butter filling and bake for 25 minutes. Remove and cool before continuing.

Cut the tart into 12 pieces and serve, spooning some of the Mango Custard on top of each.

The mid-nineteenth century saw a great influx of German immigrants into the Hill Country of Texas around current-day Austin. Trying to escape unstable economic, political, and social conditions back home, the immigrants were attracted by the massive opportunity they saw here.

By 1860, the Germans had established themselves as an influential ethnic group, founding such towns as New Braunfels and Fredricksburg. These towns still have street signs in German as well as English.

The German tradition of sausage-making and curing meats in smokehouses was most likely the forerunner of barbecue. The word "barbecue" itself, however, comes from a Veracruz Indian dialect, *barbacoa*, which refers to a slow cooking process in stone-lined pits.

germanic

hill country cuisine

molasses grilled quail
with corn pudding tamales and morita salsita

These corn pudding tamales go well with just about any meat or poultry. At Star Canyon, they accompany seared foie gras. The long, slow roasting of the corn is essential to the flavor of this dish. A by-product of making sugar, molasses is the syrup remaining from sugar cane juice after sucrose crystallization.

QUAIL

$1/2$ cup soy sauce

$1/4$ cup dark beer

2 tablespoons dark molasses

Zest of 1 lemon, minced

Zest of 1 orange, minced

1 tablespoon chopped fresh lemon verbena or fresh lemon thyme

$1/4$ cup finely diced ginger

2 garlic cloves, crushed

8 boneless quail, 3 to 4 ounces each

Corn Pudding Tamales

Morita Salsita (page 21)

CORN PUDDING TAMALES

8 cups fresh corn kernels

$1^3/4$ cups masa harina

$1^1/4$ cups very hot water

$1/2$ cup plus 2 tablespoons vegetable shortening, chilled

2 teaspoons salt

1 teaspoon baking powder

$1/4$ cup cold chicken stock (page 33)

$1/3$ cup maple syrup

Salt to taste

10 large corn husks, soaked in water for 30 minutes

QUAIL (YIELDS 4 SERVINGS)

Combine the soy sauce, beer, molasses, citrus zests, lemon verbena, ginger, and garlic thoroughly in a large bowl. Add the quail; marinate for 1 to 2 hours, turning occasionally.

While the tamales are steaming, prepare the grill (page 4) or, alternatively, preheat the broiler. Remove the quail from the marinade; reserve the marinade. Season the quail with salt to taste. Grill for 2 to 3 minutes on each side, brushing with the marinade. The molasses may caramelize and look burned, but the flavor is very pleasant.

Place the tamales on serving plates and slice open the top of each tamale from end to end. Gently push the ends together, as for a baked potato. Cut each quail in half lengthwise and place on the tamales. Spoon 1 tablespoon Morita Salsita on each tamale.

CORN PUDDING TAMALES

Preheat the oven to 350°F.

Process the corn in the bowl of a food processor for 3 minutes or until smooth. Place the purée in a baking pan and bake for 1 hour or until the corn is dry, stirring every 15 minutes. Remove from the oven and refrigerate until completely chilled.

Place the masa harina in the bowl of an electric mixer. Using the paddle attachment with the mixer on low speed, slowly add the water in a constant stream until the dough forms a ball. Continue to mix on high speed for 5 minutes. Remove the dough from the bowl, roll out to $1/2$-inch thickness on a cookie sheet, and refrigerate until completely chilled, about 1 hour.

Return the masa to the bowl and beat for 5 minutes on high speed.
Slowly add the shortening in 2-tablespoon increments. Continue
to beat until smooth and light, about 5 minutes. Scrape the
sides of the bowl and reduce to low speed, continuing to beat.

Combine the salt, baking powder, and chicken stock in a small
bowl. Slowly add the stock mixture to the masa, pouring in a
constant stream. Combine thoroughly. Whip on high speed for
5 minutes. Add the cooled corn mixture, maple syrup, and salt.

Drain the corn husks and pat dry. Tear 16 ($^{1}/_{6}$-inch-wide) strips
from 2 of the husks for tying the tamales. Divide the dough
evenly among the 8 remaining husks. Spread the dough in the
center of the husks, leaving 1 inch at each end uncovered.
Roll the corn husks so that the dough is completely enclosed.
Twist and tie each end with the reserved strips.

Steam the tamales in a conventional steamer or in a strainer or
vegetable basket set in a saucepan. Cover with a tight-fitting
lid to ensure that little or no steam escapes while cooking. Steam
for 30 to 35 minutes; the water should always be lightly boiling.
The tamales are done when the dough comes away easily from
the husk. Allow the tamales to cool slightly before serving.

barbecued brisket
with the fixin's

Texas barbecue evolved from the German migration of the mid-nineteenth century. They brought with them their techniques for brining, curing, and smoking. The indigenous beef, tomatoes, and chiles eventually became part of the mix. Brisket of beef is the perfect cut for barbecuing, as it needs long, slow heat to become tender. If it ain't smoky, it ain't Texas barbecue. The fixin's are purely Texan too.

BRISKET

$^1/_4$ cup salt

2 tablespoons freshly ground black pepper

2 tablespoons paprika

1 tablespoon cayenne powder

1 4-pound beef brisket, untrimmed

Ranch Barbecue Sauce

Mashed Potato Salad with Pickled Jalapeños and Black Olives

German Lager Baked Beans

BRISKET (YIELDS 1 TEXAS SERVING OR 4 TO 6 YANKEE SERVINGS)

To prepare the brisket, combine the salt, pepper, paprika, and cayenne in a large bowl. Trim all but a $^1/_8$-inch layer of fat from the brisket and place in a large glass or ceramic dish. Sprinkle the spice mixture over the meat, rolling to coat completely. Marinate, chilled, for at least 24 hours.

Prepare the smoker (page 7). Soak 6 to 8 large chunks of aromatic hardwood (such as hickory or mesquite) in water for 20 minutes. Place a pan of water in the bottom of the smoker. Build a fire in the smoker with charcoal and let it burn down until uniformly covered with white-gray ash, about 20 to 30 minutes. Spread out the coals; add the soaked hardwood chunks and let burn for 5 minutes. Place the brisket on the grill over the water pan. Place a shallow pan underneath the meat to catch the drippings and cover the smoker. Keep the fire stoked every 30 minutes, adding more charcoal or soaked wood chunks as needed.

After 2 hours, remove the meat and stoke the fire, adding more soaked wood. Add more water to the pan as needed. Return the meat and smoke for 5 to 6 more hours or until fork-tender, maintaining a temperature of 190°F to 225°F. Place the brisket on a board and slice as thinly as possible. Place the slices in a clean, nonreactive saucepan and add the Ranch Barbecue Sauce. Heat through. Serve with Mashed Potato Salad with Pickled Jalapeños and Black Olives and German Lager Baked Beans.

Alternatively: If you don't have a smoker or the time it takes to tend a fire, preheat the oven to 325°F. Sear the brisket on both sides in a large pan. Bake for $2^1/_2$ to 3 hours. Place the cooked brisket on a carving board and slice as thinly as possible. Place the slices in a clean, nonreactive saucepan. Add the Ranch Barbecue Sauce and heat through.

(continued)

barbecued brisket

barbecued brisket *(continued)*

RANCH BARBECUE SAUCE

1 teaspoon corn oil

2 onions, peeled and chopped

3 jalapeños, minced with seeds

6 garlic cloves, minced

$1/2$ cup firmly packed light brown sugar

$1/2$ cup cider vinegar

2 tablespoons fresh lemon juice

$1/2$ cup strong black coffee

2 tablespoons pure chile powder (page 15)

2 cups ketchup

2 tablespoons Dijon mustard

1 teaspoon salt

MASHED POTATO SALAD WITH PICKLED JALAPEÑOS AND BLACK OLIVES

12 medium-size red-skin potatoes

2 pickled jalapeños, chopped

$1/4$ cup chopped kalamata olives

2 teaspoons grainy mustard

$1/2$ cup mayonnaise (page 30)

1 teaspoon chopped fresh cilantro

1 teaspoon chopped fresh oregano

2 large eggs, hard-boiled and diced

Salt to taste

GERMAN LAGER BAKED BEANS

$1 1/4$ cups pinto beans, soaked overnight and drained

1 medium onion, finely diced

1 ham hock

$5 1/2$ cups chicken stock (page 33)

1 tablespoon olive oil

2 jalapeños, stemmed, seeded, and diced

1 tablespoon cumin

1 tablespoon pure chile powder (page 15)

1 12-ounce bottle German lager beer

1 cup diced tomatoes

2 tablespoons chopped fresh cilantro

Salt to taste

RANCH BARBECUE SAUCE

Heat the corn oil in a large enamel or stainless steel saucepan. Sauté the onions, jalapeños, and garlic until lightly caramelized, about 3 minutes.

Whisk in the remaining ingredients and bring to a boil, stirring constantly. Reduce the heat and simmer, covered, for 30 minutes. Strain the sauce through a medium strainer; pour over the sliced brisket.

MASHED POTATO SALAD WITH PICKLED JALAPEÑOS AND BLACK OLIVES

Boil the potatoes until tender; drain. Combine the potatoes with the jalapeños, olives, mustard, mayonnaise, cilantro, oregano, and eggs in a large bowl; mash with a potato masher or beaters. Season with salt. Chill until ready to serve.

GERMAN LAGER BAKED BEANS

Combine the beans, half the onion, the ham hock, and stock in a large saucepan. Bring to a boil, then reduce to a simmer for 2 hours or until the beans are tender.

Heat the oil in a sauté pan until lightly smoking. Add the remaining onion, jalapeños, cumin, and chile powder. Sauté for 3 minutes or until the onion starts to caramelize. Add the beer, tomatoes, and cilantro and cook for 1 more minute. Add the mixture to the beans and season with salt to taste.

pork tenderloin
with pickled red cabbage and green tomato chutney

This is the perfect winter dish for the season when cabbage is abundant and tomatoes are not yet ripe.

Pork tenderloin is best when prepared with simple, quick-cooking techniques, as you'll see from this recipe.

PORK TENDERLOIN

4 pork tenderloins (8 to 10 ounces each), trimmed of fat

Salt and freshly ground black pepper to taste

1/4 cup clarified butter or vegetable oil

Picked Red Cabbage

Green Tomato Chutney (page 25)

PICKLED RED CABBAGE

1/2 head red cabbage, cored and thinly sliced

1/2 medium onion, peeled and finely diced

1 small serrano, seeded and minced

1 tablespoon whole-grain mustard

1 teaspoon prepared horseradish

Pinch of ground cloves

Pinch of ground cinnamon

Pinch of ground allspice

1 cup cider vinegar

1/2 cup sugar

1 1/2 teaspoons salt

1/2 cup water

PORK TENDERLOIN (YIELDS 4 TO 6 SERVINGS)

Cut each tenderloin into 6 medallions; season with salt and pepper. Heat the butter in a large skillet over medium heat. Sauté the pork for about 3 minutes on one side; turn and cook for 2 minutes on the other. Remove from the pan and serve with Pickled Red Cabbage and Green Tomato Chutney.

PICKLED RED CABBAGE

Combine all the ingredients in a small saucepan over high heat and bring to a boil. Reduce the heat and simmer until the cabbage is tender, about 1 hour, stirring occasionally. Chill until ready to use.

pepita and chile-crusted venison loin

pepita and chile-crusted venison loin

with red wine–poached pears, gorgonzola croutons, and arugula

Pepitas, or pumpkin seeds, are used extensively in Hispanic cooking. The venison loin pairs perfectly with another time-honored combination, pears and blue cheese. If venison is not available, substitute beef tenderloin for equally tasty results.

VENISON

1/2 cup pumpkin seeds, toasted and ground (page 5)

2 serranos, minced with seeds

2 tablespoons chopped fresh cilantro leaves

1/4 cup all-purpose flour

3/4 cup bread crumbs

1 tablespoon pure chile powder (page 15)

2 teaspoons salt

2 tablespoons milk

1 large egg, beaten

1 loin of venison (2 to 3 pounds), cleaned

1 tablespoon olive oil

4 to 6 cups arugula, cleaned

Vinaigrette (see Red Wine–Poached Pears and Vinaigrette)

3 ounces Gorgonzola or blue cheese

6 croutons, about 2 inches long

Red Wine–Poached Pears

1/4 cup walnut halves, toasted (page 5)

VENISON (YIELDS 6 SERVINGS)

Preheat the oven to 400°F.

Combine the pumpkin seeds, serranos, cilantro, flour, bread crumbs, chile powder, and salt in a medium bowl. Combine the milk and egg in another medium bowl.

Dip the venison loin in the egg wash and roll in the bread crumbs, coating generously.

Heat the olive oil in a medium sauté pan over high heat until lightly smoking. Place the loin in the pan and sear on all sides. Place in a baking dish and bake for 15 to 18 minutes for medium rare.

Remove the venison from the oven and let rest for 5 to 7 minutes. Place the arugula in a large bowl and dress with Vinaigrette.

Spread the Gorgonzola on the croutons and warm slightly in the oven. Slice the venison loin and serve with the salad, poached pears, and Gorgonzola croutons. Garnish with the toasted walnuts.

(continued)

pepita and chile-crusted venison loin (continued)

**RED WINE–POACHED PEARS
AND VINAIGRETTE**

3 cups dry red wine

$^3/_4$ cup good-quality port

3 cloves

$^3/_4$ cup sugar

3 ripe Anjou or Bartlett pears, peeled,
halved, and cored

3 tablespoons raspberry vinegar

1 small shallot, chopped

1 teaspoon roasted garlic purée
(page 4)

$^1/_2$ cup walnut oil

3 tablespoons vegetable oil

Salt to taste

RED WINE–POACHED PEARS AND VINAIGRETTE

Combine the wine and port in a saucepan just large enough to
hold the pear halves. Add the cloves and sugar and bring to a
boil. Reduce the heat to low and add the pears, cut side down.
Let simmer for 10 to 15 minutes or until tender when pierced
with a knife. Remove the pears and set aside to cool. Pour off
all but 1 cup of the poaching liquid and reduce it to several
tablespoons over high heat.

Place the reduced liquid in a blender and add the raspberry vinegar,
shallot, and garlic. Blend until smooth. Add the oils in a steady
drizzle. Season with salt to taste.

chile-crusted wiener schnitzel
with lemon-caper butter sauce

This is obviously a Texas variation on an Austrian-German theme. By 1860, the Germans had established
themselves as an influential ethnic group in central Texas. I like to think of Wiener Schnitzel as
nothing more than a Chicken Fried Steak Deluxe.

WIENER SCHNITZEL

2 pounds veal cutlets, $1/4$ inch thick

1 cup fresh lemon juice (about 1 pound lemons)

$1/2$ cup all-purpose flour

2 tablespoons pure chile powder (page 15)

2 teaspoons salt

2 large eggs

2 tablespoons milk

2 cups bread crumbs

Vegetable oil for frying

Lemon-Caper Butter Sauce

LEMON-CAPER BUTTER SAUCE

1 cup dry white wine

$1/4$ cup fresh lemon juice (about 2 lemons)

Zest of 2 lemons

2 small shallots, chopped

2 garlic cloves, smashed

3 black peppercorns

1 bay leaf

$1/2$ pound unsalted butter (2 sticks), cut into tablespoons

$1/4$ cup capers, chopped

WIENER SCHNITZEL (YIELDS 4 TO 6 SERVINGS)

Marinate the cutlets in the lemon juice for 1 hour; remove and pat dry. Combine the flour, chile powder, and salt in a medium bowl. Combine the eggs and milk in another medium bowl; beat well. Place the bread crumbs on a plate. Begin the breading process by thoroughly dredging the veal in the flour mixture. Dip into the egg mixture and finish by coating evenly with the bread crumbs. Repeat this process for each piece of veal.

Preheat the oven to 200°F.

Pour enough oil in a large skillet to come $1/8$ inch up the side. Heat the oil until lightly smoking. Carefully place as many cutlets as will fit into the pan without overlapping. Fry on each side for 3 minutes or until completely golden brown. Remove to a paper towel–lined cookie sheet and hold warm in the oven until finished with all the cutlets. Serve with Lemon-Caper Butter Sauce.

LEMON-CAPER BUTTER SAUCE

Combine the wine, lemon juice, lemon zest, shallots, garlic, peppercorns, and bay leaf in medium saucepan and reduce to 2 tablespoons. Reduce the heat to the lowest setting. Add the butter pieces one at a time, whisking constantly and waiting for each piece to almost completely incorporate before adding the next. Do not let the sauce get too hot or it will break; the finished sauce should have a silky, creamy consistency. If serving immediately, remove from the heat as soon as all the butter is incorporated, and strain into a serving container. (Alternatively, the sauce can be kept warm in a double-boiler set over barely simmering water.) Stir in the capers and serve.

mile-high lemon meringue pie
with cactus pear glaze

Sometimes there's simply no better way to end a meal—or start the day—than with a slice of sweet-tart lemon meringue pie. My mother prepared the desserts at one of our cafes in west Texas when I was growing up. This and her buttermilk pie are the ones I still dream about. Cactus pears, or "tunas," are seasonally available at Hispanic markets around the country. While their use is not integral to the success of this dish, they make a nice addition. Oddly enough, I didn't realize their potential for creativity until I tasted a cactus pear sorbet many years ago at the famous Michelin three-star restaurant, Troigros, in Roanne, France. Needless to say, it was an incredible honor to get to work with Pierre Troigros a year later.

CRUST

1 1/2 cups all-purpose flour

1/4 teaspoon salt

1/2 cup vegetable shortening

4 to 5 tablespoons ice water

1 large egg white

CRUST (YIELDS ONE 9-INCH PIE)

Preheat the oven to 425°F.

Combine the flour and salt in a medium bowl. Add the shortening and incorporate with your fingertips until the mixture resembles very coarse cornmeal. Sprinkle 3 to 4 tablespoons of the water over the flour mixture in tablespoon increments, stirring constantly with a fork. Form the dough into a ball and let rest, chilled, for 1 hour.

Roll out the dough into a circle of 1/8-inch thickness on a lightly floured surface. Place the dough in a 9-inch pie pan; trim and crimp the edges. Place the shell in the freezer for 20 minutes.

Remove the shell from the freezer and prick the bottom and sides with a fork. Press the foil snugly over the bottom and sides of the crust. Pour rice or dried beans over the foil and bake in the oven for about 6 minutes.

Whisk together the egg white and remaining tablespoon of water in a bowl.

Remove the foil from the pan and brush the sides and bottom of the crust with the egg wash. Bake for an additional 8 to 10 minutes. Let cool before adding the pie filling.

LEMON FILLING

1 1/2 cups sugar

5 tablespoons cornstarch

Pinch of salt

1 1/2 cups hot tap water

4 large egg yolks

1/4 cup fresh lemon juice (about 2 lemons)

1 tablespoon lemon zest

2 tablespoons unsalted butter (1/4 stick)

MERINGUE

7 large egg whites, at room temperature

Pinch of cream of tartar

Pinch of salt

3/4 cup sugar

ASSEMBLY

2 lemons, peeled with a knife and sectioned with the membrane removed

CACTUS PEAR GLAZE

6 cactus pears, peeled and chopped

Juice of 3 limes

1/4 cup water

2 tablespoons sugar

LEMON FILLING

Combine the sugar, cornstarch, and salt in a large saucepan and add the water, whisking continuously, to make a smooth paste. Place the pan over medium heat and slowly bring to a boil, continuing to stir. Cook and stir until thickened, about 1 minute. Whisk the egg yolks in a medium bowl, gradually adding about half the hot sugar mixture. Slowly pour the egg mixture back into the saucepan and continue to whisk until smooth. Stir in the lemon juice, lemon zest, and butter. Return the pan to the heat and bring to a boil for 1 minute to thicken, stirring constantly. Remove from the heat and let cool completely.

MERINGUE

Preheat oven to 375°F.

Combine the egg whites, cream of tartar, and salt in a large bowl. Whip until the whites form soft peaks. Slowly incorporate the sugar, whisking until the meringue is glossy and forms stiff peaks.

ASSEMBLY

Fill the cooled pie shell with Lemon Filling, spreading out evenly. Place the reserved lemon segments on top of the custard. Spread the Meringue evenly over the slices, piling it as high as possible and making sure it touches the crust all the way around to prevent shrinking. Create decorative peaks and valleys with a spatula. Bake for approximately 10 minutes, checking to make sure the meringue does not burn. Serve the Mile-High Lemon Meringue Pie with Cactus Pear Glaze.

CACTUS PEAR GLAZE

Place all the ingredients in a small saucepan and bring to a boil. Reduce to a simmer and cook for 20 minutes. Remove from the heat and strain to remove the seeds. Chill and serve.

german chocolate cake

This is a cake I remember with great fondness. It was usually thought of as the cake of celebration: birthdays, anniversaries, a life achievement like graduation. Research on the name leads me to believe that it's not actually of German derivation, which I assumed for so long, but instead comes from a creation of the German Sweet Chocolate company.

CAKE

1 4-ounce package Baker's German sweet baking chocolate

$1/2$ cup water

2 cups all-purpose flour

1 teaspoon baking soda

$1/4$ teaspoon salt

$1/2$ pound unsalted butter (2 sticks), softened

2 cups sugar

4 large eggs, separated

1 teaspoon vanilla extract

1 cup buttermilk

Frosting

FROSTING

1 12-ounce can evaporated milk

$1^1/2$ cups sugar

$3/4$ cup unsalted butter ($1^1/2$ sticks)

4 large egg yolks, slightly beaten

$1^1/2$ teaspoons vanilla bean, split in half lengthwise and scraped

1 7-ounce package shredded, sweetened coconut (about $2^2/3$ cups)

$1^1/2$ cups chopped pecans, toasted (page 5)

CAKE (YIELDS ONE 9-INCH CAKE)

Preheat the oven to 350°F. Line the bottoms of three 9-inch round cake pans with wax paper.

Heat the chocolate and water in a heavy 1-quart saucepan over very low heat, stirring constantly until the chocolate is melted and the mixture is smooth. Remove from the heat. Combine the flour, baking soda, and salt in a medium bowl.

Beat together the butter and sugar in a large bowl with an electric mixer on medium speed until light and fluffy. Add the egg yolks, one at a time, beating well after each addition. Stir in the chocolate mixture; add the vanilla. Add the flour mixture alternately with the buttermilk, beating after each addition until smooth. Beat the egg whites in another large bowl with an electric mixer on high speed until stiff peaks form. Gently fold into the batter. Pour the batter into the wax paper–lined pans.

Bake for 30 minutes or until the cakes spring back when lightly touched in the center. Remove from the oven and immediately run a spatula around the sides of the pans to loosen the cakes. Cool 15 minutes. Remove from the pans and remove the wax paper. Cool completely on wire racks. Spread frosting between the layers and over the top of the cake.

FROSTING

Combine the evaporated milk, sugar, butter, egg yolks, and vanilla in a large saucepan. Cook, stirring frequently, over medium heat about 12 minutes or until thickened and golden brown. Remove from the heat and stir in the coconut and pecans. Cool to room temperature to reach a desired spreading consistency.

Central Mexico, the region surrounding Mexico City,
is a beautifully diverse area, with some of the
country's most stunning landscapes represented.
The nation's capital, twenty-three million and
counting, rests on Altiplano, a high plateau
between the Sierra Madre Occidental and Oriental
ranges. The surrounding area, scattered with lush
valleys, rushing rivers, and pre-Columbian ruins,
is home to Mexico's silver center.

Back in Mexico City, though, one can find products
    from every region. Its extensive markets are
    a microcosm of Mexico as a whole, offering a
    snapshot of all that makes up this rich country.

But you don't have to limit your search for good
    food to the markets: Well known for being one of
    the most cosmopolitan cities in the world, Mexico
    City boasts sophisticated restaurants of all kinds.
    Most would agree, however, that it's Mexico City's
    quaint and lively taquerias and cantinas that
    better define Mexico's unique style of cooking,
    eating, and living.

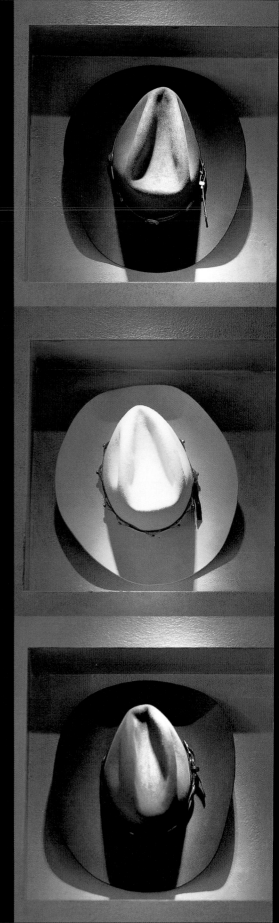

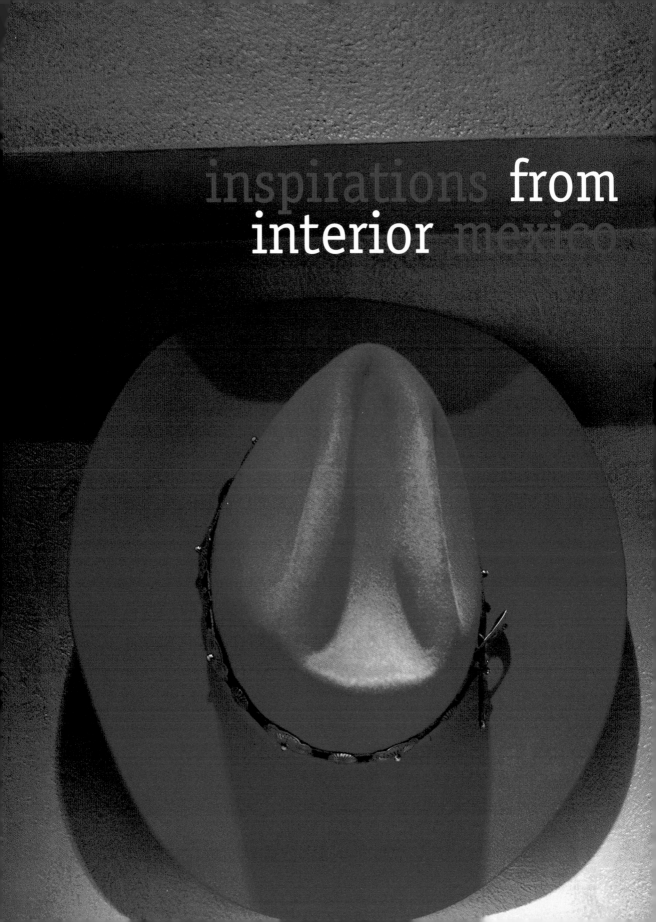

inspirations from interior mexico

roast poblano–tomatillo soup
with hoja santa

This delicious soup gets its flavor from some of my favorite ingredients—roasted poblanos, tomatillos, and that sassafras-flavored herb, hoja santa—all blended beautifully with the saltiness of the queso montasio.

SOUP

1/4 cup all-purpose flour

4 tablespoons unsalted butter, softened (1/2 stick)

3 poblanos, roasted, peeled, and seeded (page 14)

1 onion, finely diced

12 tomatillos, peeled and quartered

3 garlic cloves, minced

1 1/2 cups chicken stock (page 33)

1/2 cup cream

2 cups milk

1 cup fresh cilantro leaves

1 cup chopped hoja santa

10 ounces queso montasio

Salt and freshly ground black pepper to taste

Yellow Pepper Sauce

Pico de Gallo (page 20)

YELLOW PEPPER SAUCE

2 yellow bell peppers, roasted, peeled, and seeded (page 14)

3 tablespoons sherry vinegar

3 tablespoons olive oil

Salt and freshly ground black pepper to taste

SOUP (YIELDS 4 TO 6 SERVINGS)

Mix the flour and the butter into a smooth paste.

Combine the poblanos, onion, tomatillos, garlic, chicken stock, cream, and milk in a heavy saucepan. Bring to a boil, then reduce heat and let simmer for 5 minutes. Add the flour paste, stirring continuously to dissolve until the soup begins to thicken. Stir in the cilantro, hoja santa, and queso montasio. Pour the soup into a blender and purée to the desired texture (smooth or coarse). If puréed to a smooth texture, strain before serving. Season with salt and pepper. Drizzle with the Yellow Pepper Sauce and serve with Pico de Gallo.

YELLOW PEPPER SAUCE

Combine the roasted bell peppers with the sherry vinegar in a blender and purée until smooth. Slowly drizzle in the olive oil, continuing to blend to create an emulsion. Season with salt and pepper.

tortilla soup
with epazote

In some form or other, this soup can be found in every region of Mexico. You could say it's the national soup.

10 guajillos, stemmed and seeded

2 quarts chicken stock (page 33)

2 cups vegetable oil for frying

3 corn tortillas, julienned

4 tomatoes, roasted whole with the seeds

2 tablespoons olive oil

1 medium onion, diced

4 garlic cloves, minced

2 tablespoons minced fresh epazote

Salt and freshly ground black pepper to taste

1 cup chopped cooked chicken

1/2 pound fresh mozzarella cheese, shredded

Whole cilantro leaves for garnish

2 avocados, diced

Lime quarters, for garnish

(YIELDS 6 SERVINGS)

Slice 4 of the guajillos into thin rings. Bring a small pot of water to boil. Remove the water from heat and add the remaining 6 guajillos. Let soak for 30 minutes to soften. Drain.

Heat the chicken stock in a large saucepan. Heat the vegetable oil in a medium sauté pan to 375°F or until lightly smoking. Fry the tortillas until crisp, about 10 seconds. Remove from the oil and drain on paper towels. Quickly fry the sliced guajillos in the same oil to crisp them. Remove from the oil and drain on paper towels.

Place the roasted tomatoes, softened guajillos, and 2 cups of the warmed stock in a blender and purée for at least 1 minute or until the guajillos are completely broken down.

Heat the olive oil in a large saucepan over high heat. Sauté the onion and garlic until the onion is translucent. Add the puréed tomato mixture, remaining stock, and epazote. Bring to a simmer and season with salt and pepper.

Divide the chicken among 6 serving bowls and ladle the broth over the chicken. Garnish each bowl with fried tortilla strips and guajillo rings, shredded mozzarella, cilantro leaves, diced avocado, and a lime quarter.

pork tenderloin with ensalada de tomate verde

(*ensalada de tomate verde* courtesy of Chef Diana Kennedy)

This is a most surprisingly delicious and crisp salad. Maria Williams said she did not know the origin of the recipe but she had enriched it with trimmings to her taste. I think it is best served—as it was to a friend of mine on a ranch near San Miguel de Allende—as a botana with drinks and a pile of hot corn tortillas.

PORK TENDERLOIN

1 teaspoon ground cumin

1 teaspoon coriander

10 black peppercorns

2 teaspoons sesame seeds

1 tablespoon ginger

1 tablespoon roasted garlic (page 4)

1 tablespoon honey

2 teaspoons fresh mint, minced

$1/4$ cup sesame oil

2 chiles de arbol, ground

1 tablespoon tamarind paste

$1/2$ cup fresh orange juice
(about $1 1/2$ medium oranges)

2 pounds pork tenderloin, cut in 1- x 2-inch cubes

Salt and freshly ground black pepper to taste

ENSALADA DE TOMATE VERDE

1 pound (450 g) tomates verdes

2 serrano chiles or to taste, finely chopped

2 tablespoons, finely chopped white onion

$3/4$ cup (188 ml) roughly chopped cilantro

2 to 3 tablespoons olive oil

salt to taste

THE TOPPING

$1/2$ cup (125 ml) queso fresco, crumbled, queso añejo, or finely grated Romano

2 ounces (60 g) chicharrón, broken into small pieces

1 large avocado, diced

PORK TENDERLOIN (YIELDS 6 TO 8 SERVINGS)

In a dry sauté pan, toast the cumin, coriander, black peppercorns, and sesame seeds for about 1 minute. In a medium mixing bowl, combine the toasted items with the ginger, garlic, honey, mint, sesame oil, chiles de arbol, tamarind paste, and orange juice. Place the pork cubes on skewers, 4 to 5 pieces per skewer. Pour the marinade over the skewers and let marinate for a few hours or overnight if possible.

Prepare a medium-hot grill (page 4). Remove the skewered pork from the marinade and season with salt and pepper. Grill to desired doneness. Serve with the Ensalada de Tomate Verde.

ENSALADA DE TOMATE VERDE • SRA. MARIA REDONDO DE WILLIAMS

Remove the husks from the tomates verdes (tomatillos), rinse well, and dry before chopping them roughly. Mix with the rest of the ingredients. Just before serving, top with the cheese, chicharrón, and avocado.

tinga de pollo

Tinga is a dish that gets prepared a lot at Star Canyon for what we call "family meal," a staff lunch prepared by one of our prep cooks from Mexico. Tasty but simple, it's really just a tomato-based stew usually served with rice.

2 tablespoons olive oil for browning

1 whole chicken, cut into 8 pieces

Salt and freshly ground black pepper to taste

4 ounces chorizo

2 baking potatoes, peeled, diced, and blanched for 5 minutes

4 garlic cloves, minced

1 medium onion, diced

1 medium carrot, peeled and diced

1 stalk celery, diced

3 cups tomatoes (about 4 medium tomatoes), diced with the seeds

2 chipotles in adobo, chopped

$2/3$ cup chicken stock (page 33)

2 cups cooked white rice

Cilantro leaves for garnish

2 avocados, peeled and sliced for garnish

$1/4$ cup grated queso fresco for garnish

(YIELDS 4 SERVINGS)

Preheat the oven to 350°F.

Heat the oil in a sauté pan until lightly smoking. Season the chicken with salt and pepper, and brown it on all sides. Place the chicken in an ovenproof dish and keep warm. In the same sauté pan, cook the chorizo, breaking it up with a fork to render the fat. Add the potatoes, garlic, onion, carrot, and celery, and cook for 1 minute. Add the tomatoes and chipotles and cook for 1 minute more. Deglaze with the stock, scraping the pan to release any flavorful browned bits. Pour the mixture over the chicken and bake for 40 to 45 minutes.

To serve, place the hot rice in the center of a platter. Arrange the chicken pieces around the rice, pour the sauce over the top, garnish with the cilantro and avocado, and sprinkle with the queso fresco.

chile-crusted plátanos rellenos

chile-crusted plátanos rellenos
stuffed with venison picadillo and accompanied by avocado, jícama, and watercress salad

Plantains have been called the potato of Mexico. For this recipe you should pick plantains that are fully ripe and blackened. While picadillo is a staple in both Mexico and Texas, the use of venison betrays a decidedly Texan influence.

PLÁTANOS RELLENOS

4 ripe plantains, dark golden to black in color

1/2 teaspoon salt

Vegetable oil for greasing and frying

1 cup Venison Picadillo

Tortilla–Chile Crust

Avocado, Jicama, and Watercress Salad

PLÁTANOS RELLENOS (YIELDS 4 SERVINGS)

Cut 1/2 inch off each end of the plantains. Make four vertical cuts through the skin and just barely into the flesh. Peel away the skin, from top to bottom, one strip at a time. The riper the plantain, the easier it is to peel.

Put the peeled plantains and salt in a large saucepan. Add enough water to cover and bring to a boil. Continue to cook for 30 to 45 minutes until the plantains are fork-tender. Drain and set aside to cool slightly. Mash the plantains with a fork, and when cool enough to handle, divide into 4 equal parts.

Oil your hands. Pat each portion into an oval shape about 1/2-inch thick. Place 2 tablespoons picadillo on the oval. With both hands, bring the edges of the oval together to enclose the filling. Dredge the rellenos in the Tortilla–Chile Crust and set aside until ready to fry.

Pour enough vegetable oil to come 1/2 inch up the sides of a small, deep frying pan. Heat to 365°F or until the surface ripples and lightly smokes. With an oiled, long-handled spoon, carefully place each plantain piece in the hot oil. Pan fry, turning to brown evenly, for 6 to 8 minutes. Drain on paper towels.

Serve with Avocado, Jicama, and Watercress Salad.

(continued)

chile-crusted plátanos rellenos (continued)

VENISON PICADILLO

3 tablespoons olive oil

2 small onions, diced

2 garlic cloves, minced

1 1/2 pounds ground lean venison

1/2 pound ground pork

3 medium-size ripe tomatoes, blanched, peeled, seeded, and diced (page 5)

2 red bell peppers, roasted, peeled, seeded, and diced (page 14)

3 jalapeños, seeded and minced

1 apple, peeled, cored, and chopped

1/2 cup raisins, plumped in tequila

1 cup slivered almonds, blanched and toasted

1/2 teaspoon ground cloves

1/2 teaspoon ground cinnamon

1 teaspoon ground cumin

1/2 cup red wine

1/2 cup chicken stock (page 33)

TORTILLA–CHILE CRUST

1 cup oil for frying

4 corn tortillas

1/3 cup masa harina

1/2 teaspoon ground cumin

1/8 teaspoon cayenne powder

1/2 teaspoon pure chile powder (page 15)

1 teaspoon kosher salt

AVOCADO, JÍCAMA, AND WATERCRESS SALAD

2 cups watercress, washed and large stems removed

1 jícama, peeled and finely julienned

Serrano–Lime Vinaigrette

2 avocados, peeled and sliced

SERRANO–LIME VINAIGRETTE

Juice of 2 limes

3 serranos, thinly sliced

1/4 teaspoon kosher salt

Freshly ground black pepper to taste

1/2 cup olive oil

VENISON PICADILLO

Heat the olive oil in a large skillet until lightly smoking. Add the onions and garlic, and sauté over medium-high heat 2 to 3 minutes or until the onions are translucent. Add the venison and pork. Continue to cook about 5 minutes, breaking the meat up with a fork until it is cooked through.

Stir in the tomatoes, bell peppers, jalapeños, apple, raisins, almonds, cloves, cinnamon, and cumin, and continue to cook for 2 more minutes.

Add the wine and stock, reduce the heat, and simmer for 20 to 30 minutes. Set aside 1 cup of the picadillo for stuffing. You can freeze the rest for later use. It is delicious as a stew served simply with warm tortillas.

TORTILLA–CHILE CRUST

Pour the oil in a heavy pot over medium heat. Heat to 350°F or until lightly smoking. Fry the tortillas in batches just until crisp, about 1 minute. Drain on paper towels and cool completely. Grind the cooled tortillas in a food processor until the consistency of cornmeal. Stir in the remaining ingredients. Store in an airtight container if not using right away.

AVOCADO, JÍCAMA, AND WATERCRESS SALAD (YIELDS 6 SERVINGS)

Toss the watercress and jícama together in a medium mixing bowl. Drizzle with Serrano Lime Vinaigrette and toss. Carefully fold in the avocado slices.

SERRANO–LIME VINAIGRETTE

Combine the lime juice, serranos, salt, and pepper in a small bowl. Drizzle the olive oil in a steady stream, whisking constantly to emulsify. Toss gently with the salad or refrigerate until ready to use.

filete meztli

y salsa del sol (courtesy of Chef Americo Circuit and Patricia Quintana)

A signature offering from my friend Americo Circuit's restaurant in Dallas, La Valentina de Mexico, this beautiful dish represents night and day. Meztli comes from the ancient Aztec word for the moon, and del sol is Spanish for the sun. The contrast of the two makes for a beautiful presentation.

TENDERLOIN FILLETS

2 garlic cloves, minced

$1/2$ cup finely chopped parsley

4 tablespoons Worcestershire sauce

1 teaspoon freshly ground black pepper

$1/4$ cup olive oil

4 8-ounce beef tenderloin fillets

Salt to taste

Meztli Salsa

Salsa del Sol

4 large epazote sprigs

SALSA DEL SOL

$1/2$ pound of ricotta cheese

$1/4$ medium onion sliced

2 garlic cloves, chopped

2 serrano chiles, chopped

$1/2$ cup milk

1 cup heavy cream

1 cup sour cream

Salt to taste

MEZTLI SALSA

$1/4$ cup olive oil

2 tablespoons butter

$1/2$ cup finely chopped white onion

1 teaspoon finely chopped garlic

2 serranos, finely chopped

2 medium tomatoes, finely chopped

9 ounces frozen, canned, or fresh huitlacoche

6 ounces mushrooms (chanterelle, morel, etc.), finely chopped

3 tablespoons finely chopped cilantro

3 tablespoons minced fresh epazote

Salt to taste

TENDERLOIN FILLETS (YIELDS 4 SERVINGS)

Combine the garlic, parsley, Worcestershire sauce, and pepper in a small bowl. Whisk in the olive oil. Place the fillets in a shallow dish and pour the marinade over them, turning once to coat. Let marinate for 2 to 3 hours in the refrigerator.

Prepare a medium-hot grill (page 4). Season the tenderloins with salt. Grill the tenderloins for 4 minutes on each side for medium-rare to medium.

Ladle the Salsa del Sol on a serving plate. Spoon some of the Meztli Salsa in the middle of the Salsa del Sol, making sure that both sauces are visible for contrast. Place a fillet on top of the Meztli Sauce and garnish with the epazote sprigs.

SALSA DEL SOL

Place all the ingredients except the salt in a blender and process until smooth, about 2 minutes. Season with salt to taste.

MEZTLI SALSA

Set a heavy skillet over medium-high heat. Add the oil and butter to the hot skillet and sauté the onion and garlic until light brown. Add the serranos, tomatoes, huitlacoche, mushrooms, cilantro, and epazote. Season with salt to taste. Cook over medium heat, stirring often, until the sauce reduces and thickens. Reseason with salt to taste.

braised lamb and sweet potato chile rellenos
with pomegranates

Chile rellenos is a Mexican-inspired dish that lends itself to creative interpretation. The fillings can be as simple as cheese to as refined as lobster. This version, inspired by the classic chiles en nogada, makes a perfect cold weather dish. The braised lamb used here also tastes great simply served on a crispy fried tortilla.

SWEET POTATO CHILE RELLENOS

1 pound sweet potatoes (about 3 medium potatoes), cut in half

2 tablespoons chicken stock (page 33)

Salt and fresh ground black pepper to taste

1 teaspoon corn oil

$2/3$ cup diced onion

$1/2$ cup diced carrot

2 slices bacon, diced

2 garlic cloves, minced

1 tablespoon fresh thyme

$1/4$ cup white wine

1 cup cooked white beans (page 7)

Braised Lamb, shredded

12 medium poblanos, roasted and peeled (page 14)

Pomegranate Crema

SWEET POTATO CHILE RELLENOS (YIELDS 6 SERVINGS)

Preheat the oven to 350°F.

Place the sweet potato halves, cut side down, on the baking sheet. Bake until just tender, about 30 minutes. Remove half the potatoes and allow to cool; continue cooking the remaining halves until very soft, about 30 minutes. (Keep the oven at 350°F if you will be baking the rellenos immediately.)

Peel the cooled sweet potato halves and dice into $1/4$-inch pieces. Peel the well-cooked sweet potato halves. Place the pulp in a food processor; add the chicken stock and purée until smooth. Season with salt and pepper to taste. Combine the diced sweet potato with the sweet potato purée in a medium bowl.

Heat the oil in a large skillet until lightly smoking. Add the onion, carrot, bacon, garlic, and thyme; sauté until the onion is translucent, about 5 minutes. Add the wine and simmer for 2 minutes. Add the sweet potato mixture and the beans, stirring to combine. Season with salt and pepper. Let cool. Gently stir in the shredded Braised Lamb.

Cut a slit in each poblano, going three-fourths of the way down the pepper. Carefully remove the seeds. Spoon $1/3$ cup of filling into each poblano and overlap the skin to close the chile. (The chiles can be prepared several days in advance up to this point and refrigerated until ready to bake.) Place cut side up on a cookie sheet and bake for 30 minutes or until warmed through.

Serve with Pomegranate Crema and garnish with some of the pomegranate seeds.

(continued)

braised lamb and sweet potato chile rellenos

braised lamb and sweet potato chile rellenos *(continued)*

BRAISED LAMB

1 tablespoon olive oil

2$^1/_2$ pounds lamb shoulder

2 tablespoons salt

1 medium onion, chopped

1 medium carrot, chopped

1 stalk celery, chopped

1 tablespoon ground cumin

$^1/_4$ teaspoon ground canela

2 bay leaves

$^1/_2$ cup red wine

1$^1/_2$ cups chicken stock (page 33)

POMEGRANATE CREMA

1 pomegranate, quartered

$^1/_3$ cup sour cream

BRAISED LAMB

Heat the oil in a large pan until lightly smoking. Season the lamb with the salt, add to the pan, and brown all sides. Remove the meat and add the onion, carrot, celery, cumin, canela, and bay leaves. Sauté the vegetables for 3 to 4 minutes or until golden brown. Deglaze with the red wine and reduce to a glaze, about 5 minutes. Return the meat to the pan and add the stock. Bring to a boil, then reduce to a low simmer. Cover and allow to cook for 2$^1/_2$ to 3 hours. Remove the lamb and allow to cool. Shred the cooled meat, discarding any fat or gristle. Strain the cooking liquid and reserve.

POMEGRANATE CREMA

Squeeze the juice of 3 pomegranate quarters into a small saucepan. Reduce to a syrupy glaze over medium heat, about 3 minutes. Scrape the glaze into a medium bowl, then whisk in the sour cream. Remove the seeds from the reserved pomegranate quarter for garnish.

chicken stewed with pineapples and pasillas

The vivid color of the chiles and other ingredients explains the Mexican name for this casserole, Manchamanteles, which translates as "tablecloth stainer." No bets here as to how many cooks' aprons, napkins, and tablecloths bear the signature mark of these tasty chiles.

1 2$\frac{1}{2}$-pound chicken, cut into 8 pieces

Salt and freshly ground black pepper to taste

4 tablespoons vegetable oil for frying

$\frac{3}{4}$ cup sesame seeds

1 teaspoon cumin seeds

1 teaspoon whole allspice

4 whole cloves

1 canela stick

4 large tomatoes, roasted whole until soft

2 medium onions, roasted to lightly caramelize

10 garlic cloves, roasted (page 4)

2 pasillas, stemmed, seeded, toasted, softened in 1 cup boiling water, and drained

1 cup chicken stock (page 33)

3 ounces Mexican chocolate, roughly chopped

1 teaspoon chopped fresh rosemary

1 teaspoon chopped fresh oregano

1 tablespoon chopped fresh marjoram

1 ripe pineapple, peeled, cored, and sliced

2 ripe pears, peeled, cored, and sliced

$\frac{1}{2}$ cup chopped walnuts, toasted

(YIELDS 8 SERVINGS)

Preheat the oven to 350°F.

Season the chicken thoroughly with salt and pepper. Heat the oil in a heavy skillet over medium-high heat until lightly smoking. Brown the chicken on all sides for about 3 to 5 minutes. Remove from the pan and keep warm.

Heat a heavy skillet over medium-high heat; toast the sesame seeds, cumin, allspice, cloves, and canela for 1 minute. Place the toasted sesame seeds and spices in a blender. Add the tomatoes, onions, and garlic, puréeing on high for about 2 minutes to completely break down the spices. Add the softened pasillas, chicken stock, and chopped chocolate, continuing to purée until smooth. Place the chicken in a casserole dish. Pour the puréed sauce over the chicken, top with the rosemary, oregano, marjoram, pineapple slices, and pear slices. Cover and bake for 45 minutes to 1 hour. Serve garnished with the chopped walnuts.

quail with rose petal and dried cherry sauce
with a butternut squash purée

This is a take-off on the Quail with Rose Petal Sauce from the classic novel and movie Like Water For Chocolate. The rose essence adds an intriguing, mysterious element to the Dried Cherry Sauce.

QUAIL WITH ROSE PETAL SAUCE

8 whole quail, cut into quarters

Salt and freshly ground black pepper to taste

Flour for dredging

1/4 cup olive oil

1/4 cup peeled and minced carrot

1/4 cup minced celery

2 whole shallots, minced

4 garlic cloves, minced

1 cup dried cherries, divided

1 cup port wine

2 cups dark poultry stock (page 33)

1 tablespoon rose water

2 tablespoons guajillo paste (page 15)

1 tablespoon unsalted butter, chilled

Petals from 4 organic red roses

Roasted Butternut Squash

Butternut Squash Purée

4 sprigs fresh thyme leaves

ROASTED BUTTERNUT SQUASH

1 butternut squash, peeled and sliced into 1 1/2-inch-thick disks

2 tablespoons unsalted butter (1/4 stick)

2 tablespoons brown sugar

Salt and freshly ground black pepper to taste

QUAIL WITH ROSE PETAL SAUCE (YIELDS 4 SERVINGS)

Preheat the oven to 350°F.

Season the quail pieces with salt and pepper and toss in the flour, shaking off any excess. Heat an ovenproof sauté pan over medium-high heat and add the oil. Brown the quail on both sides, about 2 minutes. Remove and keep warm. Add a little more oil if needed and sauté the carrot, celery, shallots, garlic, and half of the cherries.

Deglaze the pan with the port, scraping the bottom to release any browned bits. Add in the stock. Stir in the rose water and the guajillo paste. Bring to a simmer and then put the quail back into the pan and baste with the sauce. Place in the oven and cook for 10 minutes. Remove the quail from the pan and keep warm. Strain the sauce through a fine sieve and season with salt and pepper to taste. Return the sauce to the pan. Add the remaining cherries to the sauté pan and gently stir in the chilled butter.

Julienne half of the rose petals. Keep all of the petals chilled.

To serve, place a roasted butternut squash round in the center of each plate. Top the squash with some Butternut Squash Purée and stack the quarters of 2 whole quail on the purée. Spoon some of the sauce over the quail and sprinkle with the whole and julienned rose petals. Garnish with a sprig of thyme and serve.

ROASTED BUTTERNUT SQUASH

Preheat the oven to 350°F.

Place the sliced squash in a baking dish, dab with the butter, and sprinkle with the sugar. Season with salt and pepper.

Cover and roast for 30 minutes or until knife-tender, but not too soft. Remove the cover and increase the heat to broil. Broil in the oven until lightly browned on top.

(continued)

quail with rose petal *and* dried cherry sauce

quail with rose petal and dried cherry sauce *(continued)*

BUTTERNUT SQUASH PURÉE

6 ounces smoked bacon, chopped

1 pound butternut squash, peeled, seeded, and cubed

6 tablespoons brown sugar

4 tablespoons unsalted butter ($^1/_2$ stick)

1 teaspoon chopped fresh Italian parsley

1 teaspoon chopped fresh chives

Salt and freshly ground black pepper to taste

BUTTERNUT SQUASH PURÉE

Preheat the oven to 500°F.

Place the bacon in a heavy baking dish and cook until crisp. Add the remaining ingredients, mix well, and cover. Bake for 30 minutes. Remove the cover and cook for an additional 15 minutes. Remove from the oven. When cool enough to handle, purée in a food processor until smooth.

Reheat before serving.

torta de piña de los virreyes
pineapple rice torte

(courtesy of Chef Diana Kennedy)

Some years ago I was writing a commentary on a fascinating cookbook that I have in my collection, La Cocinera Poblana, Volumes I and II (published in Puebla, 1877) and came across this recipe, which I have reconstructed (rather than adapted). Even I, who do not particularly like sweet rice desserts (having had my fill of rice pudding as a child in England), fell for this one. It is not as cloyingly sweet as many of the "convent" desserts of Mexico—most of which come from Spain and Portugal—and has a good crunchy texture from the pineapple and almonds. Be careful not to overcook the rice so that it becomes mushy; nor, of course, should it be too al dente. When cooked, the torta should be about $1^{3}/_{4}$ inches high, so you will need an ovenproof dish that will accommodate it, ideally 8 by 8 by 2 inches. It can be eaten the same day that it is made, but it is also good, in fact better, after ripening for a day or so in the refrigerator. Always serve it at room temperature, not cold, and pour the syrup as you serve or 5 minutes beforehand. The syrup should also be at room temperature.

(SERVES 8 TO 10)

2 cups water

2 cups grated piloncillo or dark brown sugar

1 2-inch cinnamon stick, broken up

grated rind of $^{1}/_{2}$ lime

3 cups pineapple in $^{1}/_{4}$-inch dice plus any juice that exudes

3 tablespoons fresh lime juice

1 tablespoon unsalted butter

5 ounces (about $^{3}/_{4}$ cup) uncovered short-grain rice, cooked, drained and cooled

1 ounce (scant $^{1}/_{3}$ cup) almonds, skinned, slivered, and toasted

2 ounces (rounded $^{1}/_{3}$ cup) raisins

4 extra-large eggs, separated

1 egg white

1 ounce (about $^{1}/_{4}$ cup) pine nuts

1 tablespoon sifted confectioners' sugar

Put the water, sugar, and cinnamon into a saucepan and heat, stirring until the sugar has melted. Add the lime rind and bring to a boil; continue boiling for about 10 minutes. Add the pineapple and its juice to the sugar and cook over medium heat until transparent and partially soft—about 10 minutes. Drain the pineapple and set aside to cool. Return the juice to the pan and cook over high heat with the lime juice until it has reduced to about $1^{1}/_{4}$ cups and is syrupy—about 15 minutes. Set aside to cool. Heat the oven to 375°F and place a rack on the top rung. Liberally butter the ovenproof dish.

Mix the cooled rice, pineapple, almonds, and raisins together well and set aside. Beat the egg whites to soft peaks (when the bowl is turned upside down, they will not fall out), but not too dry. Beat in the egg yolks and, when mixed well, gradually stir in the rice/raisin mixture. Carefully spoon into the prepared dish, sprinkle with the pine nuts, and bake until the eggs are set and the top puffy and golden, about 20 to 25 minutes. Dust with the confectioners' sugar and set aside to cool. Serve each portion with plenty of the cool syrup (see note above).

sweet potato tamales
with bourbon–caramel sauce and pecan brittle

This dessert brings a little bit of Mexico to great Southern cooking. If there's a better combination than sweet potatoes, pecans, bourbon, and caramel, I haven't found it yet.

TAMALES

1 sweet potato (about 12 ounces)

1³/₄ cups masa harina

1¹/₄ cups very hot water

¹/₂ cup plus 2 tablespoons butter, chilled

1¹/₂ teaspoons salt, plus additional to taste

1 teaspoon baking powder

¹/₄ cup orange juice

3 tablespoons maple syrup

¹/₂ cup light brown sugar

Pinch of nutmeg

¹/₄ teaspoon ground cinnamon

¹/₂ teaspoon ground allspice

1 cup raisins

1 pound dried corn husks, soaked in water

Bourbon–Caramel Sauce

Pecan Brittle

TAMALES (YIELDS 10 SERVINGS)

Preheat the oven to 350°F. Bake the sweet potato for 30 to 45 minutes, until fork-tender. Let cool slightly, then peel the potato and purée it with a food mill, potato ricer, or food processor.

Place the masa harina in the bowl of an electric mixer fitted with a paddle attachment. On low speed, slowly add the water in a constant stream until the dough forms a ball. Continue to mix on high speed for 5 minutes. Remove the dough from the bowl and allow to cool completely in the refrigerator for about 30 minutes. Return the masa to the bowl and beat for 5 minutes on high speed. Slowly add the butter in tablespoon additions while beating. Continue beating until smooth and light, about 5 minutes. Stop the mixer to scrape the sides of the bowl, reduce to low speed, and continue to beat. Combine the salt, baking powder, and orange juice in a small bowl. Slowly drizzle the orange juice mixture into the masa, combining thoroughly. Whip on high speed for 5 minutes longer. Whip the puréed sweet potato into the masa. Beat in the maple syrup, brown sugar, nutmeg, cinnamon, allspice, and raisins. Continue to beat for 3 additional minutes until completely lightened.

Drain the corn husks and pat dry. Divide the dough and corn husks into 10 equal portions. Tear 20 (¹/₆-inch-wide) strips from 2 or 3 of the husks for tying the tamales. Place about 2 tablespoons of the tamale dough on top of each husk, then roll the corn husks so that the dough is completely enclosed. Twist and tie each end with the reserved strips. Repeat the procedure for remaining tamales. Steam the tamales in a conventional steamer or in a strainer set in a saucepan covered with a tightly fitting lid that allows little or no steam to escape while cooking. Steam for 30 to 35 minutes; the water should always be lightly boiling. The tamales are done when the dough comes away easily from the husk.

BOURBON–CARAMEL SAUCE

1 cup sugar

$^1/_4$ cup water

1 cup heavy cream

2 tablespoons bourbon

PECAN BRITTLE

1 cup sugar

2 tablespoons water

$^3/_4$ cup pecans halves

Place the tamales on serving plates and slit open lengthwise. Pour Bourbon–Caramel Sauce over the top and around the tamale, and garnish with bits of Pecan Brittle.

BOURBON–CARAMEL SAUCE

Bring the sugar and water to a boil in a heavy saucepan. The mixture will begin to caramelize. To avoid crystallization, wash down the sides of the pan with a clean pastry brush dipped in water. Continue to cook until the mixture is a dark golden color. Remove the caramel from the heat and carefully stir in the cream and bourbon a little at a time. (The mixture will foam up at first from the heat of the caramel.) Serve warm or refrigerate in an airtight container.

PECAN BRITTLE

Bring the sugar and water to a boil in a heavy saucepan. Swirl or stir gently to dissolve the sugar. To avoid crystallization, wash down the sides of the pan with a clean pastry brush dipped in water. Continue to cook until the mixture is a deep amber color and registers 300°F on a candy thermometer.

Place the pecans on a lightly oiled baking sheet; pour the caramel over the pecans. Let cool completely, about 1 hour. Break the brittle into to small to medium bits to serve with the tamales.

capirotada
with natilla sauce

Capirotada is Mexico's version of the familiar bread pudding. The tortillas lining the bottom of the casserole make it easy to serve, and the toasty masa flavor marks this dish as unmistakably Mexican.

CAPIROTADA

Unsalted butter for greasing,
  plus 2 tablespoons for toasting

3 cups milk

1/4 cup piloncillo or brown sugar

1 vanilla bean, split in
  half lengthwise and scraped

1 canela or cinnamon stick

1 tablespoon cornstarch

1 egg yolk

1/2 cup oil for frying

2 ripe plantains, peeled
  and cut into 18 bias slices

6 corn tortillas

1 loaf brioche or challah bread,
  crust removed and sliced

1 cup raisins

1 1/4 cup dried cherries

1/4 cup rum

Natilla Sauce

CAPIROTADA (YIELDS 6 SERVINGS)

Preheat the oven to 350°F. Butter a small loaf pan.

Combine the milk, piloncillo sugar, vanilla bean, and canela stick in a medium saucepan. Bring to a simmer. Whisk the cornstarch with the egg yolk. Pour a little of the hot milk into the mixture to stabilize the temperature, then pour the tempered mixture back into the milk. Return to a low simmer, continuing to stir until the mixture thickens slightly, about 3 minutes. Remove from the heat and allow to cool.

Heat the oil in a skillet until lightly smoking and brown the plantain slices on both sides. Drain on paper towels. While the oil is still hot—adding more if needed—add the tortillas and lightly fry to soften, then drain on paper towels. Keep covered so they do not get firm or dry. Layer the tortillas on the sides of the loaf pan. Butter and toast the bread slices until lightly brown, and divide the slices into 3 stacks. Plump the raisins and cherries with the rum, then drain.

Place the first layer of the bread on top of the tortillas covering the bottom of the pan. (Remember, the tortillas will be the top when removed.) Place 9 of the plantain slices and half of the raisins and cherries on top of the bread. Slowly pour 1 cup of the milk mixture over the top: Add another layer with the bread, plantains, fruit, and 1 more cup of milk mixture. Top with the last stack of bread and the last cup of milk mixture. Cover with foil and bake for 30 minutes. Remove the foil and bake for another 10 minutes. Remove from the oven and allow to cool before cutting into 6 slices. Serve with Natilla Sauce spooned around and over the slices.

NATILLA SAUCE

4 cups milk

$2/3$ cup sugar, plus $1/4$ cup sugar

1 vanilla bean, split in half lengthwise and scraped

9 egg yolks

3 egg whites

$1/4$ cup Myers's dark rum

1 cup almonds, toasted and ground

NATILLA SAUCE (YIELDS 6 SERVINGS)

Combine the milk, $2/3$ cup sugar, and vanilla bean in a heavy saucepan and bring to a boil. Beat the egg yolks until thick, then strain the hot milk mixture into the yolks a little at a time, stirring until fully mixed. Pour the egg–milk mixture back into the saucepan and cook over very low heat for 2 to 3 minutes or until thick enough to coat the back of a wooden spoon. Strain through a fine sieve and let cool completely. Whip the egg whites with the $1/4$ cup sugar until they hold soft peaks. Fold the egg whites, rum, and almonds into the cooled mixture. Serve immediately or cover and refrigerate until ready to use.

pastel de cinco leches
with candied almonds

This dish is a variation on the classic Nicaraguan dessert known as tres leches.
Mine takes the concept a few steps further, creating tres leches y dos mas.

**PASTEL DE CINCO LECHES
WITH CANDIED ALMONDS**

5$^1/_2$ cups almonds, blanched

2 cups sugar, divided

$^1/_4$ teaspoon lemon zest

$^1/_4$ teaspoon orange zest

14 eggs, separated

$^1/_2$ teaspoon ground canela

1 cup goat's milk

1 cup coconut milk

$^1/_2$ cup cajeta (page 69 or available in Hispanic markets)

1 tablespoon water

$^1/_2$ tablespoon cornstarch

Icing

Candied Almonds

PASTEL DE CINCO LECHES WITH CANDIED ALMONDS (YIELDS 12 TO 16 SERVINGS)

Preheat the oven to 350°F. Place parchment or wax paper circles to cover the bottoms of two 10-inch cake pans and lightly spray with nonstick cooking spray. Combine the almonds with $^1/_4$ cup of the sugar in a food processor and grind until pulverized.

Combine the remaining 1$^3/_4$ cups sugar with the lemon zest, orange zest, and egg yolks in a mixer. Beat until the mixture is light and fluffy. Fold in the ground almond mixture and the canela.

In a separate mixing bowl, whip the egg whites until stiff. Fold one-fourth of the whites into the almond mixture to lighten it, then gently fold in the remaining whites.

Divide the batter between the two pans and bake for 40 to 50 minutes or until the top is golden brown and the center is firm to the touch. Place parchment or wax paper on sheet trays and cool the cakes upside down in the pans until cool.

Combine the goat's milk, coconut milk, and cajeta in a bowl. Using a pastry brush, soak each layer of the cooled cake with $^1/_4$ cup of the mixture. When you touch the top of the soaked cakes, liquid should be evident. Place the remaining soaking liquid in a small saucepan over low heat.

In a small bowl, whisk the water and cornstarch until smooth. When the soaking liquid begins to steam, but has not yet reached a simmer, whisk in the cornstarch mixture. Continue to stir, cooking until the sauce coats the back of a spoon.

Ice the bottom layer of the soaked cake. Place the top layer on the bottom layer, and ice the whole cake. Sprinkle the candied almonds on sides and top of cake.

To serve, place a slice of cake on a dessert plate and spoon with the thickened sauce.

ICING

2 cups heavy cream

$1/4$ cup powdered sugar

1 cup sour cream

Candied Almonds

CANDIED ALMONDS

4 cups sliced blanched almonds

1 egg white, whipped
    until light and frothy

$1/2$ cup granulated sugar

ICING

Whip the heavy cream and powdered sugar until soft peaks form.

Add the sour cream and continue whipping until stiff peaks form.

CANDIED ALMONDS

Preheat the oven to 325°F degrees.

On a baking sheet, moisten the almonds with the egg white. Sprinkle with the sugar and stir to coat. Bake for 5 minutes, remove from the oven, and stir. Return the almonds to the oven for 4 to 5 minutes or until golden brown and dry. Stir and cool. Store in an airtight container at room temperature until ready to use.

pumpkin flan
with mexican wedding cookies

You can celebrate the bounty of autumn with this Mexican alternative to Thanksgiving's pumpkin pie. Pumpkins, or calabazas, are used extensively in Mexican cooking, but never to better results than in this flan. The accompanying cookies are traditionally served at weddings and can be presented attractively in tissue paper.

CARAMELIZED PUMPKIN FLAN

1 2-pound pumpkin, cut into wedges and seeded

1 cup granulated sugar

1 tablespoon water

3 tablespoons brandy

2 teaspoons vanilla extract

1 tablespoon grated fresh ginger

1 teaspoon salt

$^1/_2$ teaspoon ground cinnamon

$^1/_4$ teaspoon ground allspice

$^1/_4$ teaspoon ground cloves

1$^1/_3$ cup dark brown sugar

2 cups cream

8 eggs, whisked

Mexican Wedding Cookies

CARAMELIZED PUMPKIN FLAN (YIELDS 8 SERVINGS)

Preheat the oven to 350°F.

Place the pumpkin wedges in a baking dish with a little water on the bottom. Cover and roast for 30 to 45 minutes or until fork-tender. Remove from the oven and let cool. (Keep the oven heated for later use.) Peel the pumpkin and purée with a food mill, potato ricer, or food processor.

Set aside 8 (6- to 8-ounce) ramekins. Combine the granulated sugar and water in a heavy saucepan. Bring to a boil. As it begins to caramelize and turn an amber color, wash down the sides of the pan with a clean pastry brush dipped in water. When the caramel turns a dark amber color, distribute evenly among the ramekins.

Combine the puréed pumpkin with the brandy, vanilla, ginger, salt, and spices. Combine the brown sugar and the cream in a medium saucepan over medium-high heat. Bring to a boil, then turn off the heat. Slowly pour the cream into the whisked eggs, a little at a time, until completely mixed.

Stir the cream mixture into the pumpkin mixture until thoroughly combined. Pour the mixture evenly into the ramekins. Bake, covered, in a water bath for 40 to 45 minutes. Remove and refrigerate until cold, preferably overnight. To unmold each flan, run a knife around the edge of the ramekin and turn out onto an individual serving plate. The caramel at the bottom of the ramekins should have liquified; drizzle it over the top. Serve with Mexican Wedding Cookies.

MEXICAN WEDDING COOKIES

$3/4$ cup finely chopped pecans

$1/4$ pound unsalted butter (1 stick)

1 cup sugar

1 teaspoon vanilla extract

$1 1/8$ cup cake flour, sifted

1 cup all-purpose flour, sifted

1 cup powdered sugar

MEXICAN WEDDING COOKIES (YIELDS 24 COOKIES)

Preheat the oven to 350°F.

Cream the pecans and butter together with a mixer on high speed. Add the sugar and vanilla, and continue to mix at high speed until light and creamy. Reduce speed to low. Add the cake flour and the all-purpose flour; mix thoroughly. Shape the dough into balls using 1 to $1 1/2$ tablespoons of dough per ball. Bake on a greased baking sheet for 12 to 15 minutes. After baking, remove the cookies from the pan while still warm and toss them in the powdered sugar to coat.

discovering oaxaca and

Oaxaca is perhaps my favorite region in all of
Mexico. Its terrain ranges from sweeping, fertile
central valleys to rugged mountain ranges; from
tropical jungles hiding Mayan temples to the
sunny, sandy beaches of the Pacific Ocean. This
diversity in landscape is mirrored by the diversity
of its food.

Maguey plants dot the Sierra Madre del Sur
mountain ranges and produce the world-famous

its pacific coast

and mysterious *mezcals*—all still made in the
centuries-old tradition by hand (and by donkey).
Corn remains the staff of life for Oaxaca, as it has
for centuries past. The Oaxacan chocolate made
from cocoa beans, canela, almonds, and sugar
is unsurpassed for its quality and flavor. This
delectable chocolate combined with exotic chiles
creates the foundation for Oaxaca's famous
"seven moles."

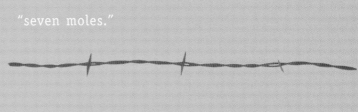

grilled shrimp
with tamarind–orange marinade
and charred tomato chipotle salsa

Tamarind is a global ingredient you find from India and Asia to Mexico.
Its pleasant bitter-sweetness has an affinity for orange.

GRILLED SHRIMP

16 large shrimp, peeled
   and deveined

Tamarind–Orange Marinade

Salt and freshly ground black pepper
   to taste

Charred Tomato Chipotle Salsa

1 bunch cilantro leaves

TAMARIND–ORANGE MARINADE

1 cup tamarind paste

$1^1/_2$ cups fresh orange juice
   (4 to 5 medium oranges)

2 tablespoons minced orange zest

2 teaspoons minced lemon zest

2 serranos, minced

4 garlic cloves, minced

$^1/_2$ cup olive oil

2 tablespoons honey

CHARRED TOMATO CHIPOTLE SALSA

12 Roma tomatoes

2 tablespoons olive oil

$^1/_2$ onion, diced

6 garlic cloves

$^1/_2$ cup chipotle purée (page 15)

2 tablespoons brown sugar

1 tablespoon red wine vinegar

1 tablespoon fresh lime juice
   (about 1 medium lime)

2 tablespoons freshly chopped basil

1 cup mayonnaise (page 30)

Salt and freshly ground black pepper
   to taste

GRILLED SHRIMP (YIELDS 4 SERVINGS)

Soak 4 wooden skewers in water overnight or use metal skewers. Place 4 shrimp on each skewer. Pour the Tamarind–Orange Marinade over the shrimp and let marinate a few hours or overnight.

Prepare a hot grill (page 4). Remove the shrimp from the marinade and season with salt and pepper. Grill for about 2 minutes per side, until the shrimp are done—firm to the touch and pink.

Serve the shrimp on the skewer (or remove them if you like) with Charred Tomato Chipotle Salsa and fresh cilantro leaves.

TAMARIND–ORANGE MARINADE

Mix the tamarind paste with the orange juice, orange zest, lemon zest, serranos, and garlic. Drizzle in the olive oil and honey and whisk until fully incorporated.

CHARRED TOMATO CHIPOTLE SALSA (YIELDS 1 QUART)

Heat a cast-iron skillet until very hot. Add the whole Roma tomatoes, turning occasionally until they begin to blacken on all sides. When they are roasted, remove the tomatoes from the pan and slice the stem ends off.

Heat the olive oil in a medium pan until lightly smoking. Sauté the onion and garlic for 5 minutes or until lightly brown. Put the tomatoes and the onion–garlic mixture through a meat grinder. (You can use a food processor, but the salsa will not be as vibrantly red. The processor whips air into the salsa, thereby lightening the color.) Stir in the chipotle purée, brown sugar, vinegar, lime juice, and basil. Fold in the mayonnaise. Season with salt and pepper. Serve immediately or store, covered, in the refrigerator until ready to use.

tortilla casserole
with refried pintos, wild mushrooms, and queso oaxaca

This recipe is a variation of the classic dish chilaquiles, *made from layers of leftover tortillas, cheese, and salsa. It makes a great side dish to any poultry or meat recipe.*

1/2 cup olive oil

1 tablespoon minced garlic, plus 4 garlic cloves

1 tablespoon minced shallot

1 pound assorted wild mushrooms (hedgehog, black trumpet, crimino, or portobello), thinly sliced

Salt and freshly ground black pepper to taste

1/2 pound tomatillos, blanched and peeled (page 5)

1/2 onion, sliced

2 serranos, stemmed

1 cup chicken stock (page 33)

1 bunch cilantro leaves, chopped

2 tablespoons chopped fresh epazote leaves

8 corn tortillas, fried crisp

2 cups Refried Pinto Beans

1/2 pound queso Oaxaca, grated

REFRIED PINTO BEANS

1 cup pinto beans, cleaned, soaked overnight, and drained

1/2 cup vegetable oil

Salt to taste

(YIELDS 6 TO 8 SERVINGS)

Preheat the oven to 350°F.

Heat the oil in a large skillet over medium-high heat until lightly smoking, and sauté the minced garlic and shallot for about 1 minute. Add the wild mushrooms, season with salt and pepper, and sauté for 5 more minutes.

Heat a cast-iron skillet until very hot. Add the tomatillos, onion, garlic cloves, and serranos, dry roasting about 10 minutes until they blacken slightly. Shake the pan occasionally to distribute the heat evenly. Combine the dry-roasted items in a blender with the chicken stock. Purée until smooth. Stir in the cilantro and epazote; season with salt.

Crush 4 of the fried tortillas into an 8-inch square casserole dish. Layer the tortillas with half of each of the Refried Pinto Beans, mushrooms, puréed sauce, and queso. Crush the remaining 4 tortillas over the queso and repeat the layers. Bake for 20 minutes or until golden brown. Serve hot.

REFRIED PINTO BEANS

Place the beans in a large pot and cover with enough water to come 2 inches above the beans. Bring to a boil, lower to a simmer, and cover. Let cook for 1 1/2 to 2 hours, checking the liquid level periodically and adding water as needed to keep the beans constantly covered.

Drain the cooked beans thoroughly. Heat the oil in a skillet until lightly smoking. Add the drained beans and mash with a large fork or potato masher for about 10 minutes to a rough purée. Season with salt.

flor de calabaza rellenos
squash blossoms stuffed with black beans and caciotta

Squash blossoms are completely underutilized in this country. They make a delicious appetizer when stuffed, as in this dish, and they also make a hearty soup when cooked with aromatic vegetables and chicken stock.

SQUASH BLOSSOMS

1/2 cup cooked black beans (page 7)

1 tablespoon sour cream

1 tablespoon chipotles in adobo

1 teaspoon ground cumin

1 teaspoon pure chile powder (page 15)

2 garlic cloves, roasted and minced (page 4)

6 ounces goat cheese

3 ounces caciotta cheese

1 tablespoon minced red onion

1 tablespoon chopped fresh cilantro

1 tablespoon chopped fresh basil

1 tablespoon chopped fresh marjoram

16 fresh squash, pumpkin, or zucchini blossoms

3 cups vegetable oil for frying

1 cup all-purpose flour, plus 2 cups more seasoned with salt and freshly ground black pepper

1 cup masa harina

4 eggs, whisked with 1/4 cup water

Yellow Tomato Pico de Gallo

YELLOW TOMATO PICO DE GALLO

3 medium yellow tomatoes, seeded and finely diced (page 5)

1 tablespoon chopped fresh cilantro

1 garlic clove, minced

1/4 cup minced onion

Juice of 1 lime

2 serranos, seeded and minced

SQUASH BLOSSOMS (YIELDS 4 ENTREE OR 8 APPETIZER SERVINGS)

In a food processor fitted with the metal blade, purée the black beans and sour cream until smooth. Add the chipotles, cumin, chile powder, garlic, and both cheeses. Process to mix completely. Remove and fold in the red onion and chopped herbs. Fill a pastry bag with the mixture and carefully pipe about 1 1/2 tablespoons into each squash blossom. Gently press the blossoms together to completely enclose the mixture. Refrigerate the stuffed squash blossoms until ready to fry.

Heat the vegetable oil in a deep-sided frying pan until lightly smoking. Combine the all-purpose flour with the masa harina. Roll each blossom in the seasoned flour, then the egg wash, then the flour and masa mixture. Drop each blossom into the hot oil and fry until crisp and golden brown, 20 to 30 seconds. Drain on paper towels and keep warm. Serve with Yellow Tomato Pico de Gallo.

YELLOW TOMATO PICO DE GALLO

Toss all ingredients together in a small mixing bowl and let stand for about 30 minutes to blend the flavors.

flor de calabaza rellenos

pastel de carne del istmo
isthmian-style meat loaf with potato purée
(courtesy of Chef Zarela Martinez)

No one can say that this meat loaf is boring! It absolutely explodes with intense flavors, including various smoked, canned, or pickled ingredients that are popular in the Isthmus of Tehuantepec. This dish is a favorite there at the parties accompanying the velas (patron saints' fiestas) of the neighborhoods and towns in and around Juchitán. The demanding part of this dish is dicing and chopping almost a dozen ingredients. Luckily most of them— everything from the olives through the almonds—can be chopped a few hours ahead and set aside until you need them. When I visited the Isthmus of Tehuantepec at the season of spring parties accompanying the local velas (saints' day festivals), I found this vividly seasoned dish being served everywhere. It also turned out to be one of the regular Sunday offerings at Venancia Toledo Hernandez's food stand in the Isthmian town of Ixtepec. She gave me her recipe and now everyone I've served it to in New York is in love with the brassy, sensuous flavors.

1/2 cup brined green olives (one 3-ounce jar), either pitted or pimiento-stuffed, finely chopped

One 2 1/2-ounce jar pimientos, drained and finely chopped

2 canned chipotle chiles en adobo, minced

2 canned pickled jalapeño chiles, seeds removed, minced

1/2 cup blanched almonds

4 ounces slab bacon, or 2 to 3 thick slices, cut into 1/3-inch dice

4 ounces boiled ham, cut into 1/3-inch dice

4 ounces smoked sausage (I use kielbasa), finely chopped

1 large onion, finely chopped

3 garlic cloves, minced

2 cups plain dry bread crumbs

One 5-ounce can evaporated milk

1 pound lean ground pork

1 pound lean ground beef

1 large egg, lightly beaten

One 3 1/2-ounce can deviled ham

3 tablespoons mayonnaise

1 tablespoon prepared mustard

3 tablespoons minced Italian parsley (leaves only)

(YIELDS ABOUT 10 SERVINGS)

Preheat the oven to 350°F.

Combine the olives, pimientos, chipotles, and pickled jalapeños; set aside.

Spread the almonds on a baking sheet and bake until fragrant and lightly browned, 10 to 15 minutes. Remove from the oven and chop coarsely. Set aside.

If desired, these prepared ingredients can be left at room temperature for 3 to 4 hours and the oven again preheated to 350°F when you resume work.

Place the bacon in a heavy medium-size skillet with 2 tablespoons water. Cook over medium-high heat, stirring frequently, for 5 minutes, until the water has evaporated and some of the fat has rendered out. Scoop out the bacon and set aside. Strain the fat from the first pan (which will now have a salty residue on the bottom) into a large clean skillet set over medium-high heat. Add the partly cooked bacon along with the ham and sausage. Cook, stirring frequently, until lightly browned, about 3 minutes. With a slotted spoon or spatula, scoop out the cooked mixture into a bowl, letting as much fat as possible drain back into the pan. Pour off and discard all but about 2 tablespoons of the fat. Add the onion and garlic; cook over medium-high heat, stirring often, until the onion is translucent, about 5 minutes. Add to the mixture.

PURÉE DE PAPAS (POTATO PURÉE)

6 medium russet or other starchy potatoes (about 2$\frac{1}{2}$ to 3 pounds), scrubbed and quartered but unpeeled

2 medium carrots, peeled and cut into $\frac{1}{4}$-inch dice

1 cup tiny new peas, fresh or frozen

$\frac{3}{4}$ cup Mexican crema (available in Hispanic markets) or heavy cream

1 large egg, beaten

2 teaspoons prepared yellow mustard, or to taste

4 tablespoons ($\frac{1}{2}$ stick) unsalted butter

1 medium onion, finely chopped

$\frac{1}{4}$ cup minced Italian parsley leaves

One 3-ounce jar pickled pearl onions, drained

One 3-ounce jar ($\frac{1}{2}$ cup) pitted green brined olives, drained and sliced

$\frac{1}{4}$ cup (or to taste) pickled jalapeño chiles, drained and finely chopped

Freshly ground black pepper

$\frac{1}{2}$ teaspoon salt (optional)

Place the bread crumbs in a medium-size bowl, add the evaporated milk, and let sit for 5 to 10 minutes to absorb the liquid while the cooked mixture cools slightly.

Place the ground pork and beef in a very large mixing bowl. Add the soaked bread and beaten egg; mix lightly. Add all the other ingredients and mix as thoroughly as possible with your hands.

Shape the mixture into two roughly oval loaves and place on a baking sheet or on a rack set in a roasting pan. (Alternatively, you can pack the mixture firmly into two 9- x 5-inch Pyrex loaf pans.) Bake until golden brown, about 1 hour. Serve hot or (as in the Isthmus) at room temperature.

PURÉE DE PAPAS (POTATO PURÉE) (6 SERVINGS)

Prepare the vegetables. Have ready a medium-size saucepan of boiling salted water. Add the potatoes and cook until barely tender, 12 to 15 minutes. Lift out, letting them drain well, and peel. Set aside. Add the diced carrots to the water and cook just until crisp-tender, about 4 minutes. Scoop out with a strainer or slotted spoon, letting them drain well, and set aside. Add the peas and cook until barely tender, about 3 minutes; remove and drain.

In a large bowl, mash the potatoes with a potato masher. Add the crema and beat with a wooden spoon to eliminate most of the lumps. Add the egg and mustard, continuing to beat until the mixture is smooth and fluffy.

Preheat the oven to 350°F.

In a medium-size skillet, melt the butter over medium-high heat until fragrant and sizzling but not browned. Add the onion and cook, stirring, until the onion is translucent, about 3 minutes. Add the parsley, cook for 1 minute longer, and beat the mixture into the mashed potatoes. Stir in the carrots, peas, pickled onions, olives, and jalapeños. Taste for seasoning and add the pepper and optional salt. Transfer the mixture to a buttered 2-quart baking dish and bake 20 minutes. Serve at once.

tres masas

tres masas

Clayudas are great thin tortilla "pizzas" from Oaxaca. Although the toppings are limited only by the cook's imagination, typically they have chorizo and a good stringy cheese like queso Oaxaca. I think of quesadillas as kind of a Mexican sandwich made from tortillas. The fillings can easily be as varied as those of American sandwiches. The combination of wild mushrooms and goat cheese may well be my favorite.

clayudas

2 tablespoons unsalted butter ($^1/_4$ stick)

1 large white onion, thinly sliced

Salt and freshly ground black pepper to taste

1 pound chorizo sausage

4 12- to 14-inch flour tortillas

1 cup Cilantro Pesto (page 213)

$^1/_2$ pound queso Oaxaca or queso fresco

(YIELDS 4 SERVINGS)

Preheat the oven to 350°F.

Melt the butter in a sauté pan over medium-high heat. Caramelize the onion slices and season with salt and pepper to taste. Remove the onion and sauté the chorizo, breaking up the meat with a fork as it cooks.

Bake the tortillas until crisp and light brown, about 5 minutes. Spread a thin layer of Cilantro Pesto on each. Top with the chorizo and caramelized onion. Sprinkle with cheese, and return to the hot oven until the cheese melts and the edges brown slightly. Cut into wedges to serve.

totopos with barbecued mussels

TOTOPOS

Barbecued Mussels

2 cups oil for frying

1 pound fresh masa dough

1 red bell pepper, roasted, peeled, seeded, and julienned (page 14)

1 yellow bell pepper, roasted, peeled, seeded, and julienned (page 14)

1 tablespoon olive oil

1 tablespoon sherry vinegar

Salt and freshly ground black pepper to taste

1 cup Black Bean Refrito (substitute black beans for pintos in Refried Pinto Bean recipe on page 138)

1 bunch romaine lettuce, sliced into a chiffonade

$^1/_4$ cup grated Parmesan cheese

TOTOPOS (YIELDS 6 SERVINGS)

Let the barbecued mussels cool slightly after cooking. Remove the meat from the shells. Strain the liquid and reserve a few tablespoons.

Heat the frying oil in a heavy saucepan to 375°F or until lightly smoking.

Divide the masa dough into 12 equal balls. Flatten in a tortilla press. Fry the tortillas in the oil 1 at a time, pressing down with a spatula to keep them from puffing up. Drain on paper towels.

Toss the mussels with the bell peppers, olive oil, sherry vinegar, and reserved barbecued mussel liquid. Season with salt and pepper.

Spread 1 tablespoon of the Black Bean Refrito on each tortilla. Top with some of the romaine chiffonade, 2 mussels, and Parmesan cheese for garnish.

(continued)

tres masas *(continued)*

BARBECUED MUSSELS

1 tablespoon olive oil

24 black mussels, scrubbed and debearded

1/2 tablespoon minced fresh garlic

1/2 bottle Mexican dark beer

1/2 cup Ranch Barbecue Sauce (page 138) or your favorite smoky BBQ sauce

2 scallions, minced

BARBECUED MUSSELS

Heat a large sauté pan over high heat. Add the olive oil, mussels, and garlic, tossing to coat. Deglaze with the beer and the barbecue sauce, cover, and cook quickly—about 2 minutes or until the mussels open. Toss out any mussels that do not open on their own and stir in the scallions.

wild mushroom and goat cheese quesadillas

QUESADILLAS

3 tablespoons olive oil

1 small carrot, julienned

1 small red bell pepper, julienned

1 small yellow bell pepper, julienned

1 small red onion, thinly sliced

Salt and freshly ground black pepper to taste

1 pound fresh masa dough for tortillas (available in Hispanic markets) or 8 fresh corn or flour tortillas

Grilled Wild Mushrooms

1/2 pound goat cheese

1 cup Avocado Crema

1/2 cup Pico de Gallo (page 20)

GRILLED WILD MUSHROOMS

1/4 cup olive oil

1/4 cup balsamic vinegar

2 tablespoons soy sauce

1 tablespoon freshly grated ginger

1 teaspoon minced garlic

4 portobello mushrooms, cleaned and stemmed

Salt and freshly ground black pepper to taste

AVOCADO CREMA

2 avocados, peeled and seeded

1 cup sour cream

Juice of 2 limes

1 bunch cilantro, stemmed

1 teaspoon kosher salt

QUESADILLAS **(YIELDS 8 SERVINGS)**

Heat the 3 tablespoons olive oil in a large sauté pan until slightly smoking. Sauté the carrot, bell peppers, and red onion about 2 minutes or until slightly softened. Season with salt and pepper. Remove and cool slightly.

Heat a comal or flat-top griddle over medium heat. Divide the masa dough into 8 portions and flatten in a tortilla press, being careful not to press too thin. Place the dough on the griddle and cook until light brown. Flip the dough over. Top half of each tortilla with the grilled mushroom strips, carrot–pepper mixture, and goat cheese. Fold the other half down against the filling, pressing lightly so it sticks together. Flip over one more time, cooking the tortilla on the griddle until golden brown on both sides. Serve the finished quesadillas with Avocado Crema and Pico de Gallo.

GRILLED WILD MUSHROOMS

Make a marinade for the mushrooms by combining the olive oil, balsamic vinegar, soy sauce, ginger, and garlic. Toss the mushrooms in the marinade and refrigerate overnight for best results.

Prepare a hot grill (page 4) or preheat the broiler. Drain the marinated mushrooms, season with salt and pepper, and grill for 3 minutes per side. Cool slightly, then slice into strips.

AVOCADO CREMA

Combine all the ingredients in a food processor and process until smooth and very green. Serve immediately or refrigerate in an airtight container.

marinated arrachera
with grilled corn avocado relish

Arrachera is skirt steak, or diaphragm muscle, that has been charcoal-grilled. It is traditionally served with tortillas and salsas, and I'm sure this is the inspiration of the better-known Texas fajitas.

ARRACHERA (SKIRT STEAK)

Skirt Steak Marinade

Grilled Corn Avocado Relish

$2^1/_2$ pounds skirt steak

Salt and freshly ground black pepper to taste

$^1/_2$ pound queso Oaxaca or caciotta, grated

SKIRT STEAK MARINADE

$^1/_2$ cup chipotle purée (page 15)

1 tablespoon ground cumin, toasted

2 tablespoons pure chile powder, toasted (page 15)

$^1/_4$ cup Worcestershire sauce

$^1/_2$ ounce Mexican beer

$^1/_4$ cup soy sauce

2 tablespoons brown sugar

GRILLED CORN AVOCADO RELISH

2 ears grilled corn, kernels cut off cob (about 1 cup)

2 tomatoes, peeled, seeded, and diced (page 5)

4 tomatillos, peeled and diced

2 cups cooked and drained black beans (page 7)

1 large jalapeño, minced with the seeds

1 tablespoon roasted garlic purée (page 4)

Juice of 1 lime

1 tablespoon minced fresh cilantro

1 tablespoon olive oil

2 avocados, peeled, pitted, and diced

Salt to taste

ARRACHERA (SKIRT STEAK) (YIELDS 6 TO 8 SERVINGS)

Prepare the marinade and the relish. Pour the marinade over the skirt steak and marinate overnight in the refrigerator.

The next day, prepare a hot grill (page 4) or preheat the oven to broil. Remove the skirt steak from the marinade, wiping off any excess. Season with salt and pepper; the soy in the marinade may have provided adequate salt for the meat. Grill or broil to desired doneness. Remove from the heat and keep warm.

Heat a nonstick griddle over high heat. Place the grated cheese in 6 to 8 flat circles on the hot griddle, as in preparing hash browns. Continue cooking until golden brown on the bottom, then flip to cook the other side. Once golden brown on both sides, remove the cheese circles to parchment or wax paper. Wrap each circle around a rolling pin to create a "taco" shell.

Slice the meat and fill the "tacos." Top with Grilled Corn Avocado Relish and serve.

SKIRT STEAK MARINADE

Combine all ingredients thoroughly.

GRILLED CORN AVOCADO RELISH (YIELDS 3 TO 4 CUPS)

Thoroughly combine the corn, tomatoes, tomatillos, black beans, jalapeño, garlic purée, lime juice, cilantro, and olive oil in a medium bowl. Fold in the avocados and season with salt. Let stand 30 minutes at room temperature to blend the flavors.

mole poblano de guajolote

dark and spicy mole with turkey (courtesy of Chef Rick Bayless)

After comparing dozens of recipes for Pueblan mole, I've come up with this version, which re-creates the rich-tasting complexity of what you'll be served in Mexico's gastronomic capital. Even with all the huge mounds of prepared mole pastes available in the Puebla market, many of the fonda *and restaurant cooks still insist on preparing their own from scratch. Which underscores Paco Ignacio Taibo's opinion: "Its recipe isn't a recipe, but recipes . . . For mole there are as many recipes as there are imaginations." It's a remarkable dish. And it's worth the effort.*

THE MEAT
A 10- to 12-pound turkey

THE CHILES
16 medium (about 8 ounces total) dried chiles mulatos

5 medium (about 2¹/₂ ounces total) dried chiles anchos

6 (about 2 ounces total) dried chiles pasillas

1 canned chile chipotle, seeded (optional)

(YIELDS 12 TO 15 SERVINGS WITH 3 QUARTS OF SAUCE)

The turkey. If your butcher won't cup up your turkey, do it yourself: Cut the leg-and-thigh quarters off the body of the turkey, then slice through the joint that connects the thigh to the leg. Cut the two wings free from the breast. Then set the turkey up on the neck end and, with a cleaver, cut down both sides of the backbone and remove it. Split the breast in half. Reserve the back, neck, and innards (except the liver) to make the broth. Cover the turkey pieces and refrigerate.

The setup. As with any recipe calling for 26 different ingredients, half the battle is won by getting yourself properly set up. Organize the ingredients as follows: stem, seed, and carefully devein the dried chiles, reserving 2 teaspoons of the seeds; tear the chiles into flat pieces. If using the chipotle, seed it and set aside. Make measured mounds of sesame seeds, coriander seeds, almonds, raisins, and onion. Lay out the garlic, tortilla and bread. Place the tomato in a large bowl and break it up, then add the chopped chocolate to it. Pulverize the remaining spices, using a mortar or spice grinder, then add to the tomato and chocolate. Have the lard or oil and broth at ready access.

Toasting the seeds. In a medium-size skillet set over medium heat, dry-roast the chile, sesame and coriander seeds, one kind at a time, stirring each until it has lightly browned. Add to the tomato mixture.

(continued)

mole poblano de guajolote

mole poblano de guajolote *(continued)*

THE NUTS, SEEDS, FLAVORINGS, AND THICKENERS

$1/4$ cup sesame seeds, plus a little extra for garnish

$1/2$ teaspoon coriander seeds

$1/2$ cup lard or vegetable oil, plus a little more if needed

A heaping $1/3$ cup (2 ounces) unskinned almonds

$1/3$ cup (about 2 ounces) raisins

$1/2$ medium onion, sliced

2 cloves garlic, peeled

1 corn tortilla, stale or dried out

2 slices firm white bread, stale or dried out

1 ripe, large tomato, roasted or boiled, cored and peeled OR $3/4$ 15-ounce can tomatoes, well drained

THE SPICES

$2/3$ 3.3 ounce tablet (about 2 ounces) Mexican chocolate, roughly chopped

10 black peppercorns (or a scant $1/4$ teaspoon ground)

4 cloves (or about 1/8 teaspoon ground)

$1/2$ teaspoon aniseed (or a generous $1/2$ teaspoon ground)

1 inch cinnamon stick (or about 1 teaspoon ground)

TO FINISH THE DISH

$1/4$ cup lard or vegetable oil

About $2^1/2$ quarts poultry broth (page 33), preferably made from turkey

Salt, about 2 teaspoons (depending on the saltiness of the broth)

Sugar, about $1/4$ cup

Frying and reconstituting the chiles. Turn on the exhaust fan to suck up the pungent chile fumes. Measure $1/4$ cup of the lard or oil into the skillet and, when hot, fry the chile pieces a few at a time for several seconds per side, until they develop a nut-brown color. Remove them to a large bowl, draining as much fat as possible back into the skillet. Cover the chiles with boiling water, weight with a plate to keep them submerged, soak at least 1 hour, then drain and add the chile chipotle.

Frying the almonds, raisins, onion, and garlic. Heat the remaining $1/4$ cup of lard or oil in the skillet, add the almonds and stir frequently until browned through, about 4 minutes. Remove, draining well, and add to the tomato mixture. Fry the raisins for a minute or so, stirring constantly as they puff and brown. Scoop out, draining well, and add to the tomato mixture. Cook the onion and garlic, stirring frequently, until well browned, 8 to 9 minutes. Press on them to rid them of fat, and remove to the mixing bowl with the tomato and other fried ingredients.

Frying the tortilla and bread. If needed, add a little more fat, then fry the tortilla until browned, break it up and add to the mixing bowl. Lay the bread in the pan, quickly flip it over to coat both sides with fat, then brown it on both sides. Tear into large pieces and add to the tomato mixture.

Puréeing the mixture. Stir the mixture thoroughly and scoop $1/4$ of it into a blender jar, along with $1/2$ cup of the broth. Blend until very smooth, adding a little more liquid if the mixture won't move through the blades. Strain through a medium-mesh sieve. Purée the 3 remaining batches, adding $1/2$ cup broth to each one; strain.

Puréeing the chiles. Purée the drained chiles in 3 batches, adding about 1/2 cup of broth (plus a little more if needed) to each one; strain through the same sieve into a separate bowl.

Frying the turkey. Heat $1/4$ cup of the lard or oil in a large (at least 8-quart) kettle over medium-high. Dry the turkey pieces with paper towels and brown them in the lard in several batches, 3 or 4 minutes per side. Remove to a roasting pan large enough to hold them comfortably. Set aside at room temperature until the sauce is ready.

(continued)

Frying and simmering the sauce. Pour off the excess fat from the
    kettle, leaving a light coating on the bottom. Return to the heat
    for a minute, then add the chile purée and stir constantly until
    darkened and thick, about 5 minutes. Add the other bowlful of
    purée and stir several minutes longer, until the mixture thickens
    once again. Mix in 5 cups of broth, partially cover, reduce the heat
    to medium-low and simmer gently 45 minutes, stirring occasionally.
    Finally, season with salt and sugar and, if the sauce is thicker than
    heavy cream, thin it with a little broth.

Baking the turkey. Preheat the oven to 350°F. Pour the sauce over the
    turkey, cover the pan and bake until the bird is tender, about 2
    hours. Remove the turkey from the pan and spoon the fat off the
    sauce (or, if serving later, refrigerate so the fat will congeal and be
    easy to remove).

Presentation. Let the turkey cool, skin it and cut the meat from the
    bones in large pieces, slicing against the grain; layout the meat in
    2 or 3 large baking dishes.

Shortly before serving, pour the sauce over the turkey, cover and
    heat in a 350°F over for 15 to 20 minutes.

Immediately before you carry the mole to your guests, spoon some
    sauce from around the edges over the turkey to give it a glistening
    coat, then sprinkle with sesame seeds.

cascabel-crusted crabcakes

cascabel-crusted crabcakes
with grilled nopales and orange salad

Crabcakes have made their way onto menus across the country over the past decade. This version ties them directly to Mexico. The cascabel, one of my favorite chiles, gets its name from the sound it makes when shaken. It rattles like a snake and has a little of the same venomous bite.

CRABCAKES

6 tablespoons clarified butter

$1/2$ cup minced onion

$1/2$ cup minced celery

$1/4$ cup minced red bell pepper

$1/4$ cup minced yellow bell pepper

2 garlic cloves, minced

2 pounds fresh lump crabmeat (preferably Gulf Coast), shell and cartilage removed

1 tablespoon minced fresh thyme

2 tablespoons minced fresh basil

1 tablespoon Worcestershire sauce

$1/2$ cup crumbled queso fresco

1 cup fresh bread crumbs

4 eggs, lightly beaten

$1/2$ teaspoon cayenne powder

3 teaspoons dry mustard

Salt to taste

Cascabel Crust

Grilled Nopales and Orange Salad

CASCABEL CRUST

$1/4$ cup vegetable oil for frying

8 corn tortillas

4 cascabels, toasted whole, stemmed, and seeded

1 cup masa harina

$1/2$ teaspoon salt

CRABCAKES (YIELDS 6 SERVINGS)

Heat 2 tablespoons of the clarified butter in a sauté pan and cook the onion, celery, red and yellow peppers, and garlic over medium-low heat to soften, about 3 minutes. Place in a bowl and allow to cool. When cool, add the crabmeat and gently toss to combine. Add the thyme, basil, Worcestershire sauce, queso fresco, bread crumbs, eggs, cayenne, and dry mustard. Toss carefully to mix and bind, add salt to taste, and form into 6 cakes. Roll each cake in the Cascabel Crust. Heat the remaining clarified butter in a large sauté pan and sauté the cakes for 2 to 3 minutes per side. Serve warm with Grilled Nopales and Orange Salad.

CASCABEL CRUST

Heat oil to 350°F or until lightly smoking in a small sauté pan. Fry the tortillas, one at a time, until crisp. Drain on paper towels and allow to cool. Place the toasted and seeded cascabels in a spice grinder and process to a powder. Combine the ground cascabels with the masa and salt in a medium bowl. Place the tortillas in a food processor and process until coarsely ground. Add the masa mixture, and pulse to mix thoroughly. If not using immediately, store in an airtight container.

(continued)

cascabel-crusted crabcakes *(continued)*

GRILLED NOPALES AND ORANGE SALAD

2 nopales (cactus pads), thorns removed

1 tablespoon clarified butter

Salt and freshly ground black pepper to taste

1 cup oil for frying

4 corn tortillas, julienned

$1/4$ cup fresh orange juice (about 1 medium orange)

1 tablespoon white wine vinegar

1 teaspoon chipotle purée (page 15)

$1/4$ teaspoon salt

3 oranges, peeled with a knife and sectioned with the membrane removed

$1/4$ cup lightly packed fresh cilantro leaves

GRILLED NOPALES AND ORANGE SALAD (YIELDS 6 SERVINGS)

Cut each nopal into $1/2$-inch slices, being careful to leave 2 inches at the base intact to make a "fan." (These cuts will help prevent the pads from being slimy.) Rub the cactus pads with the clarified butter, season with salt and pepper, and grill for 3 minutes per side. Set aside to cool, then cut into julienne strips. Heat the oil to 350°F or until lightly smoking and fry the tortilla strips in batches until golden brown and crisp. Drain on paper towels.

Combine the orange juice, vinegar, chipotle purée, and $1/4$ teaspoon salt in a small bowl to make a dressing. Carefully toss the cactus with the orange sections, cilantro, fried tortillas, and dressing.

crab salad chile rellenos
with smoked corn vinaigrette and black bean chayote relish

This unusual relleno, served cold, serves well both as an excellent appetizer and as an accompaniment to a main course of fish. Chayote is a wonderfully earthy vegetable that has a delicious crispness when served raw.

CRAB SALAD CHILE RELLENOS

1 pound fresh lump crabmeat (preferably Gulf Coast), shell and cartilage removed

2 serranos, seeded and minced

1/2 cup pumpkin seeds, roasted (page 5)

2 tablespoons chopped fresh basil

3/4 cup roasted corn kernels (1 to 2 ears corn) (page 5)

1 red bell pepper, roasted, peeled, seeded, and julienned (page 14)

Smoked Corn Vinaigrette, divided

Salt to taste

4 poblanos, roasted, peeled, and carefully seeded (page 14)

Black Bean Chayote Relish

SMOKED CORN VINAIGRETTE

2 ears corn, shucked and silks removed

1/2 shallot, chopped

1 garlic clove

1 tablespoon white wine vinegar

1/2 cup chicken stock (page 33)

1/4 cup olive oil

1/4 cup corn oil

Salt to taste

BLACK BEAN CHAYOTE RELISH

1 cup cooked black beans, cooking liquid reserved (page 7)

1 chayote, peeled and diced

1 mango, peeled and diced

1/4 cup roasted corn kernels (1/2 to 1 ear corn) (page 5)

1 tablespoon chopped fresh cilantro

1 teaspoon olive oil

Juice of 1 lime

Salt to taste

CRAB SALAD CHILE RELLENOS (YIELDS 4 SERVINGS)

Toss the crabmeat with the serranos, half of the pumpkin seeds, the basil, the roasted corn kernels, the bell pepper, and half of the Corn Vinaigrette. Season with salt. Fill each poblano with one-fourth of the crabmeat mixture.

Serve each chile relleno on a plate with the remaining Corn Vinaigrette and garnish with the remaining pumpkin seeds. Top with Black Bean Chayote Relish, and drizzle with the reserved black bean liquid.

SMOKED CORN VINAIGRETTE

Prepare the smoker (page 7) and lightly smoke the corn for 10 minutes. Cut the corn kernels off the cobs. Combine the corn kernels with the shallot, garlic, vinegar, and chicken stock in a blender or food processor; process until smooth. With the machine running, slowly drizzle in the olive oil and corn oil until emulsified. Season with salt.

BLACK BEAN CHAYOTE RELISH

Reduce the cooking liquid from the beans almost to a syrup and set aside.

Toss the cooked and drained black beans with the chayote, mango, corn, cilantro, olive oil, and lime juice. Season with salt. Let stand for 20 to 30 minutes. Served chilled or at room temperature.

black-eyed pea crabmeat gorditas
with tequila–orange vinaigrette

This recipe brings together two strong influences in Texas cooking—Southern and Mexican. I happen to love the combination of crabmeat and black-eyed peas, using them together as often as possible. Even without the gorditas, this makes a great salad.

GORDITA FILLING

1 1/2 cups black-eyed peas, soaked overnight and drained

1 quart ham hock broth or water

Salt to taste

4 slices bacon, diced

1 pound fresh Gulf Coast lump crabmeat, shell and cartilage removed

1 medium-size red bell pepper, seeded and finely diced

1 medium-size yellow bell pepper, seeded and finely diced

1 medium-size poblano, seeded and finely diced

1 small red onion, minced

3 scallions, thinly sliced

1 medium tomato, seeded and diced

1 teaspoon chopped fresh marigold mint

1 teaspoon chopped fresh chervil

1 cup Tequila–Orange Vinaigrette, plus additional for drizzling

8 Gorditas

2 oranges, peeled with a knife and sectioned with the membrane removed

Fresh cilantro springs for garnish

GORDITA FILLING (YIELDS 16 GORDITAS OR 8 GORDAS)

Place the drained black-eyed peas in a large saucepan with the ham hock broth and bring to a boil. Reduce the heat and simmer for 45 to 60 minutes or until tender. Toward the end of the cooking time, taste the peas and season with salt as needed. Drain the peas, cool, and set aside.

Cook the bacon over medium-high heat in a large skillet until all of the fat is rendered and the bacon is crispy-brown. Drain the bacon on paper towels, then dice. Combine the bacon, crabmeat, bell peppers, poblano, onion, scallions, tomato, marigold mint, chervil, and drained peas in a large bowl. Add the Tequila-Orange Vinaigrette, stirring just to combine. Let stand at room temperature for about 30 minutes to allow the flavors to meld. Meanwhile, prepare the gorditas.

Slit the gorditas open with a small knife. Stuff each gordita with 2 to 3 tablespoons crabmeat mixture. Garnish with orange sections and cilantro, and drizzle with additional Tequila–Orange Vinaigrette.

(continued)

black-eyed pea crabmeat gorditas

black-eyed pea crabmeat gorditas *(continued)*

TEQUILA–ORANGE VINAIGRETTE

Juice of 1 lemon

Juice of 2 oranges

2 tablespoons tequila

2 tablespoons sugar

1 teaspoon orange zest

2 tablespoons champagne vinegar

$1/4$ cup corn oil

$1/4$ cup olive oil

Salt to taste

GORDITAS

1 pound fresh masa harina

2 tablespoons lard or vegetable shortening

1 teaspoon salt

$1/4$ cup all-purpose flour

$1/2$ teaspoon baking powder

Vegetable oil for frying

TEQUILA–ORANGE VINAIGRETTE

Combine the lemon juice, orange juice, tequila, and sugar in a small saucepan over medium-low heat; cook until reduced to 2 tablespoons. Transfer to a small bowl and add the orange zest and champagne vinegar. Combine the oils in a measuring cup. While whisking the vinegar mixture, drizzle the oils in a steady stream. Add salt to taste.

GORDITAS

Combine the masa harina, lard, salt, flour, and baking powder in the bowl of an electric mixer; mix thoroughly. Divide the dough into 16 equal ball-shaped portions. (Or, divide the dough into 8 equal ball-shaped portions to make gordas, the larger version of gorditas.) Press out to $1/8$ inch with a tortilla press lined with lightly oiled plastic wrap.

Pour enough oil in a frying pan to come $1/2$ inch up the side. Heat the oil to 350°F or until just barely smoking over medium heat.

Place a comal or skillet over medium-high heat for 5 minutes. Cook each gordita for 30 seconds on each side or until lightly browned.

Carefully place the gorditas, 3 or 4 at a time, in the pan of hot oil. Brown on one side, turn with tongs, and brown on the other side. When puffed and crispy, remove from the oil and drain on paper towels until cool.

lace cookie tacos
with a kaleidoscope of fruit and caramel

This delicious dessert has been on a menu in one of my restaurants for the past 15 years. What began as a rather French dessert ended up as a facsimile of a Mexican staple. Whether served as a cookie cup or a taco, this dessert is one of the most satisfying endings to a good meal that I know.

LACE TACOS

1 cup finely ground almonds

$^3/_4$ cup sugar

8 tablespoons unsalted butter (1 stick), room temperature

4 teaspoons flour

2 tablespoons milk

1 cup heavy cream

2 tablespoons confectioners' sugar

1 tablespoon vanilla extract

1 cup fresh raspberries

1 cup fresh blackberries

1 cup stemmed, sliced fresh strawberries

1 cup diced fresh mango or papaya

Caramel Sauce

CARAMEL SAUCE

$^1/_3$ cup granulated sugar

1 cup light brown sugar

$^1/_4$ cup pure maple syrup

$^1/_4$ cup dark corn syrup

1 cup heavy cream

LACE TACOS (YIELDS 12 SERVINGS)

Preheat the oven to 350°F. Combine the almonds, sugar, butter, flour, and milk in a mixing bowl and stir to a smooth dough.

Cut wax paper or parchment paper into 4 (6-inch) squares and place on a large cookie sheet. Place 1 tablespoon of the cookie dough in the center of each square. Wet your fingers thoroughly with cold milk or water and flatten the dough. Continue wetting fingers and patting dough until it is so thin that it becomes transparent; the dough should be in rounds about 3 inches across.

Bake in the oven for 12 minutes or until the cookies are golden brown and have spread to about 5 inches in diameter. Remove from the oven and let stand for about 45 seconds. Remove the cookies from the paper. Mold each one on a rolling pin to resemble a fried taco shell. When hardened and cooled, remove from the rolling pin. Repeat the procedure until 12 cookies have been molded.

In a medium mixing bowl set over a larger bowl of ice water, whip the cream with an electric mixer. Sprinkle in the confectioners' sugar and continue to whip until the mixture resembles thin sour cream. Add the vanilla and whip until soft peaks form; do not overwhip.

Fill each "taco" with 2 tablespoons of the whipped cream and some fruit. Serve each on top of a dollop of Caramel Sauce.

CARAMEL SAUCE

Mix all the ingredients in a heavy saucepan. Cook over high heat until the mixture reaches 200°F on a candy thermometer. Let cool for 20 minutes, and skim the surface if necessary.

mango rum cake
with horchata ice cream

Pound cakes are from a great American tradition of baking. This is my version of the creation gone south and tropical. Horchata is that great agua fresca *made from rice that is served everywhere in Mexico. I've taken it a step further by freezing it to make ice cream, a refreshing variation on an already refreshing theme.*

CAKE

1³/₄ cup cake flour

¹/₂ teaspoon salt

¹/₂ teaspoon baking soda

¹/₂ teaspoon ground cinnamon

¹/₂ teaspoon nutmeg

¹/₄ pound unsalted butter (1 stick)

1¹/₄ cups sugar

¹/₂ cup sour cream

¹/₂ cup mango purée

3 eggs, lightly beaten

1 teaspoon vanilla

1 tablespoon grated ginger

¹/₄ cup Meyer's dark rum

HORCHATA ICE CREAM

¹/₂ cup uncooked white rice

5 cups water, divided

1¹/₂ cups slivered almonds, blanched

1 canela or cinnamon stick

3 cups coconut milk

¹/₂ cup sugar

CAKE (YIELDS 1 LOAF CAKE)

Preheat the oven to 300°F and lightly oil a 9-inch loaf pan.

Sift the flour, salt, baking soda, cinnamon, and nutmeg together in a large mixing bowl. In another mixing bowl, cream together the butter, sugar, and sour cream with an electric mixer, whipping until lemon colored, approximately 3 minutes. Beat in the mango purée, eggs, and vanilla. Beat in the ginger and rum. Fold into the dry ingredients until well combined. Pour into the loaf pan and bake for 40 to 50 minutes or until a toothpick inserted in the center comes out clean.

To serve, top each slice of cake with a scoop of Horchata Ice Cream.

HORCHATA ICE CREAM

Place the rice in a spice or coffee grinder and grind to a powder. Heat 3 cups of water to a boil in a medium saucepan. Add the rice, almonds, and canela stick. Stir until smooth, then remove from the heat. Place in a container covered with cheesecloth and refrigerate overnight.

Remove the canela stick. Place the rice mixture in a blender with the remaining 2 cups of water. Purée until smooth, about 5 minutes to extract the flavors. Pass the purée through a mesh strainer. Add the coconut milk and sugar, and thin with more milk if desired. Serve over ice as a refreshing drink, or for serving with the Mango Rum Cake, freeze in an ice cream machine according to the manufacturer's directions.

tres atoles
with pecans and vanilla, with mexican chocolate, and with blackberries

In Mexico, atoles are to tamales what milkshakes are to hamburgers in the United States. Made from a base of masa, these thick and satisfying drinks of milk, fruit, nuts, and chocolate have been enjoyed in Mexico since long before the Spaniards came.

atole base

1/2 cup masa harina

1/2 cup water

2 cups hot milk

(YIELDS 3 SERVINGS)

Combine the masa harina and water into a smooth paste. Add to the hot milk, and stir to incorporate.

pecans and vanilla atole

Atole Base

1 vanilla bean, split in half lengthwise and scraped

1 tablespoon light brown sugar

2 cups toasted pecan pieces, ground

Milk for thinning (optional)

Purée the atole base, vanilla, brown sugar, and pecans in a blender. Strain through a chinois. Thin with milk if necessary.

mexican chocolate atole

Atole Base

3 ounces Mexican chocolate, grated

5 tablespoons piloncillo or light brown sugar

Milk for thinning (optional)

Stir the chocolate and sugar into the atole base until melted and dissolved. Strain through a chinois. Thin with milk if necessary.

blackberry atole

Atole Base

2 cups fresh blackberries

4 tablespoons honey

Milk for thinning (optional)

Purée the atole base, berries, and honey in a blender. Strain through a chinois. Thin with milk if necessary.

a taste of the

yucatán

To most Americans, the Yucatán peninsula is best known for its crystal-clear waters and stunning beaches. Understandably so, as any sun-worshiping vacationer can attest.

But the Yucatán is so much more than beautiful scenery. Its rich heritage can be glimpsed in Mayan ruins such as Chichén Itzá and Uxmal, which attract visitors from all over. Of particular interest to me, however, the cuisine of the Yucatán is some of the most distinctive in the country.

Yucatán cooking takes its influence more from the Caribbean than from Mexico, offering a multitude of *recados*, or spice blends, that form the very essence of the Yucatán flavor profile. The food of the Yucatán can be some of the spiciest around, primarily because of its dependence on a Caribbean mainstay, the fiery Scotch bonnet.

coco relleno

Prepare this dish ahead and take it with you the next time you go to the beach, lake, or swimming pool.
It is typical beach fare in the coastal regions of Mexico, particularly in the Yucatán peninsula area.

3 coconuts

4 garlic cloves

1 habanero, sliced in half

1 pound rock shrimp

1 pound bay scallops, cleaned

6 tomatillos, husks removed
and chopped

2 tablespoons rum

1 cup lightly packed fresh cilantro
leaves, plus more for garnish

3 tablespoons chopped mint

1/4 cup olive oil

2 tablespoons cider vinegar

1 small red onion, sliced into thin
rings

2 mangos, peeled, seeded, and diced

2 medium cucumbers, peeled, seeded,
and sliced into half moons

Kosher salt to taste

2 tablespoons fresh lime juice
(1 to 2 medium limes)

(YIELDS 6 TO 8 SERVINGS)

For each coconut, poke a hole through two of its eyes with an ice pick to drain the coconut water out. Pour the coconut water through a fine mesh strainer and reserve. Break the coconuts in half and wipe clean. Place the reserved coconut water in a heavy saucepan over medium heat. Add the garlic and habanero and cook until the liquid is reduced by half. Add the shrimp and scallops and poach for 1 to 2 minutes or until just firm. Remove from the pan and let cool. (Also, if you prefer a less spicy dish, remove the habanero from the cooking liquid.) Bring the liquid to a boil again. Add the tomatillos and rum, cooking for 3 minutes. Pour the liquid and tomatillos in a blender; add the cilantro, mint, olive oil, and vinegar. Purée until smooth.

Place the puréed mixture in a medium bowl over ice to cool. After chilling, toss with the chilled seafood, red onion, mango, and cucumber. Season with salt and lime juice.

To serve, place the shrimp mixture in the halved coconut shells and garnish with cilantro leaves.

fish tacos
with creamy cabbage slaw and pineapple pico

One of my favorite botanos, or snacks, in Mexico is a fish taco. The creamy slaw lends a perfect texture to the taco while the sweet and acidic pineapple pico gives the flavor a perfect balance.

FISH TACOS

Marinade

2 pounds sea bass fillets

Salt and freshly ground black pepper to taste

12 to 16 fresh corn tortillas, steamed until soft

Creamy Cabbage Slaw

Pineapple Pico

Cilantro leaves for garnish

MARINADE

$^1/_2$ cup soy sauce

2 tablespoons brown sugar

1 12-ounce bottle Mexican beer

4 garlic cloves, roasted and minced (page 4)

CREAMY CABBAGE SLAW

2 cups shredded white cabbage

1 red bell pepper, julienned

1 yellow bell pepper, julienned

$^1/_2$ red onion, thinly sliced

1 jalapeño, finely minced

$^1/_4$ cup mayonnaise (page 30)

1 tablespoon fresh lime juice (about 1 medium lime)

1 teaspoon sugar

1 tablespoon horseradish

2 tablespoons chiffonade of fresh basil

Salt and freshly ground black pepper to taste

PINEAPPLE PICO

1 pineapple, peeled, cored, and diced

1 serrano, seeded and finely minced

$^1/_2$ red onion, diced

3 tablespoons chopped fresh cilantro

1 tablespoon chopped fresh mint

1 tablespoon fresh lime juice (about 1 medium lime)

FISH TACOS (YIELDS 6 TO 8 SERVINGS)

Marinate the sea bass for a few hours; drain and season with salt and pepper. Prepare a hot charcoal grill (page 4) and grill the sea bass fillets for 3 to 5 minutes per side—they will flake when done. Cut or flake the fillets into 2- to 3-inch pieces and serve on warm tortillas with the Creamy Cabbage Slaw and Pineapple Pico. Garnish with the cilantro leaves.

MARINADE

Combine all the ingredients in a blender and purée until completely smooth.

CREAMY CABBAGE SLAW

Toss all the ingredients together in a large mixing bowl. Let stand for 30 minutes to blend the flavors.

PINEAPPLE PICO

Toss all the ingredients together in a medium mixing bowl. Let stand for 30 minutes to blend the flavors.

ceviche with shrimp, oranges, and popcorn

The inspiration for this recipe came from the Ecuadorian tradition of serving orange-infused shellfish with large bowls of freshly-popped popcorn and fried corn nuts.

1 large yellow tomato, roasted, peeled, and chopped

2 jalapeños, seeded and diced (page 14)

1 yellow bell pepper, roasted, peeled, and chopped (page 14)

$1/2$ onion, roasted and chopped

$3/4$ cup fresh lime juice (8 to 10 medium limes)

$1/2$ cup fresh orange juice (about $1^1/2$ medium oranges)

2 pounds rock shrimp or medium shrimp, peeled, deveined, and coarsely chopped

Salt to taste

$1/4$ cup tomato juice

1 tablespoon sugar

Tabasco sauce to taste

1 red onion, thinly sliced

2 tablespoons chopped fresh chives

2 tablespoons chopped scallions

$1/4$ cup chopped fresh cilantro

$1/2$ cup freshly popped popcorn

$1/4$ cup fried corn nuts

(YIELDS 8 TO 12 SERVINGS)

Combine the tomato, jalapeños, bell pepper, roasted onion, and lime and orange juices in a blender and process until smooth. Bring a large pan of water to a boil. Blanch the shrimp for about 30 seconds, then cool in ice water to stop the cooking process. Drain the shrimp and let dry thoroughly. Combine the shrimp and the blended liquid in a large mixing bowl. Season with salt.

Add the tomato juice, sugar, Tabasco, red onion, chives, scallions, and cilantro. Let the shrimp marinate for at least 2 hours. Serve with popcorn and corn nuts.

ceviche with shrimp, oranges, and popcorn

shrimp chili chalupas
with papaya–habanero salsa
(courtesy of Chef David Garrido)

This shrimp chili is so good, your friends and family will be lucky if there's any left to put on the chalupas at dinnertime. Try to control yourself! Shrimp Chili Chalupas: Use the shrimp chili mixture as a topping for chalupas and garnish with a dollop of sour cream and Papaya–Habanero Salsa. Shrimp Chili Nachos: If you ate too much of the shrimp chili to make tacos, put what's left on tortilla chips and call them nachos. The salsa is a great marinade because papain, an enzyme present in papaya, is a natural meat tenderizer. We use the salsa to marinate fajitas, but it also tastes great with lobster, crab, and shrimp dishes.

SHRIMP CHILI CHALUPAS

1 tablespoon olive oil

16 medium-sized shrimp, peeled, deveined, and cut into small chunks

1 onion, diced

2 tablespoons roasted garlic purée (see page 4)

2 cups diced, seeded tomatoes

1/4 cup minced fresh Mexican marigold mint or marjoram

2 tablespoons chipotle purée (page 15)

Salt

8 freshly fried corn tortillas

1 cup Papaya–Habanero Salsa

PAPAYA–HABANERO SALSA

1 ripe papaya, halved, seeded, and peeled

1/2 habanero chile, seeded and minced

1/4 teaspoon sugar

2 tablespoons fresh lemon juice

1 tablespoon olive oil

1 yellow tomato, seeded and finely diced

1 red bell pepper, roasted, peeled, stemmed, seeded, and finely diced (see page 14)

1/2 cup coarsely chopped fresh cilantro

1 tablespoon minced fresh mint

Salt

SHRIMP CHILI CHALUPAS (MAKES 8 TACOS)

In a medium-sized skillet, heat the olive oil over high heat. Add the shrimp and onion and sauté for 2 minutes or until the shrimp are opaque. Add the garlic purée, tomatoes, marigold mint, and chipotle purée and cook for 1 minute. Season to taste with salt. Remove from the heat.

Divide the shrimp chili among the 8 chalupas. Garnish each disk with Papaya–Habanero Salsa.

PAPAYA–HABANERO SALSA (MAKES 2 1/2 TO 3 CUPS)

Dice half of the papaya and set it aside. Cut up the other half, place in a blender, and add the habanero chile, sugar, lemon juice, and olive oil. Purée until smooth. Transfer the purée to a nonreactive bowl and add the reserved diced papaya, tomato, bell pepper, cilantro, and mint. Mix well and season to taste with salt. Let stand for 15 minutes to allow the flavors to blend before serving.

annatto rice
with wild mushrooms and black bean–prosciutto refrito
(*annatto rice with wild mushrooms* courtesy of Chef David Garrido)

Bright orange rice and silky wild mushrooms are an exceptional combination that will light up any plate. This is one of the richest refried bean recipes we've ever tried. We call for it in lots of other recipes. If you can't bear to use prosciutto (it's very expensive), substitute thin slices of the best smoked ham you can afford.

ANNATTO RICE WITH WILD MUSHROOMS

1 cup Texmati rice, basmati rice, or other long-grain white rice

$^1/_2$ cup annatto oil

2 cloves garlic, minced

$^1/_2$ onion, finely diced

1 small carrot, peeled and finely diced

1 celery stalk, finely diced

1$^1/_2$ cups wild mushrooms such as morels or chanterelles, thinly sliced

Fresh corn kernels from 1 ear of corn

1 teaspoon ground cinnamon

2$^1/_2$ cups chicken stock

Salt

BLACK BEAN–PROSCIUTTO REFRITO

1 cup black beans, soaked overnight and drained

6 cups ham hock broth or chicken broth (page 33)

$^1/_2$ cup red wine (Burgundy or Cabernet)

$^1/_2$ cup chopped onion

2 garlic cloves, minced

3 tablespoons vegetable oil or lard

$^1/_3$ cup julienned prosciutto

3 pickled jalapeños, seeded and diced

Salt to taste

2 tablespoons chopped fresh cilantro leaves

Sour cream (optional)

ANNATTO RICE WITH WILD MUSHROOMS (MAKES 2$^1/_2$ CUPS)

Rinse the rice briefly in cold water and drain. In a large saucepan, heat the annatto oil over medium heat. Add the garlic, onion, carrot, and celery and sauté for 2 minutes. Add the mushrooms and corn and sauté for 4 to 6 minutes or until the onion is translucent and the mushrooms are tender. Add the rice and cinnamon and stir for 1 to 2 minutes or until the rice is well coated with the oil.

Heat the chicken stock to a boil, add it to the rice mixture, and reduce the heat to low. Cook, uncovered, for 20 minutes, or until the liquid is absorbed and the rice is tender. Season to taste with salt.

Serves 4 to 6 people

BLACK BEAN–PROSCIUTTO REFRITO

Rinse the beans in cold water. Bring the stock and wine to a bowl in a large pan. Add the beans, onion, and garlic. Bring the liquid back to a boil, lower the heat, and simmer for 1$^1/_2$ hours. Drain the beans and transfer the cooking liquid to a clean pan set over high heat. Reduce the liquid to $^1/_2$ cup.

Heat the oil in a medium sauté pan over medium-high heat until lightly smoking. Add the cooked beans, prosciutto, and jalapeños. Mash with a potato masher to a rough purée. Add the reserved bean liquid and bring to a boil. Reduce the heat and, stirring constantly, let simmer until the beans are a bit thinner than the desired consistency. (They will thicken as they sit.) Season with salt to taste, garnish with cilantro, and finish with a dollop of sour cream if desired.

shrimp taquitos

shrimp taquitos
with mango barbecue sauce and avocado–tomatillo salsa

We serve thousands of these little tacos at Star Canyon. I prefer rock shrimp, which has a similarity in texture and taste to lobster, but have also used any number of other varieties with great success. Mangos bring a tropical fruitiness to barbecue, one of the four major food groups in Texas. The Mango Barbecue Sauce complements all types of other dishes too, particularly seafood, chicken, and duck. The combination of mango, mustard, and habaneros makes a surprisingly compatible trinity.

TAQUITOS

1 tablespoon olive oil

1 pound rock shrimp, peeled and deveined

1/2 medium onion, diced

1/2 cup seeded, diced red bell pepper

1/2 cup seeded, diced yellow bell pepper

1/2 cup seeded, diced poblano

1/2 cup shredded Chihuahua cheese

3 tablespoons chopped fresh cilantro

2 tablespoons ancho purée (page 15)

Salt to taste

16 flour tortillas, cut into 4-inch circles and warmed

Mango Barbecue Sauce

Avocado–Tomatillo Salsa (page 22)

MANGO BARBECUE SAUCE

1 tablespoon olive oil

1 medium onion, diced

2 garlic cloves, chopped

1 habanero, stemmed, seeded, and chopped

3 tablespoons cider vinegar

1 tablespoon light brown sugar

1 tablespoon pasilla purée (page 15)

1 mango, peeled, pitted, and puréed

1 cup chicken stock (page 33)

Juice of 2 limes

Juice of 1 orange

1 tablespoon dry mustard

1 tablespoon Dijon mustard

Salt to taste

TAQUITOS (YIELDS 16 TAQUITOS)

Heat the oil in a large sauté pan until lightly smoking. Add the shrimp, onion, bell peppers, and poblano; sauté for 2 minutes. Remove from the heat and stir in the cheese, cilantro, and ancho purée. Season with salt.

Place a heaping tablespoon of the shrimp mixture on half of each tortilla, then fold over like a quesadilla. Serve with Mango Barbecue Sauce and garnish with Avocado–Tomatillo Salsa (page 22).

MANGO BARBECUE SAUCE

Heat the oil in a small saucepan over medium heat until lightly smoking. Add the onion and sauté for 1 minute. Add the garlic and habanero, and continue to cook about 2 to 3 minutes or until the onion is translucent, stirring occasionally.

Add the vinegar, sugar, and pasilla purée; cook until thickened, about 3 minutes. Add the mango purée and chicken stock. Reduce the heat to low and simmer for 10 minutes. Whisk in the lime juice, orange juice, dry mustard, and Dijon; simmer for 3 to 5 more minutes. Strain through a fine sieve, salt to taste, and serve with the taquitos.

huachinango and red curry masa

steamed in banana leaves

Huachinango is Mexico's famous red snapper. I've infused a little Asian flavor into the masa dough that surrounds the fish, but placed it firmly back in Mexico with the classic tomato-olive–based Veracruzana Sauce.

TAMALES

1½ pounds red snapper fillet, skinned, boned and cut into 8 portions, about 3 ounces each

Salt to taste

2 tablespoons chopped fresh mint

2 large banana leaves, about 10 by 40 inches each

Red Thai Curry Tamale Masa Dough

Veracruzana Sauce

Roasted Chile Avocado Relish

RED THAI CURRY TAMALE MASA DOUGH

3 stalks lemongrass, outer leaves peeled and discarded

1¼ cups water

1¾ cups masa harina

10 tablespoons chilled vegetable shortening

1½ teaspoons salt

1 teaspoon baking powder

¼ cup chicken stock, chilled (page 33)

2 tablespoons red Thai curry paste (available in Asian markets)

TAMALES (YIELDS 8 SERVINGS)

Place the fillets on a flat work surface and season both sides with salt. Sprinkle the mint on the fillets, pressing gently so it adheres.

Cut each banana leaf crosswise into 4 even pieces, about 8 inches by 10 inches. Soften each piece over an open flame for 10 seconds on each side, being careful not to burn them. Lay out on a flat work surface. Divide the Red Thai Curry Tamale Masa Dough into 16 even portions and roll them each into a ball. Flatten each ball between 2 layers of plastic wrap with your hand or a tortilla press to a thickness of ⅛ inch. Carefully place 1 flattened masa portion in the center of each banana leaf. Spoon 1 tablespoon of Veracruzana Sauce over the top of the dough. Place 1 piece of snapper in the center of each masa disk. Spoon another tablespoon of sauce over the fish and place another flattened masa disk over the snapper to make a sandwich. Repeat for the remaining tamales. To fold the tamales, pick up the two long sides of the banana leaf and bring them together, one overlapping the other. The leaf will surround the filling. Fold the flaps on each end underneath the tamale.

Fill the bottom of a steamer or saucepan fitted with a strainer or vegetable basket with 2 to 3 inches of water. Bring the water to a boil and place the tamales in the steamer. Cover tightly with a lid of foil so that little or no steam escapes while cooking. Steam the tamales for 25 to 30 minutes over lightly boiling water, adding more boiling water as needed. The tamales are done when they feel firm—but not hard—to the touch and the dough comes away easily from the leaves. Let rest for at least 5 minutes before serving.

Unwrap the tamales and place on serving plates. Serve with Roasted Chile Avocado Relish.

VERACRUZANA SAUCE

1 tablespoon olive oil

$1/2$ cup thinly sliced onion

2 pounds tomatoes, peeled and cored

1 garlic clove, chopped

6 green olives, pitted and chopped

2 teaspoons drained capers

1 small pickled jalapeño, seeded
  and sliced

1 teaspoon jalapeño pickling juice

$1/4$ teaspoon fresh marjoram

$1/4$ teaspoon fresh thyme

1 teaspoon chopped fresh
  Italian parsley

1 bay leaf

$1/4$ cinnamon stick

1 clove

Pinch of coarsely ground black pepper

$1/4$ cup fish or chicken stock
  (page 33)

Salt to taste

ROASTED CHILE AVOCADO RELISH

$1/4$ cup olive oil

Juice of 1 lime

Salt and freshly ground black pepper
  to taste

1 red bell pepper, roasted, peeled,
  seeded, and julienned (page 14)

1 yellow bell pepper, roasted, peeled,
  seeded, and julienned (page 14)

2 jalapeños, seeded and minced

1 small red onion, thinly sliced

1 small jícama, peeled and julienned

2 avocados, peeled and sliced

RED THAI CURRY TAMALE MASA DOUGH

Bruise the lemongrass stalks with the back of a knife and mince.
  Combine the minced lemongrass with the water in a small saucepan.
  Bring to a boil over high heat, then turn off the heat. Cover the pan
  and allow the lemongrass to infuse for 15 minutes. Strain the water
  into a clean saucepan, adding more water if necessary to make $1^1/4$
  cups of liquid. Bring to a boil, remove from the heat, and set aside.

Place the masa harina in the bowl of an electric mixer fitted with a
  paddle attachment. With the machine on low speed, add the infused
  water in a slow, steady stream until the dough forms a ball. Continue
  mixing on medium speed for 5 minutes, then transfer the dough to
  a clean bowl. Refrigerate for 1 hour.

Return the masa to the bowl of the electric mixer and beat for 5
  minutes on high speed. With the machine running, slowly add the
  shortening 2 tablespoons at a time. Continue mixing for about 5 minutes, until the dough is smooth and light. Stop the mixer to scrape
  the sides of the bowl. Reduce the speed to low and continue beating.

While the dough is mixing, combine the salt, baking powder, and
  chicken stock in a small mixing bowl. Slowly add the stock mixture
  to the masa in a steady stream. Add the red curry paste and continue
  mixing until thoroughly combined. Increase the speed to high and
  mix for 5 minutes longer.

VERACRUZANA SAUCE

Heat the oil in a large skillet over medium heat. Add the onion and
  cook, stirring frequently, about 8 minutes or until golden brown.

While the onion is cooking, cut the tomatoes in half and squeeze out
  the seeds into a strainer set over a small bowl. Cut the tomato flesh
  into 1-inch pieces and place in a mixing bowl. Add all the tomato
  juice from the cutting board, as well as the juice from straining the
  seeds, to the tomatoes.

Add the garlic to the browned onion and cook, stirring, about
  1 minute. Add the tomatoes and their juice. Simmer for 5 minutes
  to reduce some of the liquid.

Combine the olives, capers, sliced jalapeño, pickling juice, marjoram,
  thyme, and parsley. Stir in the bay leaf, cinnamon stick, clove, and
  black pepper. Add the herbs and spices to the cooked and thickened
  tomatoes. Add the stock and simmer for 10 minutes. Season with salt.

ROASTED CHILE AVOCADO RELISH

Whisk the olive oil into the lime juice. Season with salt and pepper.
  Combine with the peppers, jalapeño, red onion, and jícama.
  Slowly fold in the avocado until mixed.

fritura mixta

fritura mixta

This is sort of the Mexican version of the classic Italian mixed fried plate called fritto misto. *In Mexico, a dish served with red and green sauce on the same plate is called* divorciada, *the idea being that the sauces stay separated or "divorced" on the plate. I believe the two batters in this dish would qualify as my own version of batter divorciada, though they reunite for a beautiful presentation when served in newspaper cones.*

FRITURA MIXTA
Beer Batter Base

3 tablespoons puréed chipotles in adobo

3 tablespoons Cilantro Pesto

1 quart vegetable oil for frying

2 pounds calamari, peeled, cleaned, and sliced (leave the tentacles intact)

1 medium-size sweet potato, peeled and thinly sliced

2 medium red onions, peeled, sliced into $1/2$-inch rings, and separated

2 mangos, peeled, pitted, and thickly julienned

2 avocados, peeled, pitted, and sliced

3 limes, cut into wedges or slices

BEER BATTER BASE
$1^1/2$ cups all-purpose flour, sifted

1 teaspoon kosher salt

1 cup Mexican beer, room temperature

1 cup small ice cubes

CILANTRO PESTO
2 bunches cilantro

3 garlic cloves

$1/2$ cup pine nuts, toasted

$1/2$ teaspoon kosher salt

$1/4$ cup olive oil

$1/4$ cup grated Asiago or Parmesan cheese

Salt to taste

FRITURA MIXTA (YIELDS 6 SERVINGS)
Divide the Beer Batter Base in half. Place the chipotles in adobo in one of the halves and mix thoroughly; place the Cilantro Pesto in the other half and mix thoroughly.

Heat oil in a large saucepan until hot. Dip the calamari in the chipotle batter; dip the potato slices, onion rings, mango julienne, and avocado slices in the pesto batter. Let the extra batter run off of the dipped items, and fry a few at a time until a crisp golden brown. Serve hot with the lime wedges.

BEER BATTER BASE
Combine the flour and salt in a medium mixing bowl. Lightly whisk in the beer, being careful not to overmix; a few lumps of flour are acceptable. Fold in the ice and use immediately.

CILANTRO PESTO
Place the cilantro, garlic, pine nuts, and salt in a food processor and purée. With the processor still running, drizzle in the olive oil until the pesto is smooth and bright green. Add the Asiago and pulse to mix. Adjust the seasoning with salt if necessary.

sea bass in hoja santa
with salsa verde and rose petals (courtesy of Chef Patricia Quintana)

Hoja santa is in the black pepper family and has the aroma of sassafras. In fact, it's called the "root beer" plant and it lends an almost eucalyptic flavor to fish.

VEGETABLE BROTH

10 cups water

1 onion, quartered

6 garlic cloves

1 ear corn, cut into 3 or 4 rounds

$1/2$ leek, chopped and washed

4 celery stalks, chopped

2 turnips, chopped

2 carrots, chopped

1 teaspoon black peppercorns

$1/2$ cup soy sauce

$1/2$ teaspoon salt

FISH

4 garlic cloves, roasted and puréed

1 onion, roasted and puréed

8 tablespoons olive oil

1 jalapeño, diced with seeds

$3/4$ cup reduced vegetable broth, chilled

20 hojas santas (to cover the bottom of the steamer), plus 16 hojas santas, steamed or blanched (for wrapping fish)

10 $1/2$-pound fillets fish (bass or red snapper)

Salt and freshly ground black pepper to taste

Salsa Verde

Petals from 4 organic yellow roses

VEGETABLE BROTH (YIELDS 5 CUPS)

Bring the water to a boil in a large pot. Add the onion, garlic, corn, leek, celery, turnips, and carrots. Season to taste with the peppercorns, soy sauce, and salt. Cook over low heat for 2 hours; strain the broth and reduce by half. Chill.

FISH (YIELDS 10 SERVINGS)

Combine the garlic, puréed onion, olive oil, and jalapeño in a small bowl. Place the broth in a steamer and bring to a boil. Cover the bottom of the steamer with hoja santa. Brush the fillets with the garlic, onion, chile and oil mixture; season with salt and pepper. Wrap each fillet with hoja santa; place all the wrapped fish in the steamer and cover with a tight-fitting lid. Cook for 10 to 12 minutes, being careful not to overcook.

Ladle the Salsa Verde on a plate and place the steamed fish on top. Garnish with the yellow rose petals.

SALSA VERDE

1$^1/_2$ onions, chopped

3 garlic cloves, peeled

1$^1/_2$ teaspoons salt

5 serranos, diced with seeds

2 jalapeños, diced with seeds

1$^1/_2$ cups tomatillos, husks removed
and roasted or boiled in hot water

$^1/_2$ cup water

$^1/_2$ teaspoon sugar

$^1/_3$ cup olive oil

$^1/_4$ cup lime juice

1 cup chopped fresh hoja santa

$^1/_2$ cup chopped fresh epazote

1$^1/_3$ cup chopped fresh cilantro

SALSA VERDE

Purée the onion, garlic, salt, chiles, tomatillos, water, and sugar in a
blender. Add the oil, lime juice, and fresh herbs and blend for
30 seconds longer. Reseason to taste. Serve at room temperature.

jerked brisket salpicón tacos

This recipe brings a little Jamaica to the Mexican taqueria. The spicy brisket is refreshed by the jícama, radishes, and lime juice. This salpicón, or salad, would also be delicious as a tostada.

BRISKET TACOS

Jerk Marinade

4 pounds beef brisket, trimmed

$1/4$ cup vegetable oil

Salad

16 corn tortillas

2 cups vegetable oil for frying

Fresh cilantro leaves for garnish

JERK MARINADE

8 scallions, sliced with green parts

1 medium onion, chopped

4 garlic cloves, chopped

2 habaneros, seeded and chopped

2 teaspoons chopped fresh thyme

1 teaspoon salt

1 teaspoon light brown sugar

1 teaspoon ground allspice

$1/2$ teaspoon ground nutmeg

$1/2$ teaspoon ground cinnamon

1 teaspoon freshly ground black pepper

2 teaspoons cider vinegar

$1/4$ cup vegetable oil

SALAD

1 red onion, thinly sliced

1 jícama, peeled and diced

5 radishes, julienned

1 jalapeño, minced with seeds

2 Roma tomatoes, diced

1 bunch cilantro leaves

3 tablespoons olive oil

Juice of 1 lime

1 avocado, peeled, pitted, and diced

Salt and freshly ground black pepper to taste

BRISKET TACOS (YIELDS 8 SERVINGS)

Preheat the oven to 325°F.

Rub the marinade into the brisket and let stand for 1 hour. Heat the vegetable oil in a large cast-iron skillet over medium-high heat until lightly smoking. Sear the brisket on all sides. Place in the oven and roast for $3^1/2$ to 4 hours. Remove from the oven and let cool slightly. Shred while still warm.

Add the salad to the shredded brisket, combining carefully. Divide the mixture among the tortillas, fold in half and close with toothpicks. Heat the vegetable oil in a deep-sided frying pan until lightly smoking. Fry the tacos in the hot oil until lightly crisp, about 30 seconds. Drain on paper towels, garnish with fresh cilantro leaves, and serve with your favorite taco sauce.

JERK MARINADE

Combine all ingredients in a food processor.

SALAD

Toss the onion, jícama, radishes, jalapeño, and tomatoes. Add the oil, lime juice, avocado, and cilantro leaves and gently fold together. Season with salt and pepper.

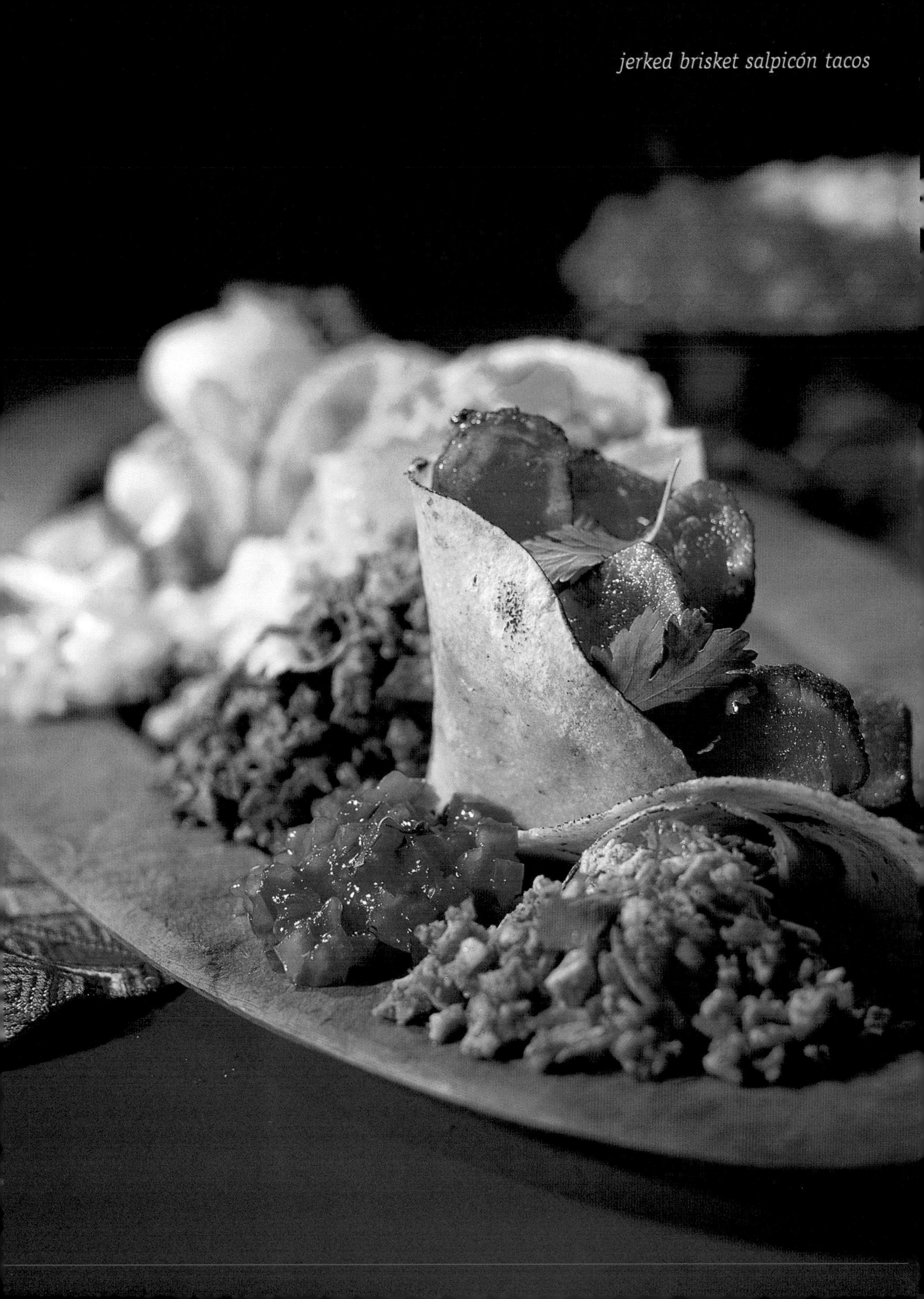

pozole de camarón

shrimp pozole (courtesy of Chef Diana Kennedy and Sra. Rafaela Villaseñor)

The most popular supper dish by far in the western states of Mexico from Nayarit down through Guerrero, especially in the hot country and coastal areas—with a few exceptions of course—is pozole. Pozole is a brothy stew of large white corn kernels and pork. Guerrero lays claim to it, and curiously, there white pozole is served in the morning and green pozole midday on Thursdays. The preparation of the corn remains much the same, but the toppings vary slightly from one region to another, and occasionally you will find chicken cooked with the pork. For local residents of Puerto Vallarta there is no pozole to compare with that of Señora Rafaela Villaseñor. Many years ago, to support a growing family, she sold her pozole and gorditas de res on the street corner just below where she lived. Now, apart from her growing take-out business, she will prepare large quantities to order for special occasions. For the devout who shun meat during Lent she prepares a red pozole with shrimp both fresh and dried. While this pozole is made in many communities along the coast of Colima and Jalisco, it was her recipe that I found most satisfying.

1 pound (450 g) prepared corn for pozole

2 quarts (2 l) plus 1¼ cups (313 ml) or more water as needed

4 ancho chiles

4 guajillo chiles

4 cloves

⅛ teaspoon cumin seeds

4 garlic cloves, roughly chopped

3 tablespoons olive oil

8 ounces (225 g) fresh medium shrimp (see preparation at end of recipe)

3 ounces (85 g) dried shrimp (see preparation at end of recipe)

salt to taste

TO SERVE

Finely chopped white onion

Thinly sliced radishes

Thinly shredded cabbage

Dried oregano

Lime quarters

(YIELDS APPROXIMATELY 12 CUPS, 8 SERVINGS)

Cover the corn with 2 quarts (2 l) of the water in a large saucepan and set over medium heat to cook until the kernels open up or "flower"—about 3 hours. (If you are at a high altitude, I recommend cooking the corn in a pressure cooker for about 50 minutes.) Set aside.

Remove the stems, veins, and seeds from the chiles separately and put them in two individual piles. Cover them separately with hot water and cook over low heat for about 5 minutes. Set aside to soak for about 10 minutes to soften and become fleshy. Drain, discarding the cooking water.

Put ¼ cup (63 ml) of the water into a blender, add the cloves, cumin, and garlic, and blend thoroughly. Add another ½ cup (125 ml) of the water and few of the anchos, then blend until smooth. Add the rest of the anchos and blend again, adding only enough water to release the blades of the blender. The sauce should be quite thick.

Heat the olive oil in a heavy pan in which you are going to cook the pozole. Add the ancho sauce and fry for about 3 minutes, scraping the bottom of the pan from time to time to prevent sticking.

Add another $1/2$ cup of the water to the blender and add the guajillos
   gradually, blending thoroughly after each addition. Run this purée
   through a fine strainer into the pan, thoroughly pressing out the
   debris of tough skins.

Cook the purée of chiles over low heat, scraping the pan to prevent
   sticking, for about 5 minutes

Add the corn and the water in which it was cooked and the
   cheesecloth bag with the shrimp heads and shells. Cook slowly
   for about 15 minutes. Add the dried and fresh shrimp and cook
   for another 10 minutes. Taste for salt. Remove the cheesecloth bag,
   squeezing it well to extract as much liquid as possible.

Serve the pozole with plenty of the broth and pass the
   accompaniments separately. Note: If the broth is too strong for
   your taste, add more hot water to dilute.

PREPARATION OF THE SHRIMP

Dried: Choose the largest you can find with head and tail intact—or at
   least in the same bag. Soak in hot water for 5 minutes to remove
   excess salt. Drain and then remove the heads and feet, leaving the
   skin and tail intact for texture and flavor. Reserve the heads.

Fresh: Medium shrimp are best for this dish, but try to buy them with
   heads still intact if possible for better flavor. Remove the heads and
   reserve them; peel and devein the shrimp.

Put the dried and fresh shrimp heads along with the fresh shells into a
   piece of cheesecloth and tie tightly.

warm tropical fruit compote
with sweet corn ice cream

Years ago in a marketplace in Oaxaca, I had an ice of intensely flavored corn. Because the corn is so different in the United States, I was never able to achieve exactly the same flavor. This version gets its richness from the milk and eggs rather than the poignant corn.

FRUIT COMPOTE

2 cups vegetable oil for frying

1 teaspoon ground canela or cinnamon

$1/4$ cup granulated sugar

6 6-inch flour tortillas

Orange Syrup

2 ripe bananas, peeled and sliced in 1-inch pieces

1 papaya, peeled and sliced in 1-inch pieces

$1/2$ pineapple, peeled and sliced in 1-inch pieces

1 tablespoon chopped fresh mint

Sweet Corn Ice Cream

6 mint sprigs

ORANGE SYRUP

$1/2$ cup fresh orange juice (about $1 1/2$ medium oranges)

2 tablespoons fresh lime juice (1 to 2 medium limes)

$1/2$ cup light brown sugar

3 slices fresh ginger root

2 tablespoons Myers's dark rum

6 tablespoons unsalted butter, cut into cubes and chilled ($3/4$ stick)

SWEET CORN ICE CREAM

4 ears corn, shucked and kernels cut off the cob

4 cups milk

1 canela or cinnamon stick

$1/2$ vanilla bean, split in half lengthwise and scraped

8 egg yolks

$1/4$ cup sugar

$1/4$ cup sour cream

FRUIT COMPOTE (YIELDS 6 SERVINGS)

Heat the oil to 350°F in a small, deep pot for frying. Mix the canela and sugar in a small bowl. Place 1 tortilla at a time between 2 ladles, and submerge the ladles completely in the hot oil. Wait 10 seconds for the tortilla "cup" to set, then pull the ladles apart, allowing the tortilla cup to float in the oil and fry until crisp, about 3 minutes. Drain the cups on paper towels and sprinkle with the canela sugar while still warm.

Bring the Orange Syrup to a boil. Gently stir in the bananas, papaya, pineapple, and chopped mint. Spoon the fruit mixture into serving bowls. Place 1 tortilla cup on top of the fruit, and fill each cup with a scoop of Sweet Corn Ice Cream. Spoon some fruit and syrup over the top of the ice cream and garnish with a mint sprig.

ORANGE SYRUP

Combine the orange and lime juices in a small saucepan. Dissolve the sugar in the juice, add the ginger, and bring to a boil over medium-high heat until reduced by half. Stir in the rum, and add the cold butter a few pieces at a time until fully incorporated. Remove the ginger.

SWEET CORN ICE CREAM (YIELDS 1 QUART)

Purée the corn with the milk in a blender; transfer to a medium saucepan set over medium-high heat. Add the canela and vanilla bean. When the milk mixture reaches a boil, remove from the heat, and let infuse for 20 minutes. Strain the mixture.

Place the egg yolks in a large bowl. Add the sugar, whisking continuously until the eggs lighten in color and form a ribbon. Gradually whisk the milk mixture into the egg mixture a little at the time. Whisk in the sour cream.

Pour the egg mixture back into a saucepan and cook over very low heat until slightly thickened, about 3 minutes. Freeze in an ice cream machine according to the manufacturer's directions.

coconut–ginger floating island
with mango sauce

This recipe is an exotic, tropical spin on the French classic, île flottante.

COCONUT–GINGER FLOATING ISLAND

1 cup water

1 cup granulated sugar

$1/2$ cup roughly chopped fresh ginger

1 15-ounce can of coconut milk

$2^1/2$ cups milk

8 egg whites, at room temperature

$1/2$ teaspoon cream of tartar

$1/2$ cup brown sugar

Mango Sauce

MANGO SAUCE

2 ripe mangos, peeled and seeded

1 cup milk

1 cup heavy cream

1 vanilla bean, split in half lengthwise and scraped

6 egg yolks, at room temperature

$1/2$ cup sugar

COCONUT–GINGER FLOATING ISLAND (YIELDS 8 TO 10 SERVINGS)

Bring the water, granulated sugar, and ginger to a boil in a medium saucepan. Reduce heat and slowly reduce by half. Once reduced, strain and cool.

Combine the milks in a shallow sauté pan and bring to a simmer, being careful not to boil over.

Place the egg whites and cream of tartar in a mixing bowl and whip at high speed. When peaks begin to form, slowly add the brown sugar, whipping continuously. Drizzle in the cooled ginger syrup, and continue beating until stiff peaks form.

Scoop the egg white "islands" into the simmering milk and poach on both sides for 4 minutes per side. Remove to a cloth or paper towels, then serve immediately with Mango Sauce.

MANGO SAUCE

Place the peeled mango in a blender and purée until smooth.

Place the milk, cream, and vanilla bean in a medium saucepan, bring to a boil, and then reduce the heat to simmer.

While the milk mixture is coming to a boil, beat the egg yolks on high speed with an electric mixer while gradually adding the sugar. Continue beating until light and lemon colored. Stir the hot milk mixture into the eggs, a little at a time, until all of the milk is added. Return the egg and milk mixture to the saucepan and cook very slowly over low heat until it thickens and registers about 185°F on a candy thermometer. Strain and chill the mixture. After chilling, whisk in the mango purée.

churros with spicy fruit salsa

churros with spicy fruit salsa
and coconut ice cream

While churros can be found on the streets all over Mexico, I particularly associate these deep-fried cinnamon dough delights with festivals and revelry. They are the perfect late-night pick-me-up with a mug of strong Mexican coffee or atole.

CHURROS

1 quart water

1 teaspoon kosher salt

3 cups all-purpose flour, sifted

1 teaspoon baking powder

4 egg yolks

3 cups vegetable oil

Cinnamon Sugar Dust

Coconut Ice Cream

Spicy Fruit Salsa

CINNAMON SUGAR DUST

1 cup sugar

1 tablespoon cinnamon or ground canela

COCONUT ICE CREAM

1 cup milk

1 cup heavy cream

$2/3$ cup sugar

1 14-ounce can coconut milk

3 tablespoons dark rum

1 teaspoon vanilla extract

SPICY FRUIT SALSA

1 pineapple, peeled, cored, and finely diced

1 mango, peeled, pitted, and finely diced

1 papaya, peeled, seeded, and finely diced

1 pint strawberries, stemmed and finely diced

1 small serrano, stemmed, seeded, and minced

1 tablespoon piloncillo sugar

1 tablespoon thinly sliced fresh mint leaves

1 tablespoon passion fruit purée or juice

CHURROS (YIELDS 6 TO 8 SERVINGS)

Bring the water and salt to a boil in a large saucepan. Sift together the flour and baking powder and add to the boiling water. Turn off the heat and beat vigorously with a wooden spoon to form a stiff dough. Continue stirring until the mixture forms a ball and pulls away from the sides of the pan. Return the heat to low and cook until smooth, about 3 minutes. Remove the pan from the heat and stir in the egg yolks one at a time to form a smooth, elastic dough. Place the dough in a pastry bag fitted with a star tip.

Heat the oil in a deep pan or deep fryer. Pipe the dough onto parchment or wax paper in 5- or 6-inch straight pieces. Slide the piped dough off the paper and into the hot oil. Fry until golden brown, about 2 minutes. Drain on paper towels and sprinkle with Cinnamon Sugar Dust while still warm. Arrange 2 churros per plate, and serve with Coconut Ice Cream and Spicy Fruit Salsa.

CINNAMON SUGAR DUST

Mix thoroughly and store in an airtight container until ready to use.

COCONUT ICE CREAM (YIELDS 1 QUART)

Combine the milk, cream, and sugar in a medium saucepan set over medium-high heat. Bring to a boil, remove from the heat, and stir to dissolve the sugar. Stir in the coconut milk, dark rum, and vanilla extract. Pour the mixture into a bowl set over ice or refrigerate to cool completely. Once cooled, freeze in an ice cream machine according to the manufacturer's directions.

SPICY FRUIT SALSA (YIELDS 6 SERVINGS)

Toss the pineapple, mango, papaya, strawberries, and serrano with the sugar in a medium mixing bowl. Fold in the mint and passion fruit purée until the fruit is coated. Chill until ready to serve.

mexican chocolate tamales
with coconut and white chocolate kahlúa sauce

This dessert starts off as the ubiquitous flourless chocolate cake of the '80s before being cleverly presented as a tamale. Mexican chocolate has canela and, in most cases, almonds added during the processing of the cocoa beans. The result is a grainy but highly flavored chocolate.

TAMALES

1 cup heavy cream

1 teaspoon vanilla extract

3 ounces unsweetened chocolate, roughly chopped

$9^{1}/_{2}$ ounces Mexican chocolate, roughly chopped

5 eggs

$^{1}/_{3}$ cup sugar

$1^{1}/_{4}$ cups coconut, toasted and divided

1 package corn husks, soaked in warm water

White Chocolate Kahlúa Sauce

WHITE CHOCOLATE KAHLÚA SAUCE

1 cup heavy cream

5 ounces white chocolate, roughly chopped

2 tablespoons Kahlúa

TAMALES (YIELDS 10 SERVINGS)

Preheat the oven to 325°F.

Bring the cream and vanilla to a boil in a heavy saucepan. Add the chocolates and remove from the heat, stirring until the chocolate melts completely. Place the eggs in a mixing bowl set over simmering water and whisk until warm to the touch (about 3 minutes). Whip the eggs with the sugar at high speed for approximately 12 minutes until they have tripled in volume. Fold the chocolate mixture into the whipped eggs, a little at a time, until completely incorporated. Pour the batter into a buttered 9-inch round cake pan lined with a parchment paper circle. Bake in a water bath for 35 minutes. Remove from the oven and allow to cool for 15 minutes. Break up the baked chocolate mixture with your hands and stir in 1 cup of the toasted coconut. Divide the mixture into 10 equal portions and roll into balls.

Drain the corn husks and pat dry. Tear 20 ($^{1}/_{6}$-inch-wide) strips from 2 of the husks for tying the tamales. Spread the chocolate dough in the center of the husks, leaving 1 inch at each end uncovered. Roll the corn husks so that the dough is completely enclosed. Twist and tie each end with the reserved strips. Steam over boiling water for 5 minutes to warm. Once warmed, slit the tamales from end to end with a knife, drizzle with White Chocolate Kahlúa Sauce, and sprinkle with the remaining $^{1}/_{4}$ cup of toasted coconut.

WHITE CHOCOLATE KAHLÚA SAUCE

Bring the cream to a boil in a heavy saucepan. Stir in the chocolate and Kahlúa, remove from the heat, and continue stirring until the chocolate is completely melted.

arborio rice pudding tamales

Arborio, the rice used in the classic Italian dish risotto, makes a delicious and toothsome rice pudding. This recipe can obviously be made without the extra step of stuffing into corn husks, but the presentation is stunning.

TAMALES

$1/2$ cup Arborio rice

1 cup water

3 tablespoons sugar, divided

2 large eggs, lightly beaten

1 cup heavy cream

$1/4$ cup milk

$1/2$ teaspoon vanilla extract

$1/2$ teaspoon ground cinnamon

$1/4$ teaspoon grated nutmeg

$1/4$ cup golden raisins, soaked in rum

$1/4$ cup dried cherries, soaked in kirsch

$3/4$ cup grated white chocolate

10 large corn husks, soaked in water for at least 30 minutes

Rum Cream

RUM CREAM

2 large egg yolks

$1/4$ cup sugar

1 cup heavy cream

1 tablespoon dark rum

TAMALES (YIELDS 8 SERVINGS)

Preheat the oven to 300°F. Place the rice, water, and 2 tablespoons of the sugar in a medium saucepan and bring to a boil. Reduce the heat and simmer for 10 minutes until just al dente. Spoon the rice mixture into a large bowl and add the eggs, cream, milk, vanilla, cinnamon, nutmeg, remaining tablespoon of sugar, raisins, and cherries; mix well.

Pour the mixture into a small baking pan, cover with foil, and bake for 20 minutes. Remove from the oven, stir thoroughly, and let cool. Mix in the grated white chocolate.

Drain the corn husks and pat dry. Tear 16 ($1/4$-inch-wide) strips from 2 of the husks; these strips will be used to tie the tamales. Place the remaining husks on a work area and spread about $1/3$ cup to $1/2$ cup of the rice pudding mixture down the middle of each husk, leaving 1 inch at each end uncovered.

Roll the corn husks so that the filling is completely enclosed and tie each end of the tamales with the strips from the corn husks. Place the tamales in a steamer set over gently boiling water and steam for 5 minutes. Place the tamales on serving plates and slice open the top of each tamale from to end. Gently push the ends together, as for a baked potato. Pour Rum Cream into each tamale and serve.

RUM CREAM

Beat the egg yolks and sugar together in a small bowl and set aside.

Bring the cream and rum to a boil in a small saucepan; pour half the mixture into the yolks. Pour the egg–cream mixture back into the saucepan, stirring to incorporate. Cook, while stirring, until the mixture smoothly coats the back of a spoon, about 5 minutes. Strain and cool in a bowl set over ice.

almonds (see *nuts*)

annatto; achiote Red seeds of the tropical annatto used for coloring and seasoning. Often found in paste form, they are used extensively by the dairy industry to make cheese yellow. Annatto is a common feature of the cuisine of the Yucatán region of Mexico and parts of the Caribbean, and is marked by an earthy, slightly acidic flavor akin to green olives with a slight iodine aftertaste.

asiago (see *cheese*)

avocado A buttery-textured fruit indigenous to Mexico and Central America for 7,000 years. Ripe avocados are mild and slightly nutty in flavor, rich in minerals, and high in unsaturated fat. Two types of avocados are commonly available in North America: the Haas and the Fuerte. I prefer the more common Haas or Mexican avocado when it is ripe, which should give slightly when a thumb is pressed on the outside. The less common and much larger variety is the Fuerte, characterized by a smoother, lime-green skin, unlike its cousin, which has dark and rough-textured skin. Once cut, avocados need to be used right away as they will turn dark very quickly.

banana leaves Used extensively in South and Central America as a premodern plastic wrap for everything from tamales to fish, these leaves serve the dual purpose of sealing in moisture and imparting a tropical and herbaceous quality to the food they wrap. The leaves can be bought fresh in Latin markets or frozen in Asian markets. For fresh banana leaves, first derib, then wilt over an open flame or electric burner before using.

basil This versatile herb—a member of the mint family that originated in the Middle East—has licorice and clove overtones that combine well with the flavors of Texas. Basil is highly perishable and should not be cut until ready to use. Look for bright-green, unwilted leaves.

beans Beans have been cultivated for thousands of years in the Americas, and the varieties are too numerous to name. And no wonder their popularity: they are rich in protein and high in minerals such as calcium, iron, and phosphorus. Always sort beans carefully for dirt and rocks before cooking. To shorten cooking time, soak the beans overnight.

caciotta (see *cheese*)

cactus leaves and pears (or nopales and tunas, as they are called in Mexico) The leaves of the prickly pear cactus are spiny, paddle-like hands that dot the West Texas and the Hill Country lands. The flavor of the leaves is akin to green beans or asparagus, but with the texture of okra. To use a leaf, remove all the spines with a paring knife, julienne the leaves, and boil them twice with tomatillo husks to minimize their sliminess. Raw leaves make a great addition to salads, and they taste good grilled also. The barrel-shaped pears of the plant should be yellow to purplish-red on the outside and bright purple to red on the inside. Buy tunas that have smooth, firm flesh and are heavy for their size. After cutting off the outside layer of skin, purée the flesh and strain for drinks, jams, or syrup. Ripe pears have a watermelon smell with a slight cherry taste.

canela Also known as Mexican cinnamon or Ceylon cinnamon, canela came to Mexico from Sri Lanka via the slave traders. It is much softer and flakier—and has about half the seasoning power—than regular cinnamon, or *Cinnamomum cassia*. Like its cousin, the *Cinnamomum zeylanicum* tree derives its flavor from the inner bark. Canela is becoming more and more common in markets with its increasing popularity.

chayote Known as *mirlitons* in Louisiana, *christophenes* in France, and *chayotes* in Mexico. This unique pear-shaped vegetable from the squash family has a flavor similar to cucumber or zucchini and a texture similar to jícama or water chestnuts. A highly prized vegetable by the Aztec culture, the chayote grown on the vine can be used raw (for a refreshing crunch in salads) or pickled. Mexican cooks usually add it to soups and stews. Peeling is not necessary, and some like to eat the pit. I, however, prefer chayotes peeled and pitted.

cheese The Spanish brought cattle to the Americas, and with the cattle, they brought their cheese-making techniques to the New World. Cheese itself probably deserves an entire book, but I will give you an abbreviated tour of the cheeses I prefer. About 80 percent of the cheese I use comes from Paula Lambert's Dallas Mozzarella Company, as hers is the freshest and closest source for me. The recipes in this book call for several types of cheese, with the main varieties as follows:

asiago: Like Monterey Jack, but firmer, and with a slightly tart flavor.

caciotta: Italian cheese very similar in texture and flavor to Monterey Jack.

goat cheese: A soft, crumbly, moist cheese with a tart and earthy flavor. Fresh goat cheese is much milder than the classic aged French chèvre, which is quite pungent.

monterey jack: A semisoft cheese with high moisture content that melts easily. A good topper for many of the Mexican-influenced dishes.

mozzarella: A soft, mild cheese that becomes stringy when cooked. Always buy fresh mozzarella and use it quickly.

pecorino or parmesan: Pecorino is made from sheep's milk and can be very pricey. It is a very tangy, hard, grating cheese that is ideal for salads. Parmesan is its slightly milder, cheaper cousin made from cow's milk.

queso fresco: A fresh, moist, white Mexican cheese made from partially skimmed milk. Similar in texture to farmer's cheese, it crumbles easily and makes a fabulous garnish to many Texas foods.

queso oaxaca: A white, cow's-milk cheese also know as asadero, which appropriately translates as "roaster or broiler" for this easy-melting cheese. It is sold in a number of forms, the most common being the tightly wound balls of string cheese (quesillo), which are absolutely delicious when aged for a few weeks.

ricotta: A delicate, low-fat, no-salt cheese that is actually the by-product of making mozzarella. The whey of the mozzarella curd is used to make this soft cheese. It takes on other flavors quite well and is even good for desserts.

chocolate Cocoa beans used to be traded and used as currency by the Mayans and Aztecs, and many people today still consider chocolate to be as good as gold. Cocoa beans are harvested, fermented, and dried to create chocolate. Columbus ground the beans with sugar, vanilla, and cinnamon to create tasty drinks, which he introduced to Europe upon his return.

chorizo A fabulous way to make your breakfast eggs a little livelier. This highly spiced loose sausage is available in most Hispanic markets, but shouldn't be confused with the hard, cured, Spanish-style chorizo. Most Mexican markets make their own, but commercial varieties work well also.

cilantro People seem to either love cilantro or they will cross the Mississippi to stay away from it. I would cross the Rio Grande to get it because cilantro is as much a part of Texas cooking as beef. Like chiles, cilantro (or Chinese parsley) is addictive, and its cooling, pungent flavor fits perfectly with this food. Some people refer to cilantro as coriander, though they are technically incorrect. In actuality, coriander is the seed of the cilantro plant and has an entirely different flavor profile. The leaves are the most often used part, but don't throw away the stems: tie them into a bundle and use in soups, sauces, or stocks; remove before serving.

coconut The fruit of the coconut palm shows up most in the Gulf Coast region of Texas and is used in almost all middle-latitude coastal cuisines. I like to use the coconut milk for sauces. The lily-white meat freezes well and works best grated or shaved and toasted. Use it in desserts or as a breading for fried seafood.

coriander A commonly misunderstood spice, coriander is the seed of the cilantro plant, but should not be confused with cilantro itself. The flavor tastes slightly citrusy with a touch of sage. It often plays second fiddle to cumin to create earthy flavors in sauces, soups, and rubs in Texas food. Coriander is wonderful toasted and tastes best when ground fresh.

corn The foundation upon which all of South, Central, and North America's native cuisines are based. Every part and form of an ear of corn is used somehow in Texas cuisine. Let's start on the outside of this vegetable and work our way in.

blue corn: Usually ground into meal to make breads. It has a slightly sweeter taste than yellow corn and is used in celebrations in Mexico.

corn cobs: Don't throw them away! Fresh corn cobs, brought to a boil with water to cover, make a wonderful vegetarian alternative to chicken stock. I use it in my restaurants for an inexpensive vegetarian stock.

corn husks: Used fresh and dried as wrappers for tamales.

corn starch and corn syrup: Both are derived from modern processes and are foreign to older cuisines. It does, however, point out the incredible range of products derived from one lowly plant.

fresh kernels: Best cut straight from the cob and used immediately.

fresh masa and masa harina: After drying the posole, it is then made into fresh masa for corn tortillas. Masa harina is corn flour that is widely used for making tamales. The lime soaking gives all of these products a very distinct flavor.

grits and cornmeal: Available in many different grinds and multiple colors. Staples in many different cultures, grits and cornmeal sold in North America are from dried corn that has not been soaked in lime, giving it a different flavor from its Mexican counterparts.

huitlacoche: Also know as the Mexican truffle, it is a fungus that grows in the pozole variety of corn. We are only now beginning to understand the Aztec's love of this smoky-sweet fungus. For years farmers destroyed corn stalks infected with the grayish-black corn smut (as it is sometimes called), but recently gourmets have come to prize it as an exotic alternative to traditional mushrooms. It is now actively cultivated for restaurants and is available canned in Hispanic markets.

posole or pozole: Also know as hominy in the South, this is a larger-kerneled cousin to the sweet eating variety. It is usually harvested fully mature and dry with a high starch content. The kernels are usually soaked in a slaked lime solution to soften the tough outer shell, then dried again. Posole is popular in Mexican soups and as a side dish.

cumin or comino
Derived from a plant that is a relative of the carrot family, it looks like a skinny caraway seed. Another import from Spanish settlers, its pungent, earthy flavor and smell is a key ingredient in many Texas dishes. I prefer to toast and then grind my own, but if preground has to be used, be sure to toast it first to bring the essential oils back to life.

epazote
Stinkweed, wormweed, and pigweed—all ugly names for a beautiful herb. Considered just a weed for years by cooks north of the border, this Mexican herb is finally beginning to make a name for itself here in the States. Mexican cooks have long incorporated epazote into their dishes to bring a unique flavor to their food and to, well, defuse the explosive qualities of beans. While most parts of the country carry dried epazote, I still prefer it fresh and slightly cooked or, with younger leaves, raw in salsas. You'll have the best luck finding fresh epazote in your local Hispanic market, though you might find it growing wild in an odd place like Central Park in New York, where I stumbled upon some one afternoon.

grits (see *corn*)

hoja santa
Also called the "root beer" plant because of its primary sassafras flavor, hoja santa is a more complex herb than the familiar root, with an herbier green flavor and a spiciness betraying its membership in the black pepper family. I discovered this herb in Oaxaca several years ago. There it is used extensively in salsas and moles, and is also believed to have medicinal properties. The leaves can be used as an alternative to banana leaves as a food wrapper. They will lend the food an interesting anise flavor. Hoja santa grows up to ten feet high along the river walk in San Antonio. Despite being well-suited to the South Texas climate, it is often difficult to find, though I expect it to become more readily available in the next three to five years.

huitlacoche (see *corn*)

jícama
Known to some as the Mexican potato, this light-brown skinned tuber's similarities end there. Jícama was originally found in the Amazon Basin, then spread to Mexico. It has an affinity for salads and is best raw, with its fresh apple-turnip flavor. And its water chestnut–like texture lends itself to salsas and relishes, as you will see in this book. You will find it cooked in some recipes, but I prefer it raw, served simply with salt, chile powder, and lime juice for the perfect summer snack.

lard
As one of the very few cooking fats available in the early 1800s, lard became a key player in the development of Texas cuisine. The food police have, for the most part, eradicated lard for purportedly healthier alternatives like vegetable shortening and olive oil. Unfortunately, few things lend the same flavor to food that lard does. As my mentor and friend, Julia Child, says, "Everything in moderation." I say, use your best judgment and give it a try to rediscover an old Texas taste.

lemon verbena
Similar to lemon balm in flavor, this powerful herb brings the flavor and aroma of lemon to foods without the acidity. It is not quite inter-changeable with lemon balm, but lemon balm can be used as a substitute.

limes
Indispensable as the acid component in Texas. I recommend that you buy the smaller Mexican limes instead of the larger Persian limes, as Mexican limes produce more and sweeter juice.

macadamia nuts (see *nuts*)

mangos A tropical fruit that originated in Asian cuisines and considered sacred by some. Ripe mangos are much easier to find in grocery stores now and are indispensable in salsas, drinks, relishes, and sauces. Ripe mangos should have red-orange skin and give slightly when pressed, not to mention a heady perfume akin to gardenias. The tropical coolness of this fabulously sweet fruit is the perfect foil to the heat of chiles in Texas cuisine.

marigold mint Very similar to tarragon, but more heady in flavor with anise tones. This herb goes well in salads and works well with corn and squash, too. In Mexico, the natives consider it a medicinal herb and usually drink it as tea. In addition to all these qualities, the edible flowers make an attractive garnish.

marjoram One of many members of the mint family used in Texas cuisine. Marjoram is a highly underutilized herb that is sweeter and more complex than oregano, though many cooks use it interchangeably with oregano. In Mexico, it is called wild oregano and looks very similar to oregano.

masa harina (see *corn*)

monterey jack (see *cheese*)

mozzarella (see *cheese*)

nuts Nuts add a richness to everything from sauces to desserts. They bring a pleasant texture contrast to food and are also very nutritious. The main types of nuts used in this book include the following:

almonds: Very versatile due to their mild flavor. Very common in Texas cooking and also found in many classic mole recipes. They work very well with desserts, too.

macadamia nuts: One of the richest nuts commonly used in America. Originally cultivated in Australia from a type of evergreen tree and named after Scott John Macadam, who began their cultivation. Introduced to Hawaii in the '30s, they have become a major cash crop for the state. They should be used rather quickly, as they turn rancid quite fast.

pecans: The most widely cultivated nut in the world.

flavor and high fat content. I prefer to use them as an accent to salads and meat dishes where their flavor is a perfect addition. As with macadamia nuts, pecans are susceptible to rancidity and should be frozen in an airtight container if not used quickly.

pine nuts: Also known as pignolis or piñons, they are the priciest of the nuts I use. The main reason for this cost is the difficulty in processing. Pine nuts are the heart of the individual spines of pine cones. Harvesting is done almost exclusively by hand, and the shells must be heated to extract the meat. There are native varieties available from New Mexico and Arizona, but the majority of the American supply comes from Asia and the Middle East. I prefer to toast pine nuts before I use them. Perfect for moles and also needed for classic pesto.

walnuts: Related to pecans and also part of the hickory family, walnuts have a high fat content as well. They are the second most consumed nut in the United States. I prefer to soak them overnight in cold water to avoid any bitterness encountered in the skin. For an even richer walnut flavor, try the rarer black walnuts native to the Appalachian region.

nopales (see *cactus leaves and pears*)

oils My favorite oil for cooking is olive oil, as it imparts a unique but subtle flavor to food. A quality brand of olive oil is necessary for use in dressings and such, as its flavor has to stand alone. Peanut and/or canola are the best oils for frying, because they withstand high temperatures and are relatively flavorless. Vegetable oil is perfect for cooking delicate food that needs a neutral oil and is perfect for blending to tone down a powerful olive oil. Nut oils, such as hazelnut, walnut, and almond, are unique additions to salad dressing, but spoil easily and should be sealed well after each use.

okra This relative of the hibiscus and a staple in Southern cooking was brought to the New World by slaves longing for home. One of many vegetables from the nightshade family, its influence is most prominent in Cajun and Creole cooking, where the seed pod is used as a thickening agent in gumbo. The thickening action of okra comes from the sliminess that some consider unappetizing. If you fall into this category, try it fried, and you'll be treated with a nice (and unslimy) surprise.

onions Surprisingly, onions are a member of the lily family. I love to cook with sweet onions grown here in Texas, the Noonday and Texas Spring Sweet. The more common sweet onion, Vidalia, now grown in Georgia, is originally from Texas stock. Try one of these sweet onions on a hamburger at your next barbecue and discover how wonderfully sweet they are even raw. The standard onion I use for cooking in this book is the yellow onion, which is slightly sweeter than the white variety. Red onions are very mild and used mostly for color. As with shallots, look for dry, papery skins and firm, heavy onions.

oregano Like cilantro, this intensely flavored herb is a key ingredient to Texan and Mexican cooking. Mexican oregano, which I enjoy quite a bit, is slightly stronger than its cousin called Italian oregano. One of the most versatile mint family members, oregano should be used fresh, not dried, whenever possible.

oysters Cultivated for thousands of years dating back to the Romans, oysters thrive in estuaries and shallow bays where the salinity of ocean water is diluted slightly. The United States, Japan, and France, respectively, produce the most oysters. If you want to avoid the labor of shucking your own, you can find them preshucked, but be careful to check for shell fragments with your fingers.

papaya Papayas found in the United States are grown mostly in Hawaii, Florida, and Mexico. This fruit, not unlike the mango, is best when the skin is yellow-orange and gives slightly when pressed. The seeds in the center, though edible, are usually discarded. If you buy a papaya that is underripe, or green, place it in a paper bag in a warm place for a couple of days.

parsley I prefer the flat-leafed or Italian parsley to the steakhouse garnish craze, curly-leaf variety. In most Texas cooking you will find cilantro in lieu of parsley, but it still has its place in cooking and is great for perking up heavier dishes.

pecans (see *nuts*)

pecorino (see *cheese*)

pepitas Pepitas—often called pumpkin seeds, though they're actually from a variety of squash—have a green hue that is only slightly diminished by roasting. Pepitas have been an out-of-hand snack for hundreds of years south of the border and are the most frequently used for moles. They lend themselves best to savory dishes and are a low-calorie alternative to nuts.

piloncillo The traditional brown, unrefined sugar of Mexico. The name refers to the most common shape it is sold in, a truncated cone. The necessary amount has to be chopped from the cone, which is never easy since it is very hard (I find it is easiest to cut with a serrated knife). You can find piloncillo in most Latin American groceries and some well-stocked chain supermarkets. Dry and well-wrapped, it lasts indefinitely.

pine nuts (see *nuts*)

pomegranates Native to the Middle East, this large berry is now grown in the United States in Texas, California, and Arizona. The translucent red-pink seeds make a stunning garnish, and the flavor well complements the food of Texas. Buy unblemished fruit and be careful when cleaning them to avoid the bitter white pith. This very labor-intensive fruit is notorious for staining clothes, so don't wear your nice apron when you prepare them.

pozole or posole (see *corn*)

queso fresco (see *cheese*)

queso oaxaca (see *cheese*)

ricotta (see *cheese*)

rosemary This rustic-looking, evergreen shrub is a member of the mint family as well. It has a powerful flavor that works best when complementing food as opposed to overpowering it. The piney, lemon flavor is a perfect addition to a grilled meat, either as a skewer or thrown directly on the fire to flavor the smoke.

saffron It takes 70,000 hand-picked stigmas from the Mediterranean crocus flower to make just one pound of saffron, explaining, of course, its extremely high price. Used for its delicate flavor and brilliant yellow color, saffron came to the New World by way of the Spaniards, who, once again, made a lasting impression on the cuisine of Texas.

sage Multiple varieties of this subtle herb grow wild in Texas. It is the perfect addition to fowl, pork, game, and that American classic, stuffing. Originally, as with most herbs, it was used for medicinal purposes.

scallions

Scallions evolve into green onions, but at the scallion stage their peppery-onion flavor is much milder than the green onion's. A member of the lily family that's related to garlic and leeks, the scallion is a versatile and indispensable component to Texas cooking.

shallots

Another member of the lily family that has a flavor somewhere between onions and garlic. Buy shallots that have dry, reddish-brown, papery skins and are heavy for their size. My first introduction to the shallot was in France, where it is used extensively in French cuisine.

shrimp

The most consumed seafood product in the United States, shrimp is usually sold frozen with a per pound count (U-10, 11–15 jumbo, 15–20 large, 31–35 medium, and so on). They are sometimes even frozen on the fishing boats before they reach land to preserve their freshness. This crustacean has an incredibly sweet and succulent flesh, a flavor that comes through most with fresh shrimp. Unfortunately for Middle America, fresh shrimp are often restricted to coasts due to their very short shelflife.

sweet potatoes

A Southern staple from the morning glory family. Contrary to popular belief, sweet potatoes are not yams. Named for their high sugar content of 3 to 6 percent, they are my favorite tuber. The smaller potatoes are usually more tender and sweet.

tamarind

Another ocean-crossing plant that originated in West Africa and is now grown in Asia and Mexico. The fruit itself is the pod of an evergreen tree that is usually found in paste form. It is used extensively in Southwestern cuisines, as its pleasant bittersweet tartness complements chiles very well. A favorite of steak sauce producers, it makes fabulous glazes and marinades.

thyme

A multipurpose herb from the ever-present mint family, thyme is widely used in Texas cooking. Its clean, green-peppery flavor enhances stocks, soups, and sauces, as well as meats. Like rosemary, it can be added to the grill to provide a fragrant flavor to meats and vegetables.

tomatillos

This relative of the tomato is also in the nightshade family and is a staple of Texan and Mexican cooking. The husk should be removed and the sticky surface rinsed. Their slightly lemony flavor lends itself nicely to salsas.

tomatoes

A native to the New World whose name comes from the Aztec language. Thought to have originated in Peru, the tomato was believed poisonous by Europeans. Due to this superstition, tomatoes have become widely used only in this century. Use vine-ripened whenever possible, unless you are making my Fried Green Tomato Salad. Out-of-season tomatoes are harvested green and then exposed to ethylene gas to produce a red flesh, but never attain the flavor of "real" tomatoes. When good-quality tomatoes are not available, use a high-quality Italian canned product. Make sure you drain them first and adjust the recipe accordingly. Yellow tomatoes are becoming more and more readily available and have a sweeter flesh. They are a striking and flavorful addition to salads and salsas.

vanilla

Another Aztec addition to the culinary world, the vanilla bean derives from the orchid family. The best-quality beans are usually from Tahiti, although Mexican Papantla vanilla is also excellent. Use fresh vanilla whenever possible, and choose large, plump, soft beans.

vinegars

Vinegars, like oils, have many different characteristics and uses. I like to keep aged sherry vinegar and balsamic vinegar in my kitchen, and I also recommend keeping multipurpose vinegars, such as apple cider, red wine, and champagne, around as well. As with oils, you should be especially concerned with highest quality when making vinaigrettes and other items where the vinegar's flavor stands alone. Making your own fruit vinegars couldn't be simpler: pour good quality champagne or white wine over macerated fruit, and store in an airtight bottle for at least one month.

walnuts

(see *nuts*)

index

credits

ANNATTO RICE WITH WILD MUSHROOMS
AND BLACK BEAN PROSCIUTTO REFRITO, PAGE 207

Annatto Rice with Wild Mushrooms from *Nuevo*

Tex-Mex by David Garrido, Robb Walsh © 1998,

published by Chronicle Books, San Francisco

FILETE MEZTLI Y SALSA DEL SOL, PAGE 157

Used by permission of Americo Circuit

and Patricia Quintana

Copyright © 1999 Americo Circuit

and Patricia Quintana

MOLE POBLANO DE GUAJOLOTE, PAGE 186

From *Authentic Mexican: Regional Cooking*

from the Heart of Mexico by Rick Bayless

Copyright © 1987 by Rick Bayless

and Deann Groen Bayless

Used by permission of

William Morrow & Company, Inc.

PASTEL DE CARNE DEL ISTMO
(ISTHMIAN-STYLE MEAT LOAF), PAGE 180

Reprinted by permission of Macmillan

General Reference USA, a division of Ahsuog, Inc.

From *The Food and Life of Oaxaca:*

Traditional Recipes from Mexico's Heart

by Zarela Martinez Copyright © 1997

PORK TENDERLOIN WITH ENSALADE
DE TOMATE VERDE, PAGE 152

Ensalada de Tomate Verde

from *My Mexico* by Diana Kennedy

Copyright © 1998 by Diana Kennedy

Reprinted by permission of Clarkson N. Potter,

a division of Crown Publishers, Inc.

POZOLE DE CAMARÓN, PAGE 218

From *My Mexico* by Diana Kennedy

Copyright © 1998 by Diana Kennedy

Reprinted by permission of Clarkson N. Potter,

a division of Crown Publishers, Inc.

PURÉE DE PAPAS (POTATO PURÉE), PAGE 181

Reprinted by permission of Macmillan

General Reference USA, a division of Ahsuog, Inc.

From *The Food and Life of Oaxaca:*

Traditional Recipes from Mexico's Heart

by Zarela Martinez Copyright © 1997

SEA BASS IN HOJA SANTA WITH SALSA
VERDE AND ROSE PETALS, PAGE 214

Copyright © 1999 Patricia Quintana

Used by permission of Patricia Quintana

SHRIMP CHILI CHALUPAS WITH
PAPAYA-HABANERO SALSA, PAGE 206

From *Nuevo Tex-Mex* by David Garrido,

Robb Walsh © 1998, published by

Chronicle Books, San Francisco

TORTA DE PIÑA DE LOS VIRREYES, PAGE 165

From *The Art of Mexican Cooking*

by Diana Kennedy

Copyright © 1989 by Diana Kennedy

Used by permission of Bantam Books,

a division of Random House, Inc.

Production of the public television series

NEW TASTES FROM TEXAS
WITH STEPHAN PYLES

is made possible in part by

Radisson
HOTELS WORLDWIDE®
The difference is genuine.℠

SEAFOOD SUPPLY COMPANY
"Where The Best Chefs Fish!"

Central and South West Corporation

GALLO *of* SONOMA.